TREATME[N]
DEPRESS

Pergamon Titles of Related Interest

Becker/Heimberg/Bellack SOCIAL SKILLS TREATMENT FOR
DEPRESSION

Blanchard/Andrasik MANAGEMENT OF CHRONIC HEADACHES:
A Psychological Approach

Bornstein/Bornstein MARITAL THERAPY:
A Behavioral-Communications Approach

Hersen/Bellack/Kazdin THE CLINICAL PSYCHOLOGY
HANDBOOK

Meichenbaum STRESS INOCULATION TRAINING

Plas SYSTEMS PSYCHOLOGY IN THE SCHOOLS

Weiss/Katzman/Wolchik TREATING BULIMIA:
A Psychoeducational Approach

Yost/Beutler/Corbishley/Allender GROUP COGNITIVE
THERAPY: A Treatment Method for Depressed Older Adults

Related Journals

(Free sample copies available upon request)

CLINICAL PSYCHOLOGY REVIEW
JOURNAL OF ANXIETY DISORDERS

PSYCHOLOGY PRACTITIONER GUIDEBOOKS

EDITORS

Arnold P. Goldstein, Syracuse University
Leonard Krasner, Stanford University and SUNY at Stony Brook
Sol L. Garfield, Washington University

TREATMENT OF DEPRESSION

An Interpersonal Systems Approach

IAN H. GOTLIB
University of Western Ontario

CATHERINE A. COLBY
Children's Psychiatric Research Institute

PERGAMON PRESS
New York   Oxford   Beijing   Frankfurt
São Paulo   Sydney   Tokyo   Toronto

Pergamon Press Offices:

U.S.A.	Pergamon Press, Maxwell House, Fairview Park, Elmsford, New York 10523, U.S.A.
U.K.	Pergamon Press, Headington Hill Hall, Oxford OX3 0BW, England
PEOPLE'S REPUBLIC OF CHINA	Pergamon Press, Room 4037, Qianmen Hotel, Beijing, People's Republic of China
FEDERAL REPUBLIC OF GERMANY	Pergamon Press, Hammerweg 6, D-6242 Kronberg, Federal Republic of Germany
BRAZIL	Pergamon Editora, Rua Eça de Queiros, 346, CEP 04011, Paraiso, São Paulo, Brazil
AUSTRALIA	Pergamon Press Australia, P.O. Box 544, Potts Point, N.S.W. 2011, Australia
JAPAN	Pergamon Press, 8th Floor, Matsuoka Central Building, 1-7-1 Nishishinjuku, Shinjuku-ku, Tokyo 160, Japan
CANADA	Pergamon Press Canada, Suite No. 271, 253 College Street, Toronto, Ontario, Canada M5T 1R5

First printing 1987

Library of Congress Cataloging in Publication Data
Gotlib, Ian H.
Treatment of depression.
(Psychology practitioner guidebooks)
Bibliography: p.
1. Depression, Mental--Treatment. 2. Depression, Mental--Patients--Family relationships. 3. Family psychotherapy. I. Colby, Catherine A. II. Title.
III. Series. [DNLM: 1. Depression--therapy.
2. Depressive Disorder--therapy. 3. Interpersonal Relations. 4. Psychotherapy--methods. WM 171 G684t]
RC537.G68 1987   616.85′2706   86-25209
ISBN 0-08-033634-5
ISBN 0-08-033633-7 (soft)

Printed in Great Britain by A. Wheaton & Co. Ltd., Exeter

To our parents:
Mark and Regina, and Marvin and Margaret

Contents

Preface   ix

Chapter

1. DEPRESSION: SYMPTOMATOLOGY, EPIDEMIOLOGY,
    AND RISK FACTORS   1
    Depression   1

2. AN INTERPERSONAL SYSTEMS CONCEPTUALIZATION
    OF DEPRESSION   22
    Historical Perspective   22
    An Integrative Framework   30
    An Interpersonal Systems Conceptualization of Depression   33
    Case Example   38

3. GENERAL TREATMENT PRINCIPLES AND STRATEGIES
    CHARACTERISTIC OF INTERPERSONAL SYSTEMS THERAPY
    FOR DEPRESSION   42
    Tasks of Therapy   45
    Therapy Techniques   49
    Individual Therapy Techniques   58

4. ASSESSMENT OF DEPRESSION: A SYSTEMS PERSPECTIVE   62
    Assessing the Context of the Depression   63
    Assessment of the Individual Subsystems   70
    Interviewing the Depressed Patient   76
    Depression-associated Cautions in the Use of an
        Interpersonal Systems Approach to Treatment   81
    Marital and Family Assessment   84
    Marital-Family-associated Cautions in the Use of an
        Interpersonal Systems Approach to Treatment   91
    The Assessment Data   94

5.   STAGES OF TREATMENT I. THE ASSESSMENT STAGE   96
     Introduction and Assessment   96

6.   STAGES OF TREATMENT II. THE INTERVENTION STAGE   118
       Intervention   118
       Termination   142
       Follow-up   145

7.   CASE EXAMPLES   147
       Case 1: A Depressed Child   147
       Case 2: A Depressed University Student   153
       Case 3: A Depressed Married Woman   158
       Concluding Comments   164

Afterword   Beyond Depression: Further Applications
                 of Interpersonal Systems Therapy   166

References   171

Author Index   181

Subject Index   187

About the Authors   191

Psychology Practitioner Guidebooks List   193

Preface

Depression is the single most common psychiatric disorder seen by mental health professionals and is perhaps the most lethal. It has been estimated that one in five depressed persons receives treatment, 1 in 50 is hospitalized, and 1 in 100 commits suicide. Furthermore, the lifetime expectancy of an affective disorder has been estimated at 20%. There are many costs associated with depression. The economic costs of depression include not only direct treatment expenses, but also losses incurred through lowered productivity, job absenteeism, and permanent withdrawal from the work force. Teuting, Koslow, and Hirschfeld (1981) have estimated the costs of treatment and of loss of time at work alone to be 10 billion dollars per year.

There are other costs of depression. In children and adolescents, depression-associated difficulties in school may lead to alterations in subsequent career choices. The social costs of depression are not measurable in dollars. Indeed, it is impossible to assess the social damage caused by depression: grief and pain, marital and family conflict, physical illness, and death.

Over the last decade, there has been a growing recognition that depression is an interpersonal phenomenon, and this awareness has led researchers and clinicians to examine the role of close relationships in the etiology, course, and outcome of depression, as well as the negative impact of depression on close relationships. Thus, a growing empirical literature is emerging that assesses the marital and family relationships of depressed individuals. Paralleling this new direction of research in depression is the growing interest in general systems approaches to the treatment of psychological dysfunction. An increasing number of mental health professionals are now attending more explicitly to the social or interpersonal aspects of their clients' symptoms, and this focus is affecting the types of intervention strategies they offer.

Unfortunately, the literature examining interpersonal factors in depression is not readily available to the practising professional in a form that is clinically useful. This is particularly disconcerting given Secunda, Katz, Friedman, and Schuyler's (1973) statement, in a special National Institute of Mental Health report on the depressive disorders, that "the burden for therapy for the large pro-

portion of the depressive illnesses . . . falls squarely upon psychosocial therapeutic modalities." The purpose of this guidebook, therefore, is to integrate the
empirical literature that assesses the marital and family relationships of
depressed patients with systems-oriented intervention techniques. In outlining
this integration, we present a systems description of depression and provide the
clinician with explicit, step-by-step procedures derived from this description,
to be used in assessing and treating the depressed patient.

This guidebook consists of seven chapters and an afterword. We begin by
presenting an overview of the nature of depression. The symptomatology and
classification of the depressive disorders are described and the epidemiologic
and demographic aspects of depression, including marital status, gender, and
socioeconomic status, are discussed. In this chapter the various interpersonal
risk or vulnerability factors that have been implicated in this disorder are also
discussed. This description of depression is followed by a chapter outlining the
historical roots of family therapy and the theoretical underpinnings and principles of a general systems approach to the understanding of human functioning.
Building from an empirical foundation, which includes both the research
described in the previous chapter and our own work assessing the social supports and the marital and family interactions of depressed patients, a description of depression is developed that ascribes considerable importance to the role
played by members of the individual's social environment in maintaining or
exacerbating the depressive condition. In this context, particular attention is
paid to the development of an escalating pathogenic family interaction—a process that involves both the effects of an individual's depression on his or her
spouse and children and the reciprocal impact of the spouse and children's
behaviors on a parent's depressive symptoms. This chapter concludes with a
detailed case presentation that will be used in subsequent chapters to illustrate
various intervention strategies.

This description of depression is followed by four chapters detailing assessment, intervention, and treatment evaluation and follow-up procedures. In
Chapter 3 principles and treatment strategies for depression are outlined that are
based on an interpersonal systems conceptualization of this disorder. In Chapter
4 various approaches to an interpersonally oriented assessment of depression are
examined. DSM-III and Research Diagnostic Criteria for depression are presented and self-report measures and interview schedules for use with both
depressed adults and children are discussed. In addition, the typical individual
assessment procedure for depression is extended to include an assessment of the
social environment of depressed persons and the quality of their marriages and
family situations.

In Chapters 5 and 6 the use of the principles described in the two previous
chapters is illustrated through a detailed description of the assessment and treatment of a family with a depressed mother, from the initial telephone contact
through the treatment sessions and finally to the follow-up assessment. Proce-

dures to identify the general goals of therapy from an interpersonal systems framework are presented, with emphasis on the roles of both the therapist and the patients in constructing these goals. The rationale for involving the couple or family in therapy is discussed, and techniques for engaging the cooperation of family members in this endeavor are described. Finally, the specific use of the assessment and intervention principles and techniques described earlier is discussed.

In Chapter 7 three extended case examples are presented, through which are highlighted many of the points made and issues dealt with throughout the previous chapters. In these examples, the use of this systems approach to the treatment of depression with individuals, couples, and families is illustrated. Finally, in the Afterword, the relevance of the perspective described in this guidebook to a broader range of maladjustment is briefly discussed. We view this guidebook as a springboard to the interpersonal systems treatment of anxiety, obesity, obsessions, and other common clinical conditions. Thus, in the Afterword the ways that this interpersonal systems approach can be applied to disorders other than depression are discussed. We hope that in addition to presenting therapists with a comprehensive approach to the treatment of depression, this book will stimulate clinicians to think of ways to treat other patients in their practices from a similar perspective.

We gratefully acknowledge the support provided to the first author by the Medical Research Council of Canada (Grant MA-8574), the Ontario Mental Health Foundation (Grant 923-85/87), and the Natural Sciences and Engineering Research Council of Canada (Grant A0575). These grants were awarded for the study of the marital interactions of depressed patients, the functioning of the children of depressed mothers, and the cognitive functioning of depressed individuals, respectively. The continuing support of these agencies has greatly facilitated the preparation of this book.

Chapter 1
Depression: Symptomatology, Epidemiology, and Risk Factors

In this chapter we will examine the signs and symptoms that comprise a diagnosis of depression. In this context, the criteria necessary for an individual to be diagnosed as depressed will be presented and various types and dimensions of a diagnosis of depression will be discussed. In addition, the epidemiological factors that are most strongly associated with depression will be examined. Consistent with the orientation of this guidebook, in presenting this discussion particular attention will be paid to those epidemiological variables that are clearly interpersonal in nature. Finally, this chapter will conclude with a discussion of social and interpersonal risk factors in depression, factors that place an individual at increased risk for developing and exhibiting depressive symptomatology.

DEPRESSION

Of all the psychiatric symptoms, depression is by far the most common, accounting for 75% of all hospitalizations. It has been estimated that each year more than 100 million people in the world develop clinically recognizable depression, a prevalence ten times greater than that of schizophrenia. Furthermore, the World Health Organization believes that this number is likely to increase (Sartorius, 1979). Similarly, Weissman, Myers, and Harding (1978) estimate that over a lifetime perhaps 25% of the general population will experience at least one clinically significant episode of depression. Lehmann (1971) has observed that the death rate, from all causes, in depressed females is twice and for depressed males three times the normal rate. The difference in suicide

1

rates is even more impressive. Pokorny (1964) reported a depressive suicide rate in Texas 25 times greater than the expected level among males, and Temoche, Pugh, and MacMahon (1964) reported a suicide rate 36 times the expected level in Massachusetts. Corroborating these statistics, the National Institute of Mental Health reports that of the 22,000 suicides committed annually in the United States, upwards of 80% can be traced to a precipitating depressive episode. When one considers the various medical and diagnostic categories of which depression is an intricate part, or those with which it is frequently associated, and the number of patients who show on careful examination a masked or subclinical form, the problem of depression is truly great.

Symptoms

The term *depression* has a number of meanings; it covers a wide range of emotional states, ranging in severity from normal, everyday moods of sadness to psychotic episodes with increased risk of suicide. The most prominent features of depression in adults are a dysphoric mood and loss of interest in or failure to derive pleasure from usual activities and pastimes. In addition, as Digdon and Gotlib (1985) note, depressed children also commonly exhibit sleep disturbance, decreased school performance, and somatic complaints.

Certainly, everyone has at some time felt "sad," "down in the dumps," or "blue"—feelings of despondency and disappointment are nearly universal experiences. There are, however, specific symptoms that distinguish clinically significant, diagnosable depression from these normal, occasional feelings of sadness. These symptoms are presented in Table 1.1. As we can see from this table, clinically depressed individuals may exhibit symptoms in any of several areas of functioning. First, as already stated, there is a pronounced and persistent dysphoric affect, most often characterized by depression, anxiety, or, for some individuals, hostility. Although these emotions resemble the unhappiness experienced in normal, everyday life, they do appear to be qualitatively different. Episodes of weeping often accompany the depression, at least in its early stages. With increasing severity of depression, however, the patients may become incapable of weeping, stating that although they feel like crying, they cannot.

Depressed persons may also demonstrate behavioral disturbances involving either agitated or retarded psychomotor activity and retarded or pressured speech. Behavioral agitation, likely associated with the anxiety component of depression, is relatively uncommon. Although some depressed patients may fidget with their fingers and feet, more obvious signs of agitation, such as pacing and pressured speech, are rare. In contrast, psychomotor retardation is a much more common symptom of depression. Stooped posture, delay in responding to questioning, and monotonous voice pitch are frequent exemplars of this retardation.

Table 1.1. Symptoms of Depression

Affective	Dysphoric mood
	Anxiety
	Fearfulness
	Guilt
	Weariness
	Anger, hostility, and irritability
Behavioral Manifestations	Agitation
	Facial expression
	Psychomotor retardation
	Withdrawal
	Retardation of speech and thought
	Neglect of personal appearance
	Dependence
	Crying
Attitudes Towards Self and the Environment	Self-deprecation
	Low self-esteem
	Feelings of worthlessness
	Negative view of the world, the self, and the future
	Feelings of helplessness, pessimism, and hopelessness
	Inability to experience pleasure
	Thoughts of death or suicide
Cognitive Impairment	Decreased ability to think or concentrate
	Indecisiveness
Physiological Changes and Bodily Complaints	Weight loss or gain
	Appetite disturbance
	Sleep disturbance
	Loss of energy
	Decrease in sexual interest
	Menstrual changes
	Fatigue
	Weakness
	Indigestion
	Constipation or diarrhea
	Tension, muscle aches and headaches

With respect to cognitive functioning, depressed individuals often find it difficult to concentrate; thoughts are slowed and confused, and effective problem-solving becomes virtually impossible. Thoughts concerning the self are often centered on themes of hopelessness, helplessness, and self-devaluation. In severe cases, delusions and hallucinations congruent with these themes may be present, and the individual may experience extreme cognitive confusion or demonstrate a preoccupation with suicide.

Finally, many depressed persons exhibit vegetative or physiological symptoms of depression. Of these physical manifestations of depression, sleep disturbances are perhaps the most prominent. Most depressed persons experience insomnia combined with early morning awakening; however, this symptom may be reversed in the early stages of depression. Disturbances in gastrointestinal functioning are common and, combined with loss of appetite, often result in considerable weight loss. Depressed individuals frequently report tiredness and fatigue, even in the absence of any physical exertion, and experience a loss of sexual energy, often manifested in men by impotence and in women by frigidity or amenorrhea. In essence, it is the severity, pervasiveness, and persistence of the change in day-to-day functioning that distinguishes clinical depression from more normal feelings of sadness.

Diagnosis and Classification

Clinical depression clearly involves a wide variety of symptoms. Moreover, not all depressed persons manifest the same pattern or combination of symptoms. Because of the common nature of this disorder, and because depressed individuals frequently report also feeling anxious or hostile, it is often difficult for the clinician to make an accurate diagnosis.

The current diagnostic system in North America is the Diagnostic and Statistical Manual of Mental Disorders (DSM-III; American Psychiatric Association, 1980). This manual divides affective disorders into *Major Affective Disorders*, in which the individual exhibits a full affective syndrome; *Other Specific Affective Disorders*, in which there is only a partial affective syndrome of at least 2 years' duration; and *Atypical Affective Disorders*, essentially a residual category for those affective disturbances that cannot be classified in either of the two previous specific subclasses. Seven separate depressive and manic syndromes are listed under *Affective Disorders* in DSM-III, in addition to the two "atypical" categories. Specifically, three *Bipolar disorders* (manic, depressed, and mixed); two *Major Depression disorders* (single episode and recurrent); and two *Other Specific Affective disorders* (cyclothymic and dysthymic disorders) are described, along with *Atypical Bipolar Disorder* and *Atypical Depression*. Finally, there are four additional DSM-III categories that involve depressed affect: (a) *Adjustment Disorder with Depressed Mood*, indicating a relatively mild depressive reaction to stress; (b) *Uncomplicated Bereavement*, a normal grief reaction; (c) *Schizoaffective Disorder*, a category used when the clinician is unable to differentiate between *Affective Disorder* and either *Schizophreniform Disorder* or *Schizophrenia*; and (d) *Organic Affective Syndrome*, indicating depression due to a specific organic factor.

The two most common of these diagnostic categories seen in general clinical practice are *Major Depressive Episode* and *Dysthymic Disorder*. Although clinical instruments and schedules used to derive diagnoses of depression will be described in detail in Chapter 4, it may be helpful here to present criteria used in making these diagnoses. Table 1.2 presents the DSM-III criteria necessary to make a diagnosis of *Major Depressive Episode*. Briefly, this diagnosis essentially requires both the presence of a prominent dysphoric mood and the daily occurrence over at least 2 weeks of a minimum of 4 depressive symptoms. The

Table 1.2. DSM-III Diagnostic Criteria: Major Depressive Episode

A. Dysphoric mood or loss of interest or pleasure in all or almost all usual activities and pastimes. The dysphoric mood is characterized by symptoms such as the following: depressed, sad, blue, hopeless, low, down in the dumps, irritable. The mood disturbance must be prominent and relatively persistent, but not necessarily the most dominant symptom, and does not include momentary shifts from one dysphoric mood to another dysphoric mood, e.g., anxiety to depression to anger, such as are seen in states of acute psychotic turmoil. (For children under six, dysphoric mood may have to be inferred from a persistently sad facial expression.)

B. At least four of the following symptoms have been present nearly every day for a period of at least two weeks (in children under six, at least three of the first four).
   1. poor appetite or significant weight loss (when not dieting) or increased appetite or significant weight gain (in children under six, consider failure to make expected weight gains)
   2. insomnia or hypersomnia
   3. psychomotor agitation or retardation (but not merely subjective feelings of restlessness or being slowed down) (in children under six, hypoactivity)
   4. loss of interest or pleasure in usual activities or decrease in sexual drive not limited to a period when delusional or hallucinating (in children under six, signs of apathy)
   5. loss of energy; fatigue
   6. feelings of worthlessness, self-reproach, or excessive or inappropriate guilt (either may be delusional)
   7. complaints or evidence of diminished ability to think or concentrate, such as slowed thinking, or indecisiveness not associated with marked loosening of associations or incoherence
   8. recurrent thoughts of death, suicidal ideation, wishes to be dead, or suicide attempt

C. Neither of the following dominate the clinical picture when an affective syndrome (i.e., criteria A and B above) is not present, that is, before it developed or after it has remitted:
   1. preoccupation with a mood-incongruent delusion or hallucination
   2. bizarre behavior

D. Not superimposed on either Schizophrenia, Schizophreniform Disorder, or a Paranoid Disorder.

E. Not due to any Organic Mental Disorder or Uncomplicated Bereavement.

Source: American Psychiatric Association. *Diagnostic and Statistical Manual of Mental Disorders*, 3rd Ed., Washington, DC: APA, 1980. Used with permission.

symptoms of *Dysthymic Disorder* (Table 1.3), which was previously referred to as *Depressive Neurosis*, are similar to those of a major depressive disorder, but are less severe, are of shorter duration, and do not include any psychotic features such as delusions and hallucinations. In addition, it is important to note that the criteria for *Dysthymic Disorder* require that the individual has been bothered by these depressive symptoms at least intermittently for 2 years.

Subtypes of Depression. In addition to these diagnostic categories, numerous subtypes of depression have also been described (e.g., psychotic, neurotic, reactive, involutional, agitated, presenile, acute, and chronic). Three of the more widely used distinctions are those between unipolar and bipolar depression, between primary and secondary depression, and between endogenous and nonendogenous depression.

Table 1.3. DSM-III Diagnostic Criteria: Dysthymic Disorder

A. During the past two years (or one year for children and adolescents) the individual has been bothered most or all of the time by symptoms characteristic of the depressive syndrome but that are not of sufficient severity and duration to meet the criteria for a major depressive episode (although a major depressive episode may be superimposed on Dysthymic Disorder).

B. The manifestations of the depressive syndrome may be relatively persistent or separated by periods of normal mood lasting a few days to a few weeks, but no more than a few months at a time.

C. During the depressive periods there is either prominent depressed mood (e.g., sad, blue, down in the dumps, low) or marked loss of interest or pleasure in all, or almost all, usual activities and pastimes.

D. During the depressive periods at least three of the following symptoms are present:
  1. insomnia or hypersomnia
  2. low energy level or chronic tiredness
  3. feelings of inadequacy, loss of self-esteem, or self-deprecation
  4. decreased effectiveness or productivity at school, work, or home
  5. decreased attention, concentration, or ability to think clearly
  6. social withdrawal
  7. loss of interest in or enjoyment of pleasurable activities
  8. irritability or excessive anger (in children, expressed toward parents or caretakers)
  9. inability to respond with apparent pleasure to praise or rewards
  10. less active or talkative than usual, or feels slowed down or restless
  11. pessimistic attitude toward the future, brooding about past events, or feeling sorry for self
  12. tearfulness or crying
  13. recurrent thought of death or suicide

E. Absence of psychotic features, such as delusions, hallucinations, or incoherence, or loosening of associations.

F. If the disturbance is superimposed on a preexisting mental disorder, such as Obsessive Compulsive Disorder or Alcohol Dependence, the depressed mood, by virtue of its intensity or effect on functioning, can be clearly distinguished from the individual's usual mood.

Source: American Psychiatric Association. *Diagnostic and Statistical Manual of Mental Disorders*, 3rd Ed., Washington, DC: APA, 1980. Used with permission.

The unipolar-bipolar dichotomy, one of the most widely accepted subdivisions of depression, rests on the proposition that depressions with and without manic periods should be viewed as distinct disorders. Unipolar is commonly defined as one depressive episode or a history of only depressive episodes.* In contrast, bipolar disorder is characterized by both manic and depressive episodes, either separately or concurrently. Although the utility of the unipolar-bipolar distinction is well established and generally supported empirically, this dichotomy is not without its difficulties. For example, although the symptoms associated with manic episodes clearly differ from depressive symptoms, the distinction between unipolar depression and the depressive phase of bipolar dis-

---

*It is also possible, although much rarer, to have a unipolar diagnosis based on one manic episode or a history of only manic episodes.

order is much less clear. Furthermore, although most researchers agree that bipolar depression has a stronger genetic component than does unipolar depression, other contrasts are less striking. Finally, as Abrams and Taylor (1980) note, bipolar depressions are more similar to *endogenous* unipolar depressions than to *nonendogenous* unipolar depression (see below), and the unipolar-bipolar distinction has thus proven not to be as clear-cut as was originally hoped.

The distinction between primary and secondary depression was originally advanced by Munro (1966) and emphasized more recently by Robins and Guze (1972). The crux of this distinction essentially involved the presence or absence of a preexisting, nonaffective psychiatric disorder or incapacitating medical illnesses. Primary depression was characterized as a full depressive syndrome which met the criteria for major depression *in the absence* of other psychiatric or medical disorders. In contrast, secondary depression referred broadly to depressive symptoms occurring subsequent to or superimposed on any other psychiatric or medical disorder. This distinction was based on the recognition that depressive syndromes frequently accompany or follow certain psychiatric or physical disorders, such as alcoholism and anxiety disorder. The primary-secondary distinction has received support from a number of investigators, although as Leber, Beckham, and Danker-Brown (1985) note, the diagnosis of secondary depression identifies such a heterogeneous group of patients that the utility of the distinction is likely to be limited.

A final distinction to be considered is that between endogenous and nonendogenous, or reactive, depression. Whereas endogenous depression is characterized by severely depressed mood, depressive delusions and/or hallucinations, psychomotor retardation or agitation, pathological guilt, and disorders of sleep, appetite, and other bodily functions, these symptoms are either attenuated or absent altogether in reactive depression, which is also typically associated with an environmental precipitant. Furthermore, as will be seen in Chapter 4, endogenous depressions seem to respond better to antidepressant medication than do nonendogenous depressions. Although recent studies (Helms & Smith, 1983) support the consistency of the endogenous-reactive distinction, others (Benjaminsen, 1981) do not, and the clinical utility of this distinction also remains an unresolved issue.

We recognize that this brief description of the diagnosis and classification of depression is somewhat confusing, but unfortunately, it is nonetheless accurate. As Sinaikin (1985, p. 199) recently stated in reviewing the diverse diagnostic criteria for depression:

> It is apparent, then, that at this point in time the clinician cannot possibly hope to glean from the literature a set of discrete, mutually exclusive, and valid diagnostic categories. Rather, the clinician must be willing to tolerate some degree of diagnostic overlap, forego considerations of ultimate nosological validity, and instead judge each diagnostic category on the basis of the therapeutic and prognostic information that it conveys.

It is appropriate at this point to note that depression in this guidebook refers not necessarily to a formal clinical diagnosis but instead to a more general syndrome of depressive symptoms that includes dysphoric mood, self-devaluation, and loss of pleasure or interest in usual activities. This constellation of symptoms may be manifested to some degree by individuals suffering from a variety of disorders other than depression, such as anxiety, phobias, and alcoholism. As will be seen in the Afterword, however, the therapeutic approach outlined in this guidebook is not necessarily limited to depression, but may instead be applicable in modified forms to a diverse range of symptomatic disturbances.

Epidemiology

The following section of this chapter is devoted to a brief examination of epidemiological factors associated with depression. We hope to impart to the clinician information that will increase awareness of the diverse demographic factors that have been implicated in the expression of depressive symptoms. With a working knowledge of these variables, the therapist can be more cognizant and sensitive to the possibility of depression when assessing and treating individuals who belong in these demographic categories.

Studies in Europe and in the United States indicate that in the adult population approximately 18 to 26% of females and 8 to 12% of males have at some time in their lives experienced a major depressive episode (Weissman & Boyd, 1983), and that one-third of these individuals are hospitalized as a result of their depression. Dysthymic disorder is even more common. Therefore, there are currently between 10 and 14 million people in the United States who have a diagnosable depression (Weissman & Boyd, 1983). Again, although only a minority of individuals experience depressive symptoms of sufficient severity and persistence that they meet the strict formal diagnostic criteria of a clinical disorder, many more experience distinct depressive moods. Bradburn (1975) has estimated that 40% of the population report feelings of depression, disappointment, and unhappiness over the course of a year.

There are specific demographic variables associated with a relatively high incidence of depression. The more important of these variables will be discussed, and the manner in which each is related to depression will be indicated.

Gender. Perhaps the most consistent and robust finding in the field of depression is that depressive disorder occurs more frequently in women than in men, at approximately a 2:1 ratio (Weissman & Klerman, 1977). Although it is beyond the scope of this guidebook to attempt to account for this increased incidence of depression in women, it may be instructive to consider briefly some explanations that have been offered. We should first note that a number of investigators have suggested that the sex differences in depression may be an artifact of either differential reporting biases of males and females or differences in the ways in which males and females express depression (the depressive equivalents alternative). In general, neither of these explanations fully accounts for the observed gender differences in depression, and the interested reader is referred to Gove and Geerkin (1977) and Petty and Nasrallah (1981) for extended discussion.

In an attempt to account for the greater observed incidence of depression in females, biological theories focus on the female hormonal system, implicating estrogen and progesterone in the etiology of depression, or on a genetic predisposition to depression in females. The empirical evidence linking hormonal changes directly to depression is equivocal, and certainly not strong enough to account for the high incidence of depression in females. The support for the genetic explanation is similarly weak. Cloninger, Christiansen, Reich, and Gottesman (1978) argue that depressed *males* are more genetically deviant than are depressed females, and Merikangas, Weissman, and Pauls (1985) recently found that the relatives of male and female depressed persons were equally likely to be diagnosed as depressed. Therefore, there is currently no consistent evidence that the observed gender differences in depression are due to biological factors.

More psychosocially oriented theories focus on the sex roles of women, their lower social status, and their greater experience of role conflict in society. Gove and Tudor (1973) have suggested that the importance of the traditional female role as homemaker is decreasing, and that the gender differences in the expression of depression may be a result of this trend or of the conflicts experienced by women in choosing between work and home. In support of this postulation, Aneshensel, Frerichs, and Clark (1981) found that the greater incidence of depression in females holds only for married and employed women. An interesting formulation by Radloff (1975) maintains that the gender difference in depression is due to socialized feelings of learned helplessness among women. None of these theories, however, has received unqualified support, and the evidence is, at best, confusing.

Age. In general, the incidence of depression rises shortly after puberty, peaks between the ages of 25 and 44 years, and declines somewhat in later years (Weissman, Myers, & Thompson, 1981). With respect to gender, depression seems to first occur at a younger age in women than in men. Although the incidence of depression in women is greatest under 35 years of age and tends to decrease with age, the peak prevalence of depressive symptoms in men appears in the 45-to-65-year age range. Moreover, it appears that different types of depression are associated with different age-related patterns of incidence. For example, bipolar disorder has an earlier average age of onset (around the late 20s) than does non-bipolar depression, which has a peak incidence around the middle to late 30s.

Marital Status. The relationship between marital status and depression is complex. Gove, Hughes, and Briggs Style's (1983) review of the literature suggests that married individuals generally have better mental and physical health than do unmarried persons. Interestingly, however, this protective function of marriage appears to be more strongly operative in males than in females; Radloff (1975) reported that although there are no consistent gender differences in depression among the widowed and never married, significantly more women than men are depressed among the married and the divorced or separated. This general pattern of results, however, must be qualified by Renne's (1971) findings. Renne reported that both men and women who are unhappily married are more depressed than are their separated and divorced counterparts. The relationship between depression and marital status is further complicated by the psychological health of the spouse. Collins, Kreitman, Nelson, and Troop (1971) found that the wives of neurotic outpatients reported five times more physical and psychological problems than did the wives of matched normal controls. Although some investigators have postulated an "assortative mating" hypothesis to account for these findings (i.e., spouses of the patients were disturbed *before* they married), other findings diminish the viability of this explanation; although recently married women did not differ on measures of psychopathology, almost 50% of patients' wives married more than 17 years showed conspicuous morbidity. Therefore, it appears that living with a psychiatric patient can have a significant effect on the spouse, a finding that will have important implications for the conceptualization and treatment of depression.

Socioeconomic Status. Investigators consistently report that most depressive disorders are found more often in individuals from lower socioeconomic backgrounds than in those from higher socioeconomic classes (cf. Brown & Harris, 1978). A single exception is bipolar disorder, which is more strongly associated with a high socioeconomic status (Weissman et al., 1981). Among married women, those who have low-income, low-status jobs and young children seem to be at highest risk for developing clinically significant depression, although married working-class women who do not work outside the home and who have two or three children are also at risk.

Suicide. Over the last quarter century, there has been a worldwide increase in suicide attempts. Indeed, the suicide rate among adolescents and young adults has increased almost tenfold, to the point that now 12% of all suicide attempts in the United States are made by adolescents. At present, 55,000 suicides are reported in the United States every year. It has been estimated that between 30 and 80% of suicides are completed by persons who would have been diagnosed as having a major depression. Women, who have a greater incidence of depression than do men, also demonstrate a suicide attempt rate that is five times higher than that for men. Paradoxically, however, and likely because of the difference in suicide methods, men have a completed suicide rate three times higher than that for women.

Interpersonal Risk Factors in Depression

We have presented these findings concerning epidemiological aspects of depression to give the clinician a sense of the various ways in which diverse demographic factors are associated with this disorder. In the final major section of this chapter, this line of exploration will continue, with a discussion of risk factors and concomitants of depression that are explicitly interpersonal. Our purpose in presenting this discussion is twofold. First, we hope to demonstrate the importance of interpersonal factors in the development and maintenance of depression and, in so doing, to help the clinician become aware of the influential role played by these factors. Second, and equally important, we begin to provide the rationale and empirical basis for an interpersonal conceptualization of depression. In doing so, the stage is set and the reader prepared for the description of depression detailed in Chapter 2 and for the ensuing interpersonal assessment and treatment strategies. The following discussion will focus on the role and impact of interpersonal risk factors for depression such as the experience of early loss and parental conflict, stressful interpersonal life events and family circumstances, lack of social support, and marital discord or separation.

Effects of Early Interpersonal Experiences: I. Loss. The issue of whether early loss of a parent places an individual at increased risk for depression later in life has been the focus of long-standing controversy. Since Freud first commented on the similarity between bereavement and depression, investigators have conducted research designed to examine this relationship more systematically. Data have been generated to support both sides of the question; indeed, of four recent reviews of this literature, two concluded that there is an association between parental loss and depression (Lloyd, 1980; Nelson, 1982) and two concluded that no such relationship exists (Crook & Eliot, 1980; Tennant, Bebbington, & Hurry, 1980).

The results of many of these studies are striking. Brown (1961) found that 41% of a large sample of depressed adult psychiatric patients had lost a parent through death before the age of 15, an incidence twice that of a control group of medical patients and three times that of the general population in England. Similarly, Frommer and O'Shea (1973) found that women who had suffered separation from or the death of either parent before age 11 had an incidence of postpartum depression that was twice as great as that of women who had not. Other investigators, however, have been unable to replicate these results. Munro (1966) and Jacobson, Fasman, and DiMascio (1975) found no difference in the incidence of childhood parental death between depressed and nondepressed subjects. In a similar investigation, Abrahams and Whitlock (1969), in comparing the incidence of childhood bereavement in depressed psychiatric patients and matched general hospital outpatients, found no differences between the two groups with respect to early parental death.

It is difficult from the results of these studies to draw firm conclusions concerning the strength of the relationship between early loss of or separation from a parent and the development of subsequent depression. Certainly, numerous factors have been implicated in the etiology of depression, and consequently, one would not expect to find that all or even a majority of individuals experiencing depressive symptomatology had lost a parent early in their childhood. Moreover, the quality of the parenting received before the loss and the quality of the caretaking that replaced that lost through parental separation or death are important factors that must be considered. Nevertheless, in light of the equivocal nature of these findings, clinicians must remain sensitive to the possibility of depressive symptoms emerging or becoming exacerbated in individuals who have experienced the loss of a parent early in their childhood.

Effects of Early Interpersonal Experiences: II. Family Environment. This section focuses on the characteristics of the early family life of individuals who, as adults years later, have experienced one or more depressive episodes. To date, no research has been conducted in which children and their families were assessed and the children followed into their adult years in order to examine childhood predictors of adult depression. Consequently, in describing the childhood environments of depressed adults, we must rely in large part on retrospective research. As will be discussed, there are difficulties with the interpretation of findings from this type of study. Nevertheless, the results of such studies are remarkably consistent across methodologies in suggesting that the early lives of depressed adults were marked by discord and problematic parenting.

Two early studies form the foundation of the literature examining the childhood environments of depressed patients. Cohen, Baker, Cohen, Fromm-Reichmann, and Weigart (1954) described the results of an intensive psychoanalytic investigation of the family background, interpersonal relationships, and personality characteristics of 12 manic-depressive patients. They reported that a consistent characteristic of these families during the patients' childhoods was that they felt in some way "set apart" and socially inferior to other families. Cohen et al. (1954) also described how the patient's incessant demands and lack of empathy seemed to create feelings of hostility and frustration in those around him. Gibson (1957) replicated these findings and reported that the manic-depressive patients came from families in which there was a marked striving for prestige. Moreover, the patients were typically the children chosen in these families to be the "instruments" for their parents' prestige needs.

More recent investigations conducted from a variety of theoretical perspectives have converged to corroborate and expand the results of these two studies, suggesting that depressed individuals have had more aversive childhoods than have nondepressed persons. Raskin, Boothe, Reatig, Schulterbrandt, and Odle (1971) administered the Children's Report of Parental Behavior Inventory to depressed patients and matched nondepressed controls to assess their childhood perceptions of their own parents. The depressed patients rated their parents as less positively involved in their children's activities, less affectionate, and more negatively controlling. They also described feeling less accepted by their parents and more emotionally deprived during adolescence. Corroborating these results, Abrahams and Whitlock (1969) and Jacobson et al. (1975) found that compared with normal controls, depressed patients reported greater parental rejection and abuse, higher parental discord, and less parental affection. Interestingly, Jacobson et al. (1975) also found a higher incidence of psychiatric illness in the parents of depressed patients. Finally, Parker (1981) used the Parental Bonding Instrument (PBI) to assess self-reported parental care and overprotection in unipolar and bipolar depressed patients and matched nonpsychiatric controls. Parker found that although the bipolar depressed patients could not be distinguished from the nonpsychiatric controls, the unipolar depressed patients reported significantly less parental care and greater maternal overprotection. Furthermore, depressive experience in the nonclinical group was associated with low parental care and parental overprotection.

Studies such as these indicate that the childhood of depressed patients relative to that of nondepressed controls is more likely to have included parental rejection, abuse, inattention, family discord, and a higher rate of parental emotional disturbance. Moreover, a number of studies suggest that it is unlikely that these findings reflect a negatively distorted recall by the depressed person rather than a veridical picture of a problematic early home life. Parker (1981) reported that the patient-reported associations between low maternal care or maternal overprotection and subsequent depression were confirmed by independent reports from the patients' mothers. Furthermore, investigators examining the characteristics and functioning of parents of depressed children have found an elevated level of psychopathological disorders in these parents (Brumback, Dietz-Schmidt, & Weinberg, 1977; Puig-Antich, Blau, Marx, Greenhill, & Chambers, 1978; see Digdon & Gotlib, 1985, for a detailed review of studies in this area).

Because the families of depressed children appear to be remarkably similar to those described by depressed adults in recalling their childhood experiences, there is a high probability that the early family environments of depressed patients are indeed characterized by parental deviance, tension, and rejection or lack of involvement. We believe that there are three important implications of this body of research for the therapist who is treating a family with a depressed adult. First, the clinician must remain aware of the great possibility that the depressed person who comes to therapy has experienced a problematic or conflictful early family history. Therefore, in interviewing the depressed patient it is important that the therapist elicit a detailed history from the individual and take this early experience into consideration when conceptualizing the depressed patient's present family situation.

Second, we believe that it is important to consider negative reports made by the depressed person to be veridical perceptions, rather than statements to be dismissed as "cognitive distortions" (cf. Coyne & Gotlib, 1983, in press). There is little question that depressed individuals emit a high proportion of negative statements and often exhibit the "negative cognitive triad" described by Beck, Rush, Shaw, and Emery (1979): a negative view of the self, the world, and the future. The issue is whether these negative statements have a basis in reality. Our position is that since depressed individuals often face negative or depressing life situations, the therapist should explore these negative reports and be prepared for the possibility that they represent realistic appraisals of negative circumstances. Certainly we are not suggesting that therapies that focus primarily on the depressed person's cognitions are ineffective. Rather, we believe that this focus can be profitably expanded and complemented by an interpersonal systems approach that also attempts to change the behaviors and responses of those individuals who comprise the depressed person's immediate social environment.

The final point we wish to make here involves the children of these depressed patients. Numerous studies that have examined the functioning of children of depressed parents uniformly have found a significant impact of parental depression on the health and development of the child. (See Coyne & Gotlib, 1986, for a detailed review of these investigations.) In fact, the results of these investigations represent one important rationale for the practice of the interpersonal systems approach described in this guidebook. In light of these findings, it is imperative that the therapist treating a family with a depressed parent be sensitive to the effects of this depression on the patient's children, and be prepared to take steps to decrease the magnitude and longterm significance of these effects.

Effects of Recent Stressful Life Events. In recent years there has been a growing interest in the relationship between stressful life events and various somatic and psychological disorders. In examining the relationship between life events and depression, Paykel et al. (1969) found that depressed patients reported having experienced three times as many stressful events in the 6 months before the onset of depression as did nondepressed controls during the same period. Similarly, Paykel and Tanner (1976) reported that in the month before relapse, the number of life events reported by those formerly depressed patients who subsequently relapsed was significantly higher than that reported by patients who remained nondepressed. Both O'Hara (1986) and Paykel, Emms, Fletcher, and Rassaby (1980) found that women who experienced postpartum depression reported an elevated number of stressful life events in the prepartum and early postpartum periods. Interestingly, in addition to the *number* of life events experienced, depressed subjects in these investigations were also differentiated from nondepressed subjects by the *nature* of the events: the majority of events whose frequency discriminated between these two groups of subjects were undesirable in nature and typically involved exits of persons from the subjects' lives (cf. Paykel et al., 1969).

There is clearly a relationship between stressful life events, particularly interpersonal events, and depression. Unfortunately, the magnitude of this relationship is typically quite small, and a large portion of the variance in level of depression is therefore not accounted for by measures of cumulative stressful life events. One solution to this problem is to broaden the concept of life events to include the less dramatic but more frequent demands or hassles of day-to-day living (cf. DeLongis, Coyne, Dakof, Folkman, and Lazarus, 1982). Even with this increased explanatory power, however, it was difficult to explain why not everyone who experiences undesirable events or hassles demonstrates subsequent depressive symptomatology. In addressing this issue, investigators turned their attention to factors that may mediate the relationship between stressful life events and depression. Interestingly, one of the most viable constructs in resolving this issue has proven to be interpersonal: that of social support.

Social Support. Social support is generally defined in terms of both the size of the individual's social network and number of ties, and the individual's perception of being supported and cared for by others, wanted, and loved. In one of the first studies to suggest that social support may moderate the relationship between life events and depression, Nuckolls, Cassel, and Kaplan (1972) investigated the roles of stressful life events and social support with respect to birth complications and found an interaction between life change scores and social support. Specifically, of those women who reported high life change scores both before and during pregnancy, those who also reported high social support during this time experienced fewer birth complications than did those who reported low social support.

Subsequent research has corroborated these findings. Pearlin, Lieberman, Menaghan, and Mullan (1981) found that social support had an indirect effect on depression through its influence on such factors as level of self-esteem before the period of stress. Similarly, Monroe, Imhoff, Wise, and Harris (1983) found an interaction between social support and a desirability-undesirability dimension of stressful events in predicting depressive symptoms in a population of university students. Finally, in a major epidemiological study of depressive symptomatology in a large British community, Brown and Harris (1978) found that of all individuals who experienced a large number of stressful life events, those having a close and confiding relationship were less likely to become depressed than were those not receiving this kind of social support. In fact, Brown and Harris (1978) also identified three other social factors which, in conjunction with major life events, increased a woman's vulnerability to depression: being unemployed, having three or more children in the home, and losing a mother before age 11 (recall the findings of the literature reviewed earlier in this chapter concerning the relationship between early death of a parent and subsequent depression).

Perhaps the most impressive work examining the direct relationship between depression and social support, however, was that reported by Henderson, Byrne, and Duncan-Jones (1981) in Australia. In a large-scale study assessing the quality and quantity of interpersonal contacts reported by depressed individuals, they found that depressed persons spent as much time with their primary group as did matched nondepressed controls, but that a higher proportion of their interactions were experienced as affectively unpleasant. Moreover, compared with the nondepressed controls, the depressed subjects reported having fewer close friends and fewer contacts outside the household.

It is apparent, therefore, that a lack of supportive interpersonal relationships may act directly, or indirectly in combination with stressful life events, in contributing to the development of depressive symptomatology. Clearly, depressed individuals perceive their social relationships to be problematic in many respects. To gain a better understanding of the interpersonal relationships of depressed individuals, investigators have examined both the behavior of depressed persons engaged in social interactions and the responses of other people to these depressed persons.

The Social Behavior of Depressives

Over the last decade, increasing attention has been given to the elucidation of interpersonal processes in depression. In this context, theories have been formulated to explain the etiology or maintenance of depression in behavioral terms. Lewinsohn (1974) postulated that a low rate of response-contingent positive reinforcement — a result of the individual's poor social skills — elicits symptoms of depression. Although research has generally not supported the etiological role of poor social skills, studies have nevertheless identified various social skills deficits associated with depression. Gotlib and Asarnow (1979) found depressed persons to be less skillful than their nondepressed counterparts at solving interpersonal problems. In interactions with others, depressed persons maintain less eye contact than do nondepressed controls, are less verbally productive, speak more softly and more monotonously, and take longer to respond to others' verbalizations (Gotlib, 1982; Gotlib & Robinson, 1982). The conversational behavior of depressed persons is frequently self-focused and negatively toned; in an interpersonal situation they communicate self-devaluation, sadness, and helplessness (Biglan et al., 1985).

These studies clearly indicate that depressed individuals demonstrate an interpersonal style in social situations that differs markedly from that exhibited by nondepressed persons. Recent studies have broadened the scope of these findings by examining the behaviors of persons interacting with depressed individuals. The impetus for many of these studies was provided by Coyne's (1976b) interpersonal description of depression. Essentially, Coyne contends that depressive symptoms may be maintained or exacerbated by the responses of significant others with whom the depressed person interacts. A sequence of behavior is initiated by the depressed person's initial demonstration of depression. Individuals in the depressed person's social environment initially respond with genuine concern and support. If the depressed person's symptomatic behavior continues, however, others with whom they interact themselves begin to feel depressed, anxious, and frustrated or hostile, feelings that are communicated subtly (and mixed with positive qualifiers) to the depressed person. When the depressed individual observes these negative or discrepant messages, she or he becomes increasingly symptomatic in an attempt to regain the initial support. Unfortunately, this reaction simply makes further interactions even more aversive for others in the social environment. Coyne suggests that this "deviation-amplifying" process continues until, in the extreme, people either withdraw completely from the depressed person or have him withdrawn through hospitalization.

Studies now provide empirical support for aspects of this interactional description of depression (e.g., Coyne, 1976a; Gotlib & Beatty, 1985; Gotlib & Meltzer, in press; Gotlib & Robinson, 1982; Howes & Hokanson, 1979; Strack & Coyne, 1983). These studies suggest that depressed persons have an aversive interpersonal style to which others respond with negativity and rejection. As Coyne, Kahn, and Gotlib (in press) note, however, much of this research has been conducted with analogue populations or procedures, and neither the contribution of these findings to our understanding of the role of more intimate relationships in the development and maintenance of clinical depression, nor their implications for therapy are addressed in these studies. To examine these issues, we must turn to investigations assessing the marital and family relationships of depressed individuals.

Marital Discord

Several studies have underscored the importance of examining intimate relationships in depression. A number of investigations have provided considerable evidence of the relationship between depression and marital difficulties (e.g., Crowther, 1985). Sager, Gundlach, and Kremer (1968) estimated that one-half of all patients who seek psychotherapy do so because of marital problems; from a different perspective, Rush, Shaw, and Khatami (1980) have suggested that in at least 30% of couples experiencing marital problems, one spouse is clinically depressed. Paykel et al. (1969) found that the most frequent life event preceding the onset of depression was a reported increase in arguments with the spouse. Similarly, Vaughn and Leff (1976) found that depressed persons are more vulnerable than are schizophrenics to family tension and to hostile statements made by family members, and Schless, Schwartz, Goetz, and Mendels (1974) demonstrated that this vulnerability to marriage- and family-related stresses persists after depressed patients recover. Consistent with these results, Merikangas (1984) reported a divorce rate in depressed patients 2 years after discharge to be nine times that of the general population. Finally, as already noted, recent investigations have reported that the lack of an intimate, confiding relationship with a spouse or boyfriend increased women's vulnerability to depression (e.g., Brown & Harris, 1978).

These investigations have provided the foundation for studies that examine more systematically the marital relationships of depressed persons. Weissman et al. (e.g., Rounsaville, Weissman, Prusoff, & Herceg-Baron, 1979; Weissman & Paykel, 1974) conducted structured interviews with depressed female psychiatric outpatients over the course of their treatment, and found that they reported greatest impairment as wives and mothers, expressing problems in the areas of affection, dependency, sexual functioning, and communication. The marital relationships of depressed women were characterized by friction and hostility, and the women tended to be more dependent, less assertive, and less affectionate toward their spouses than were matched normal controls. In addition, Rounsaville et al. (1979) found that the presence of marital disputes was an important determinant of treatment outcome. Those women who came to treatment and who also had marital disputes demonstrated less improvement in their symptoms and social functioning and were more likely to relapse after a course of individual therapy. Furthermore, at a 1-year follow-up, these marital problems had persisted, even though the women were no longer severely depressed and had improved in other areas of functioning. These findings led Weissman and Paykel to conclude that " . . . the marital relation was a significant barometer of clinical status" (p. 94).

Subsequent research has corroborated Weissman's results. In one of the first observational studies of depressed patients, Hinchliffe, Hooper, and Roberts (1978) examined the behavior of 20 depressed persons interacting with their spouses and with opposite-sex strangers. Compared with the interactions of nondepressed surgical patients, couples with a depressed spouse showed greater conflict, tension, and negative expressiveness. The interactions of depressed patients were also characterized by more frequent interruptions and pauses. Interestingly, the depressed subjects were more verbally productive and tended to laugh more often with a stranger than with their spouse. After recovery, the interactions of the 10 male depressed patients were less negative, resembling those of the surgical controls; consistent with Weissman and Paykel's (1974) findings, however, the depressed women continued to show high levels of tension and negative expressiveness.

In a similar study, Hautzinger, Linden, and Hoffman (1982) assessed the interactions of 26 couples seeking marital therapy, 13 of whom had a depressed spouse. Consistent with Hinchliffe's results, Hautzinger et al. (1982) found that communication patterns in couples with a depressed spouse were more disturbed than were those in couples without a depressed partner. Spouses of depressed partners seldom agreed with their spouse, offered help in an ambivalent manner, and evaluated their depressed partner negatively. Drawing on their own similar findings, Merikangas, Ranelli, and Kupfer (1979) suggested that the behavior of the patients' spouses may be as influential in predicting clinical outcome as the patients' own symptoms and behaviors. Biglan et al. (1985) reported that in marital interactions, depressed women exhibited higher rates of depressive behavior (e.g., self-derogation and complaints) and lower rates of problem-solving behavior than did their husbands and nondepressed control spouses. Biglan et al. found further that the patients' depressive behavior appeared to be functional in reducing their spouses' aversive behavior, and suggested that these findings "underscore the importance of marital interactions in depression" (p. 432).

Finally, four recent studies found the interactions of depressed persons and their spouses to be characterized by hostility. Arkowitz, Holliday, and Hutter (1982) found that following interactions with their wives, husbands of depressed women reported feeling more hostile than did husbands of psychiatric and nonpsychiatric control subjects. Similarly, Kahn, Coyne, and Margolin (1985) reported that couples with a depressed spouse were more sad and angry following marital interactions and experienced each other as more negative, hostile, mistrusting, and detached than did nondepressed couples. Kowalik and Gotlib (in press) had depressed and nondepressed psychiatric outpatients and nondepressed nonpsychiatric controls participate in an interactional task with their spouses. The depressed patients emitted more negative and less positive behaviors than did the nondepressed controls. In the fourth study, Gotlib (1986) found that during hospitalization, the interactions of depressed male and female psychiatric inpatients and their spouses were characterized by negative affect and hostility. By discharge, the interactions of the (formerly) depressed male patients and their spouses were much more positive. Interestingly, however, although the depressed women had improved significantly with respect to their level of depressive symptomatology, the post-discharge interactions of these women and their spouses were as negative and hostile as they had been during the patients' hospitalization. (See Gotlib & Hooley, in press, for a more detailed discussion of these studies.)

The Effects of Marital/Family Therapy for Depression

These descriptions of the problematic intimate relationships of depressed persons provided the impetus for investigations assessing the efficacy of therapies for depression aimed at improving the quality of the marital or family interactions. The concept of treating depression from a marital and/or family perspective is a relatively new one; consequently, a large body of outcome studies in this area does not exist. However, successful results have been reported using marital or family approaches to the treatment of depression. Considered collectively, these studies highlight the need for the therapist to treat the marital or family context as well as the depression.

In a series of case studies, Lewinsohn and his colleagues suggested that providing patients and their spouses with feedback about their interpersonal behaviors in the home can decrease the level of depression and improve interper-

sonal relationships. Lewinsohn and Atwood (1969) and Lewinsohn and Schaffer (1971) presented cases in which feedback about interpersonal behavior
between a depressed woman and her husband was used in combination with
conjoint marital therapy to effect behavioral change. The women's MMPI-
Depression scores decreased significantly and marital communication and family interactions improved.

McLean, Ogston, and Grauer (1973) examined the effects of a behaviorally-
oriented conjoint marital therapy on the valence of the marital communications
of 10 depressed outpatients and their spouses. At a 3-month follow-up, McLean
et al. (1973) found that compared with control couples receiving antidepressant
medication, individual psychotherapy, or both, depressed couples receiving the
conjoint marital treatment demonstrated a significant reduction in depressed
mood and a reduction in the frequency of their negative interchanges.

Both Hinchliffe et al. (1978) and Rush et al. (1980) reported successfully
treating depression by involving the spouse in a cognitive couples intervention.
The sample sizes in these two investigations were small, and neither utilized a
control group; nevertheless, in both these studies the treatment clearly was
effective in ameliorating the depression and improving dysfunctional marital
interactions.

In one of the better studies in this area, Friedman (1975) conducted a 12-
week therapy program designed to assess the separate and combined effects of
amitriptyline and "marital and family oriented psychotherapy" in depressed
patients. Depressed patients were randomly assigned to treatment groups and
assessed with respect to depression symptom severity, global symptomatic
improvement, and marital and family relations. Both drug and marital therapy
showed substantial advantages over their respective control conditions (placebo
drug and minimal individual contact). Furthermore, there also appeared to be
differential effects of these two modes of treatment. Whereas drug therapy was
associated with early improvement in clinical symptoms, marital therapy was
associated with longer-term improvement in the patient's participation and performance in family role tasks, reduction of hostility in the family, and improvement in the patient's perceptions of the quality of the marital relationship.
Friedman concludes that it is possible that "the marital therapy approach is more
effective and quicker to achieve a positive effect with neurotically depressed
married patients than is either individual or peer group therapy" (p. 634).

A similar pattern of results was obtained in a pilot study conducted by Beach
and O'Leary (1986), who compared the treatment effectiveness for depression
of conjoint behavioral marital therapy, individual cognitive therapy, and a wait-
ing-list control condition. Although wives receiving behavioral marital therapy
and those receiving individual cognitive therapy both showed clinically significant reductions in depressive symptomatology, only those wives receiving the
conjoint marital therapy also showed a marked reduction in marital discord.
Interestingly, the results of Friedman's and Beach and O'Leary's studies are con-

sistent with findings from the Yale group. Weissman (1979) noted that although antidepressant medication combined with intrapsychic individual psychotherapy can reduce depressive symptomatology, it has little effect on interpersonal difficulties and social adjustment. Indeed, Weissman and Klerman (1973) reported that despite symptomatic improvement, marital difficulties were the single problem area discussed most frequently by depressed women in maintenance therapy. In a 4-year follow-up of these women, Bothwell and Weissman (1977) reported that although the women were asymptomatic with respect to depression, they continued to report problems with marital disputes.

Overall, it is clear that the marital and family relationships of depressed persons are characterized in large part by negative affect, tension, and hostility. Furthermore, evidence suggests that although individual therapy may be effective in reducing the level of depressive symptomatology, it does not ameliorate difficulties in interpersonal functioning; marital or family therapy may be indicated to both relieve symptoms and to reduce the marital/family discord of depressed persons. As we have seen, depressed individuals report experiencing more stressful life events than do nondepressed persons, and it is likely that the marital interactions of depressed persons represent a further source of stress. Although adequate social support could buffer some of the effects of this stress, the research we have reviewed suggests that depressed persons also lack support outside of their families, engendering negative reactions and eroding support from those with whom they interact.

In this chapter, we have presented the results of a large number of studies. Although the findings of these investigations will take time to assimilate, our purpose in presenting this review was to sensitize the clinician to the wide range of interpersonal factors implicated in the etiology, maintenance, course, and treatment of depression. All evidence considered, the emerging picture of the depressed individual includes a difficult early environment, stressful life events (most particularly interpersonal losses), and current problematic marital, family, and social relationships and interactions. Moreover, these interpersonal difficulties appear to persist in the absence of interventions explicitly involving the spouse or family of the depressed person. There is therefore little doubt of the importance and relevance of adopting an interpersonal perspective in understanding the pervasive enigma of depression. In the chapters that follow, we will broaden this perspective to describe an interpersonal systems approach to the treatment of this disorder.

Chapter 2
An Interpersonal Systems Conceptualization of Depression

HISTORICAL PERSPECTIVE

The emergence of an interpersonal "systems" or family approach to conceptualizing human behavior and psychopathology resulted in part from a growing dissatisfaction with traditional psychoanalysis. Questions were being raised regarding the justification of the often prohibitive length of psychoanalytic treatment, its relatively high cost, and its often seemingly negligible changes (Hoffman, 1981). Combined with this declining interest in psychoanalysis, a number of independent historical events began to converge in the decade following World War II that were instrumental in the formation of the family therapy movement.

One influence emerged from a social/cultural context as a result of a sudden reuniting of families immediately following the end of the Second World War. With husbands returning from having served overseas, many families unexpectedly found themselves experiencing serious adjustment problems, which often resulted in emotional disturbance in one or more family members (e.g., marital conflict or delinquency in children). Consequently, it was often difficult to isolate the disorder to a single individual in the family, and therapists recognized the necessity of providing treatment for the whole family in order to deal adequately with the problems underlying the disturbance.

A second major influence on the emergence of family therapy was the interpersonal school of psychiatry developed by Harry Stack Sullivan. Sullivan trained under Adolph Meyer, who conceptualized mental disorders as reaction patterns to life situations. Meyer's psychobiological approach to understanding psychiatric disorders placed considerable emphasis on the patient's psychosocial and interpersonal experiences, and his influence on Sullivan is readily apparent. Sullivan devoted his clinical work to the understanding and treatment of schizophrenia. He believed that some of his schizophrenic patients had been rendered anxious as infants by their angry or disapproving mothers. Therefore, in contrast to the dominant intrapersonal models of schizophrenia, Sullivan proposed a conceptualization of schizophrenia that had as its focus the interpersonal environment of the patient. Although he did not treat families, Sullivan's writings, and, in particular, his interpersonal framework, served to inspire subsequent family theorists and therapists.

A third influence on the development of the family therapy movement was the seminal work of the Palo Alto group, which was investigating interpersonal communication patterns in families with a schizophrenic member. These investigators introduced the double-bind theory to explain the development of this disorder. A double-bind situation exists when an individual receives contradictory messages from another person; the individual is required to respond to the communication, but because of the contradictory nature of the original message, is unable to make a correct response. Frequent exposure to this type of stressful situation causes the individual to become confused and to feel rejected, until he ultimately learns to escape this aversive situation by responding with his own incongruent messages (i.e., schizophrenic language). Although empirical support for this conceptualization of schizophrenia has been equivocal, its importance lies in its recognition of and attention to faulty or pathological communication patterns among family members and, hence, in its emphasis on the significance of the role of the family in conceptualizing the development of this disorder. Indeed, the double-bind theory provided the impetus for investigators to consider many other disorders (e.g., anorexia nervosa, agoraphobia, and obesity) from a family perspective.

A final major influence on the emergence of family therapy was the growing interest in general systems theory, with its emphasis on the interrelatedness of all elements that comprise a "system." Although general systems theory was developed in the biological sciences, its applicability to the social sciences began to be appreciated in the early 1950s. According to this theory, a complex interactional system (e.g., a family) can only be fully understood by examining the relationship among the various components. No part of a system can move or change without affecting all of the other elements in the system. The importance of general systems theory to the family therapy movement rests on its view that individuals exist and operate as part of a system rather than in isolation, and that consequently, they can only be fully understood within the context of that system. Because general systems theory is a cornerstone of family therapy, it will be discussed in greater detail below.

The early use of the term *family therapy* originated from a belief that some contact with the patient's family helped the therapist to gain a better understanding of the patient's pathological condition. Essentially, the therapist met with family members to determine the impact they had on the identified patient.

Despite family involvement, however, therapy in these early years remained focused on the intrapsychic processes of the individual. Over time, the conceptualization and increasing definition of family therapy assumed a focus that placed greater emphasis on the role of the family in the development and maintenance of symptomatology in a family member. Both the patient's symptoms and the process of treatment began to be considered in terms of the social systems of which he or she was a part. Concurrent with this shift of focus, the traditional process of isolating the patients from their interpersonal and social contexts started to wane. An *inter-* rather than an *intra*personal model of pathology gained popularity, and the field of psychotherapy experienced a growing interest in conceptualizing psychiatric disorders in terms of family dynamics. Increasing emphasis was placed on the role of the family in producing pathology, and the family unit itself was considered the "patient" in need of treatment. As we noted earlier, this new view of the family drew heavily from the theoretical tenets of general systems theory formulated by von Bertalanffy (1950, 1968).

General Systems Theory

General systems theory is based on a group of assumptions regarding the formal organizational properties of systems. The theory essentially maintains that a system is more than a collection of separate parts; consequently, a system cannot be fully understood by examining only the individual elements that comprise it, no matter how extensive the examination. Rather, to completely understand a complex system, both the relationships among its various components and the underlying set of rules that govern the system must be considered. This theoretical perspective assumes that all systems have in common certain fundamental characteristics, and that these properties can be clearly and explicitly described and defined, irrespective of their content or context.

General systems theory also proposes that all systems have self-regulating feedback mechanisms that control their functioning in order to maintain a steady state. If the level of functioning falls below a certain acceptable level, then an action is required to raise that level. Similarly, if a system's activities exceed a given point, then a corrective measure that returns the system to its previous stable state is necessary. A frequently cited example of this principle is that of a thermostat set to a certain temperature. When the temperature of the room is at the set temperature, no action is required. If the room temperature falls too low, however, the thermostat activates the furnace, which continues to operate until the temperature has returned to its set point. Similarly, if the room temperature exceeds the set point, the thermostat shuts down the furnace to allow the temperature to drop. Systems theorists maintain that families also have a built-in thermostat, or self-regulating feedback mechanism, that operates to keep them in a state of homeostasis. If the family (or one of its members) begins to deviate, the family attempts to return itself to its "normal" level of functioning. It is when these attempts at self-regulation fail that the family seeks assistance.

The relevance of general systems theory as a framework for understanding human behavior and psychopathology can best be understood by outlining in greater detail the general concepts of this perspective as they have been applied to the field of family therapy. Five principles are described below.

1. *Mutual Causality.* In contrast to psychoanalytic theory, which views pathology as originating in the intrapsychic makeup of the individual and has a marked emphasis on linear causality (i.e., some early trauma or conflict is posited to have caused the present symptom), systems theory conceptualizes pathology as originating in the relationships among family members and maintains a concomitant emphasis on circular or mutual causality (i.e., the behavior of family members is mutually reactive and interactive). From this latter perspective, the behavior of the identified patient is conceptualized as only one component or element of a recursive sequence in which everyone's communications and actions form an ongoing meaningful choreography. Because family members do not exist in isolation from one another, changes in the behavior of one member affect the other family members. Indeed, deviation in the behavior of one family member is often a reaction to some change in another member's behavior, which in turn leads to additional changes. The interactional nature of problem development and maintenance then clearly assumes a circular or mutual causality. Therefore, in this perspective the development of problems is conceptualized as interactional rather than intrapsychic, and all members of the family system, rather than only the index patient, are viewed as being involved in the creation, maintenance, and modification of family behavior patterns.

2. *System Rules.* A second important concept of general systems theory as it applies to families involves the notion of rules. Families have rules that govern the relationships among their members and that define the parameters of acceptable and unacceptable behaviors and interactions. For example, families generally have rules about how to express and deal with conflict and anger, how to treat dad if he comes home from work in a sullen mood, how much and under what conditions affection can be expressed, who makes major decisions related to family activities, and about how children are to behave when guests visit. Indeed, there are family rules related to virtually every aspect of family functioning.

If a family undergoes a change, stress, or trauma that creates disequilibrium or chaos, the family must be sufficiently flexible to redefine its parameters in order to accommodate the required change; otherwise, some form of pathology will emerge. For example, a family might have a rule that every Saturday night is "family" night, during which time a special event is planned. If the family system becomes stressed by a developing adolescent who suddenly prefers to spend Saturday night with friends, the family must change that rule or "pathology" or symptomatic behavior will develop. This pathology may take the form of a rebellious or anorectic adolescent, a depressed mother, or an abusive father. Regardless of the symptom that develops, however, it is conceptualized as reflecting a breakdown in the family system rather than in a particular individual. The individual who develops the problematic behavior is simply viewed as the one "selected" by the family, for any of a number of reasons, to serve as the symptom bearer.

3. Adaptation to Change. A third area of application of general systems theory involves the family's ability to adapt to change, essentially an indication of the family's level of health. Since the inception of the family therapy movement, several attempts have been made to classify families along a functional/dysfunctional dimension (e.g., Bowen, 1981). An example of one such effort is the circumplex model of marital and family systems (Olson, Sprenkle, & Russell, 1979), which attempts to integrate numerous related concepts of family functioning. The circumplex model provides a comprehensive framework for conceptualizing and differentiating among various levels of family functioning, and it was developed to aid the clinician in assessing the family and in generating consequent treatment objectives. Essentially, this model postulates that families can be described in terms of two characteristics: cohesion and adaptability.

Family cohesion refers to the emotional closeness family members have with one another and the degree of autonomy experienced by individuals within the family system. At one extreme of family cohesion is *enmeshment*, characterized by overidentification with the family. Members of an enmeshed family are not allowed any autonomy, as independence is perceived by the rest of the family as rejection. Relationships outside the family are limited, in part because individuals generally lack the self-confidence and trust necessary to develop close relationships and in part because such attempts are discouraged by the other family members. Finally, members of an enmeshed family tend to react similarly and with fervor to emotional events, almost as if they were all part of the same emotional system. At the other extreme of family cohesion is *disengagement*, in which families have only minimal emotional involvement with one another and function in relatively autonomous ways. These families rarely display signs of affection, often appearing noticeably cool and aloof with each other. They share very little together, including time, interests, activities, and emotional closeness. Unlike those in enmeshed families, children in disengaged families become quite independent at an early age. Because of the impoverished emotional and communicational alliances among family members, however, children in disengaged families are limited in their capacity to form close relationships.

The second dimension of family functioning is adaptability, which refers to the family's ability to make structural, role, and rule changes in response to situational and developmental demands. At one extreme of adaptability is *rigidity*.

Rigid parents adhere to an authoritarian style of parenting, and it is virtually always one parent who makes decisions in the family. Families adhere to a rigid rule system that is strictly enforced, and there is only limited opportunity to negotiate either plans or decisions among family members. At the other extreme of family adaptability is *chaos*, characterized by a lack of clear leadership. A parent will on one occasion assume a role of responsibility, but on another occasion abdicate that responsibility. Children in these chaotic families rarely know what to expect; they lack clear guidelines and boundaries from their parents. Finally, discipline in these families is inconsistent, a practice that reinforces the children's tendency to engage in endless attempts to negotiate. These negotiations, however, are often in vain because of both the lack of clear direction or leadership and the dramatic role shifts in the family with respect to the individual who assumes decision-making responsibility.

According to the circumplex model, the healthiest families are those that function midway between the extremes on both dimensions (i.e., those relatively involved or connected families who also allow individual autonomy and who are able to respond to stressful demands with an optimal balance of flexibility and structure). The importance of this conceptual framework in helping to understand families will be underscored in Chapters 4, 5, and 6, in which we discuss assessment issues, treatment goals, and strategies and techniques for intervention.

4. Function of the Symptom. A fourth area of the relevance of general systems theory to the family involves the postulation that the development of symptomatic behavior may serve a specific purpose or function within the family. A related assumption is that individuals and families that develop symptomatic behaviors vary in their "need" to maintain that dysfunctional behavior. The reasoning behind these formulations follows from a position espoused by strategic family therapists: in most cases, no matter why or how the dysfunctional behavior is triggered, it will persist only if it is maintained and supported by the individual's current behaviors and by his interactions with others. In some cases, depression in an individual may persist because of family members' well-intentioned attempts to help the depressed person return to his previous state of health. Therefore, as Watzlawick, Weakland, and Fisch (1974) propose, family members initially endeavor to cheer up the depressed person, but their attempts generally backfire, with the depressed person becoming even more depressed. Family members react to this symptomatic exacerbation by intensifying their efforts to help or cheer up the depressed person. This behavior inadvertently puts pressure on the depressed person to change, and it may have the unintended effect of making him feel inadequate, a disappointment to the family. In turn, family members may respond to any small changes either with overenthusiastic optimism or with anger and frustration at the seemingly meager improvement. The depressed person reacts to both of these responses by sinking even lower. Paradoxically, the more the family members attempt to "help" the depressed person, the more depressed and helpless she or he becomes. The following example will help to illustrate this concept.

> Mr. Hill's employer suffered a financial setback and was forced to lay off and reassign staff. Although Mr. Hill was in a senior management position and had a solid track record as a competent supervisor, he was reassigned to a non-management position. He experienced this demotion as an indication of incompetence, even though this clearly was not the case. Mr. Hill's family responded to his misfortune by pointing out to him all of his accomplishments over his 20 years with the company. Unfortunately, this reaction had the unanticipated effect of making Mr. Hill feel even more discouraged. After all, if he had achieved all of that, and it still had not been sufficient to maintain his position, perhaps he was incapable of producing the required level of work. Mr. Hill began to feel inadequate in relation to his work. In addition, as he saw his family becoming frustrated with him, he began to feel depressed about his ability to be a good husband and father as well. Mr. Hill's family became increasingly concerned about his growing depression. The more they tried to cheer him up, however, the worse his depression became until eventually Mr. Hill was hospitalized.

In other cases, an individual's symptomatic behavior can be seen as a more direct manifestation of family disturbance. As a general principle, when an individual develops a symptom (e.g., anorexia nervosa, depression, or school phobia), this behavior will continue only if it is supported by other family members who are responding in such a way as to maintain the pathology. In contrast to the process just outlined, the purpose of this type of family reaction is to preserve the family integrity and to prevent unbearable conflict from causing worse damage to the family system (e.g., a marital separation). For some families, the underlying dynamics within the family may be more threatening than is the resultant dysfunctional behavior of a family member. Because removal of the symptom would necessitate dealing with these other conflictual issues, the family has an investment in maintaining the problem behavior, and there is often considerable collaboration within the family to "hold onto" the symptomatic behavior. Thus, the development of a symptom is conceptualized as the result of a more general dysfunction within the family system (e.g., marital conflict) and an attempt to provide a distraction from that problem area. The attempt to "detour" the problem, however, ultimately *becomes* the problem. The following vignette illustrates this point.

> Mr. and Mrs. Peters had a traditional and reasonably stable marriage until Mrs. Peters decided to discard her role as a housewife and enter the working world. Mr. Peters held strong beliefs about the importance of women devoting themselves to their home and family; however, his attempts to dissuade his wife from her decision were fruitless. The months following the beginning of Mrs. Peters' job were full of alternating periods of cold silence and heated arguments. The Peters' three children were distressed by this uncharacteristic behavior of their parents, but were hopeful that it would be short-lived. As the conflict continued and intensi-

fied, however, hopes for a quick return to normal functioning waned. The children first began to plead with their parents to be nice to each other. Next, they embarked on a course of "perfect" behavior, but that too failed to have an effect. The oldest daughter, 15-year-old Stephanie, began to have trouble eating and sleeping and began to lose weight quite rapidly. When she lost 20 pounds in just over 2 months, her parents became alarmed. Their concern was genuine, as were their attempts to help her. Following discussions with their family physician, Stephanie was diagnosed as anorexic. Mr. and Mrs. Peters escalated their efforts to help their daughter overcome this potentially life-threatening condition. Their own disharmony and unhappiness seemed unimportant compared with the difficulties their daughter was experiencing. Their cohesive efforts to improve Stephanie's health began to achieve positive results. Ironically, however, as Stephanie gained weight, her parents slipped back into their negative interactive pattern. Their anger had not been resolved, merely postponed, and was resumed with greater intensity. As the stability of the family became threatened, Stephanie's anorectic condition began to worsen. Her dysfunctional behavior unknowingly became the only apparent way to keep her parents out of battle and the family intact.

5. *Involvement of the Family.* A final area of relevance in applying general systems theory to the family concerns the necessity to involve all family members in attempts to "correct" (i.e., treat) the dysfunctional system. This principle follows from the position that family members share responsibility for their problems — there are no victims and no perpetrators. Consider, for example, a family who has a 4-year-old son who becomes asthmatic.

Mr. and Mrs. Winston were an energetic couple with strong career and athletic interests. When they were informed of their son Andrew's asthmatic condition, they understandably became upset, in part because they were concerned that Andrew's condition would seriously curb their activities. A pattern emerged in this family: Whenever Andrew did not get his own way, he became upset and brought on an asthma attack. Because of the consequences to their behavior, Mr. and Mrs. Winston became reluctant to confront their son or to deny his requests. They were, however, unhappy about feeling manipulated by Andrew and began to argue over how the situation should be handled. Mr. Winston became particularly annoyed because he felt that his wife was pampering their son, and that this pampering was interfering with the time and activities he and his wife had shared together. As the frequency of their arguments escalated, and the marital relationship became less satisfying, Mrs. Winston spent an increasing amount of time and attention on Andrew. In turn, Andrew's reaction to all of this attention was to assume an inflated sense of his own importance in the family system, and consequently, to intensify his demands. His growing demands increased the frequency with which his requests were refused, however, and this in turn increased the frequency of his asthmatic attacks.

It is not difficult to see the vicious cycle that this family had generated. Although it might be easy to blame everyone in this family for their problems, it is important to realize that all members play a role in the development of a problem-maintaining cycle. This example conveys the value and, indeed, the necessity of involving the entire family in the treatment process to best assess and understand the individual's symptoms in the context of the family's organizational structure and functioning.

The broad concept of general systems theory has spawned numerous specific theories and therapies aimed at the understanding and treatment of pathological behavior in families. Although most family theorists have drawn on the tenets of systems theory in devising their own theories of family therapy, there is basically general agreement on each of the five fundamental principles just outlined. Moreover, since the 1950s, these systems therapies have been applied to virtually every clinical condition. (We present an extended discussion of this point in the Afterword.)

AN INTEGRATIVE FRAMEWORK

Although a systems approach to understanding and treating dysfunctional behavior and relationships offers advantages over a purely intrapsychic individual approach, it also has certain limitations. The primary limitation is the lack of importance accorded intrapsychic or intrapersonal factors. As Seagraves (1982) points out, general systems theory is lacking a conceptual framework that provides a position or role for individual factors. Indeed, the individual's intrapersonal dynamics are generally considered irrelevant to the understanding of dysfunctional behavior. Therefore, systems approaches can be viewed as occupying the opposite end of the continuum to individual approaches. Both are extreme positions, however, and as such, both deny aspects central to the other. On one hand, the individualist position places almost total importance on intrapsychic factors, with only minimal attention given to social and interpersonal factors. On the other hand, systems approaches attach major importance to the interpersonal context in which the individual is functioning, while largely denying the significance of individual factors.

The position that we maintain throughout this guidebook is that an approach that integrates both intra- and interpersonal factors holds considerably greater promise in providing a comprehensive conceptual model of depression than does either focus alone. Although a general systems perspective provides the core framework within which we will conceptualize depression, we have expanded that perspective to include the role of individual contributions to the disturbance. Because all systems are made up of components, it is clear that any part can have structural vulnerabilities that cause it to weaken, deteriorate, or malfunction, quite independent of the role it plays within the system proper. The individual properties of that particular component, therefore, may have played a greater role in the breakdown of the system than would be apparent from an examination of its functional relationship within the system. Within the context of a family system, the individual characteristics of the family members have an impact on the type and quality of interactional patterns within the family, a contribution that extends beyond the general systems properties of that family. Family members bring their own strengths and weaknesses to the overall system of which they are a part. Thus, although we are conceptualizing depression essentially from a systems framework, we recognize that there are also "individual" factors operative in this disorder, in the absence of which the depression might not have occurred.

The approach to assessment and treatment delineated in this guidebook, therefore, deviates from a "pure" systems approach in two important ways. First, based on the rationale outlined above, we have modified the general systems perspective to include a consideration of individual factors. Thus, the therapeutic tasks of conceptualizing, assessing, and treating the depression include attention to factors at both an individual and an interpersonal level. Second, the description of depression presented in this guidebook does not follow directly from any one specific systemic theory. Rather, we have combined the tenets of general systems theory with selected and empirically supported aspects of individual theoretical orientations to construct a working conceptual description of depression. By using a modified approach, we are able to take advantage of the knowledge offered by the various systems- and individually-oriented theories and therapies and not be confined by the limits of any one of them. The outcome of this strategy is an approach that is richer and more process-oriented in the way in which it deals with depressed individuals and families.

We are by no means the first to propose an "interpersonal systems" approach to understanding and treating depression. Other theoreticians and therapists have described, evaluated, and advocated similar procedures; consequently, the clinical utility of this perspective has already achieved some initial empirical support. For example, Klerman, Weissman, Rounsaville, and Chevron (1984) have formulated "Interpersonal Psychotherapy" (IPT) for depression, an approach aimed at reducing symptoms of depression and at improving the social functioning of depressed individuals. Although IPT addresses many of the same issues as the interpersonal systems approach described in this guidebook, the major differences between the two approaches involve the conceptualization of "the patient" and the people who are actually seen in treatment. In IPT, the patient is clearly the depressed person, and unless there are exceptional circumstances, she or he is seen alone in individual therapy. In contrast, the "patient" in our interpersonal systems approach is the couple or family with the depressed person, and unless there are exceptional circumstances, the depressed person is seen in therapy together with his or her spouse and children. We will discuss in Chapter 4 specific situations in which the depressed individual might be seen alone in treatment.

Similarly, Feldman (1985) has proposed "Integrative Multi-Level Therapy" (IMLT), an interpersonal and intrapsychic therapeutic approach designed to

treat distressed individuals, couples, and families. Briefly, Feldman conceptualizes depression as the result of processes involving both interpersonal and intrapsychic problem stimulation and problem reinforcement. For symptomatic
behavior to develop, two events must transpire. First, problem stimuli must
occur, which cause a symptom to develop. Second, the symptom or dysfunctional interactions must be followed by interpersonal or intrapsychic reinforcing
consequences, or both, such as increased attention to negative behaviors, which
increase the likelihood of the problem recurring in reaction to future problem
stimuli. Based on this model, Feldman recommends an intervention program
comprised of cognitive and behavioral strategies conducted through a combination of conjoint and individual therapy sessions.

There is, therefore, reason to consider seriously an integration of individual
and interpersonal factors in the conceptualization and treatment of psychopathology. Indeed, a number of studies have suggested that both intrapsychic
and interpersonal factors are implicated in the etiology and maintenance of such
diverse disorders as anorexia nervosa (Garfinkel et al., 1983), substance abuse
(Clark, Capel, Goldsmith, & Stewart, 1972), school phobia (Waldron, Shrier,
Stone, & Tobin, 1975), and marital conflict (Gottman, 1979). Furthermore, as
Feldman (1985) notes, procedures aimed at producing interpersonal changes
and strategies designed to affect intrapsychic functioning have both been demonstrated to effect therapeutic change.

A number of models of depression have implicated the role of intrapsychic
factors in the etiology of this disorder. Two models in particular have received
the most empirical attention. Beck (1967) invokes three sets of cognitive constructs to explain psychological aspects of depression: the cognitive triad, schemata, and cognitive distortions. The cognitive triad consists of patterns of
thinking that lead depressed persons to regard themselves, their current situation, and their future possibilities in negative terms. Schemata are generally
viewed as cognitive structures that affect the encoding, storage, and retrieval of
information. Beck postulates that the schemata used by depressed individuals
are negative in nature, leading the depressed person both to selectively filter out
positive information and to perceive negative or neutral information as being
more negative than it actually is. Most importantly, cognitive theorists postulate
that these cognitive factors play a causal role in the development of depression.

A similar model has been presented by Abramson, Seligman, and Teasdale
(1978). The learned helplessness model postulates that depressed persons have
learned that outcomes are uncontrollable, and expect that future outcomes will
also be out of their control. Persons who are prone to depression tend to attribute
negative outcomes to internal, global, and stable factors and, to a lesser extent,
positive outcomes to external, specific, and unstable causes. As in Beck's model,
these patterns of attributions are hypothesized to play a causal role in the development of depression. (For an extended discussion of the research associated
with these two models of depression, see Coyne and Gotlib, 1983, in press.)

Depression has recently been studied from an interpersonal perspective. This interest in interpersonal factors in the etiology, maintenance, and treatment of depression resulted in large part from a growing dissatisfaction with the limited ability of intrapsychic models to offer a sufficiently comprehensive explanation of this disorder. At the same time, a growing body of literature was emerging, underscoring the importance of considering interpersonal factors in depression. Perhaps the most clearly articulated interpersonal description of depression is that presented by Coyne (1976b), who contends that depressive symptoms are maintained in large part by the responses of significant others in the depressed person's environment. As we noted in Chapter 1, Coyne suggests that persistent demands for support emitted by the depressed person gradually become aversive to members of the social environment, who become increasingly annoyed and frustrated with the constant depressive symptomatic behavior. The depressed person becomes aware of these negative reactions in others and consequently becomes even more needy and persistent in emitting the depressive symptoms. Coyne suggests that this downward spiraling process may continue until members of the social environment withdraw completely from the depressed person or, in the extreme, have him withdrawn through hospitalization.

The description of depression to be presented below is derived from Coyne's conceptualization, but it emphasizes the roles played by both the individual and the members of his or her social environment in the development and maintenance or exacerbation of the depressive condition. In addition, the implications of this conceptualization in the treatment of depression are also discussed. The description that we present draws both from general systems theory, outlined herein, and from theoretical positions that attend exclusively to intrapsychic factors in the etiology of depression.

AN INTERPERSONAL SYSTEMS CONCEPTUALIZATION OF DEPRESSION

There is little question that there are multiple causes of depression. Although the conceptualization of depression presented herein describes possible etiological factors and processes, we give considerably more attention to identifying the processes by which depression may be maintained or exacerbated. The description is oriented primarily towards helping the clinician to conceptualize and understand depression as an expression, a reflection, or an indication of disturbed interpersonal interactions, most likely at the level of marital or family relationships. We believe that this description will be of value to the clinician in generating treatment goals and planning effective intervention strategies. Two assumptions are made in this description:

1. Individuals and families vary in their ability to deal with the diverse demands and stresses of daily living. This ability is determined in part by the available supports, the types of demands encountered, and the general "health" of the individual and the family (e.g., the individuals' personality characteristics, the family's degree of cohesiveness, and their ability to make adaptive changes).

2. Depression can develop from either individual (e.g., cognitive and biochemical) or interpersonal (e.g., marital/family and social) vulnerabilities or causes. If the depressive symptoms persist, however, they are likely being maintained or reinforced in some way by interactions between the individual and the social system.

Essentially, this conceptualization maintains that the first stage in the development of depression is an "event" or "stressor" that imposes a significant demand on the individual to make an adaptive change. This event can be interpersonal or intrapsychic in nature, or both, and can include such situations as a failure (perceived or real) at home, school, or work, termination of a relationship, a move to another city, separation from family, promotion to a more demanding job, illness or death of a family member, a wife planning to return to work, and the last child leaving home. It is important to note that this "event" may itself be internal (e.g., biochemical changes) or may interact with other internal factors (e.g., maladaptive cognitions) to produce depression. Thus, diathesis-stress models of depression, such as Beck's conception of an event-related activation of dysfunctional schemata and Seligman's notion of the predisposing role of attributional processes in interaction with the occurrence of negative events, are operative at this stage.

Once the individual becomes depressed and begins to exhibit depressive symptoms, two factors may converge to maintain or exacerbate the depression. The first factor is interpersonal, involving the nature and quality of the responses of others in the depressive's social environment to the individual's symptomatic behavior. As we noted earlier, compared with nondepressed individuals, depressed persons demonstrate less eye contact when interacting with others, talk less, take longer to respond to others' verbalizations, and speak more softly and more monotonously. In addition, the conversational behavior of depressed persons is frequently self-focused and negatively toned, and centered around themes of self-devaluation, sadness, and helplessness. Not surprisingly, as we have also noted, a number of investigations have demonstrated that people are more apt to reject, feel uncomfortable with, and behave negatively toward a depressed person exhibiting these symptomatic behaviors than they are a nondepressed individual. Considered collectively, the results of these studies suggest that depressives have an aversive interpersonal style to which others ultimately respond with negativity and rejection.

The second factor, which interacts with these interpersonal behavior patterns, involves the depressed individual's perceptions and interpretations of the reactions of others. Recent investigations using diverse methodologies have demonstrated that depressed persons have a tendency or "readiness" to focus on or attend to negative aspects of their environment (e.g., Gotlib & McCann, 1984; Gotlib & Cane, 1986; Lewinsohn, Lobitz, & Wilson, 1973). Although the etiological significance of this information processing style has not yet been resolved, for the purpose of conducting therapy we believe that it is more important to understand the nature of the relationship between this type of cognitive functioning and the depressed individual's interpersonal behavior.

Our position is that there is a reciprocal relationship between the cognitive style of depressed persons and their interpersonal functioning. When individuals become depressed, they exhibit depressive symptoms. This symptomatic behavior elicits negative or, at best, ambivalent responses from others in their social environment. Because of the depressed person's cognitive style, they attend closely to these negative responses; indeed, even when both positive and negative behaviors are emitted by others, the depressed person will pay more attention to the negative behaviors (Gotlib, 1983). We are not stating that depressed individuals necessarily evidence *distorted* perceptions of their environment. Rather, we are simply suggesting that depressed persons demonstrate increased accessibility and attention to realistically negative aspects of their environment, which they engendered through their own symptomatic behavior.

This focus on the negative characteristics of their environment leads the depressed person to become even more depressed, more symptomatic. Coyne (1976b) argues that this renewed display of symptoms is intended to regain the support from others that was initially offered when the depressed individual first became symptomatic. Regardless of the purpose of this exacerbation of symptoms, the point remains that these depressive behaviors lead others to become even more negative or to withdraw further. Because the depressed individual has little difficulty perceiving and focusing on these negative behaviors, the cycle worsens. Thus, not only do depressed persons engender negative, or ambivalent responses from others in their social environment, but also their tendency to focus on or attend to these negative behaviors only serves to compound the situation and increase their depression. In turn, the relationship between the depressed individuals and their friends and family is further degraded, all of which contributes to the maintenance or escalation of the negative interactional sequences described earlier.

Not all individuals who experience a stressful event become depressed, and similarly, not all those who do become depressed necessarily proceed through all of these stages. For example, some individuals or families, whom we will refer to as *flexible and healthy,* possess the resources to allow them to cope adequately with the initial "event" or stress without producing depressive symptoms. They will continue to function satisfactorily until the next stressful event, at which time they will again mobilize their resources in dealing with the demand. For example, an intact family with two young children was about to launch its youngest child into the school system. This is frequently a stressful time for a family, particularly when the mother has spent an extended period of time in the home, devoting herself to taking care of her children. Although this particular family underwent a relatively difficult period of adjustment while the mother sought and secured a position of employment outside the home, the support and health of the mother and the other family members were sufficiently strong to preclude the emergence of depressive symptoms.

In contrast to these healthy families, individuals in other families, whom we will designate as *vulnerable*, will in fact become depressed as a result of this stressful "event." The event may activate dysfunctional schemata, or may interact with the individual's depressogenic attributional style to produce the depressive symptoms. Regardless of the etiology, however, with strong and consistent support either from the family system or from external sources, these individuals and families are able to avoid the effects of the depressed person's negative cognitive style and make an adaptive change with relatively little effort. This change leads to a reduction or elimination of depressive symptoms and a return to a homeostatic, well-functioning state. The family is able to function at a satisfactory level until the next stressful event, whereupon this cycle may be repeated. The likelihood of repetition will depend on a number of factors (e.g., the skills acquired by the individual or family during the previous depressive episode to deal effectively with this new demand, the similarity between the two stressors, and the like).

Consider, as an example, a young teenager who became mildly depressed as two events—a failed exam and a rejection by her boyfriend—coincided, and who, perhaps because she attributed these events to shortcomings in her own character, was left feeling inadequate, unattractive, and distraught. She began to attend to and focus on the mildly negative behavior exhibited by her friends and family in reaction to her behavior, and because of her increased sensitivity to this behavior, she became more depressed and reached out more fervently for support. Her family was there to offer her continued support, however, and as a result of time spent with both her parents and two close friends, she was ultimately able to return to her previous healthy level of functioning. In general, although this girl was vulnerable to depression, her relatively high level of health and the family's strong cohesiveness were instrumental in preventing the depressive symptoms from deteriorating into a major depressive episode.

A third type of individual or family, whom we will refer to as *rigid and unhealthy*, is similar to the vulnerable type, in that he or she is unable to cope effectively with the initial stressor, and consequently she or he develops symptoms of depression. Unlike the vulnerable family, these families are unable (at least at this point) to deal adaptively with the depression. In these rigid and unhealthy families, the symptom may serve a major or essential role for the individual or family system. For example, a couple consisting of an assertive and controlling wife and a passive husband began to experience considerable marital disharmony. The level of conflict in their marriage became so intense that the possibility of divorce, which neither really desired, was raised. Before any decision was reached, however, the husband became severely depressed, and the issue of a possible separation was postponed in order to deal with the depression. The husband began a course of treatment, during which his wife was quite supportive. Nonetheless, a subtle, yet clear pattern began to emerge. Whenever the husband's condition began to improve, there was a noticeable corresponding increase in the marital conflict. This marital stress was immediately followed by a relapse in the husband's depression and the wife's return to her supportive role. Thus, the husband's depression became the only means by which this couple could avoid the issue of marital disharmony and keep their marriage intact. The depression began to serve an essential role in the marriage (i.e., it kept the couple together). At this point, this couple was unwittingly working together to maintain the depression in order to prevent their marriage from disintegrating.

Regardless of whether or not this couple seeks therapy, they can maintain this transactional pattern of behavior as long as the need to do so is sufficiently strong (and the alternative of marital disharmony is more threatening to the couple's integrity as a system). Therefore, there are two possible options at this point: the family/couple system can remain at its current dysfunctional *but manageable* level or the depression could worsen sufficiently to necessitate therapeutic intervention (e.g., the husband becomes suicidal). Ideally, this intervention will be oriented towards dealing with the pattern of interaction that is maintaining the depressive behavior, as well as providing individual support to the husband. This will often necessitate dealing with other issues within the couple or family. Depending on the degree of success achieved in dealing with these issues, the depression may begin to play a less important role in the family system. The family may then return to its previous level of functioning or, with a more successful intervention, to an even healthier level.

In sum, an event occurs that makes a demand on the individual(s) to adapt. Because of intrapsychic and/or interpersonal factors, some individuals are better able to adapt to this demand than are others; those who are less able to adapt begin to exhibit depressive symptomatology. This display of depressive symptoms, in turn, represents a stressor to which the spouse, family, or both must adapt. Here, too, some families are better able to adapt than are others. As we noted earlier, healthy families who have an optimal balance of cohesiveness and adaptability will cope best. Members of these families may still become depressed; the families, however, will have a higher probability of being able to find solutions to the difficulties and help ameliorate the members' depression. They are also likely to tolerate the depression longer without exhibiting disruptive effects. In contrast, families low in cohesion or adaptability are likely both to increase the probability of the occurrence of depression in one of the family members (recall the data suggesting that lack of a close relationship represents a vulnerability factor for the development of depression) and, in conjunction with the depressed member's increased attention to their negative behaviors, to exacerbate the depression when it does occur. Depression in the context of this type of marital or family system is thus more likely to be maintained and to recur.

This conceptualization of depression has important implications for the practice of therapy. The clinician must be cognizant of the interactive or reciprocal nature of depression. A depressed individual has effects on the other family members, who in turn may, in any number of ways, inadvertently reinforce or exacerbate the depression. For example, they may attempt to help the depressed individual by relieving him of all responsibilities. This action may make the depressed person feel useless and even more depressed. The family may give advice and then feel frustrated, irritated, or angry when their advice fails to have its intended effect. The depressed person, perceiving and being especially sensitive to this negative affect, may become more depressed, leading the family to feel themselves greater failures for being unable to help, and the downward-spiraling cycle will so continue until some intervention is effected in the system.

In any of these cases, to deal comprehensively with depression, the clinician must attend to both the individual and the family. An exclusive focus on only one of these components is incomplete. In terms of the individual, it is important to determine what it is that increases that person's vulnerability to depression in order to minimize the probability of relapse. Factors involving the individual clearly must be addressed. Even with a supportive family, some individuals experience repeated depressive episodes. Similarly, we cannot ignore the fact that often only one member of a family becomes depressed. It is also important to focus on the family dynamics in cases of depression. How can the depression be understood within the context of the family system? What is the family doing with the individual that may be maintaining or exacerbating the depression? What can they do differently?

The emphasis of the assessment and intervention strategies described in the following chapters is placed jointly on the individual and the family. We believe that efforts to understand and alter the relationship between the depression and the family interactions will be more successful than attempts aimed at changing either one alone. Given the high relapse rate for depression, the interpersonal risk factors associated with this disorder, and the relative failure, described earlier, of individually-oriented therapies to affect the social/interpersonal functioning of depressed patients, we believe that the interpersonal systems approach presented in this guidebook represents a promising direction for the treatment of depression.

CASE EXAMPLE

A detailed case example will provide the opportunity to conceptualize an actual depressed patient from our interpersonal systems perspective. This example will also be used in later chapters to elucidate issues of assessment and treatment.

Mrs. Maria Richardson, a 30-year-old mother of two children, was born into a European family with strong roots in traditional Italian values and practices. Her family was organized and run by her mother, who was well established as the head of the family with respect to domestic concerns. The role of Maria's father was to provide financial security for the family. He worked long, hard hours for a construction company, and because of the type of work, he was often away from home for extended periods of time. Even when his work allowed him to be home, however, he rarely spent time in family activities. His view of his family was that he knew what was best for all of them, and his children were never allowed to openly challenge his authority. If the children were ever brave enough to make a special request of their father, it had to be done by their mother. The children were not allowed to approach their father directly over potentially conflictual requests or situations. Maria remembered her father as a cold, distant, powerful, and unapproachable man. Although there were many times while she was growing up that Maria craved love and affection from her father, she felt unable to request or receive it. Moreover, there were an equal number of times when Maria felt intense anger and resentment towards her father for what she felt were unfair restrictions; yet, she was never able to stand up to him and question his rules. At such times she turned instead to her mother for comfort and support. Because of this interactional pattern and the emotional unavailability of her father, Maria developed a close relationship with her mother.

Maria's mother devoted herself almost entirely to the raising of her children, and discouraged any activities that would have allowed her children greater independence. Maria was not permitted to have much of a life outside the family, particularly with respect to dating boys. Maria's peers saw her as a quiet girl who, for the most part, kept to herself. She did not join school activities, nor was she ever a behavioral problem in school. Maria approached school projects with an intensity greater than that of most of her peers. In fact, she recalled that the lonelier she felt, the more intensely she became involved in these projects. There were several occasions while Maria was growing up when she felt depressed. In reaction to this feeling, she would fantasize about how much happier she would be when she was married and had a devoted family of her own.

When Maria was 18, she was asked out on her first real date. Her date, Michael, was almost as introverted as Maria. Michael had grown up in a matriarchal family, with poor communication between family members. He was not close to either of his parents and had become self-sufficient at an early age. As her dating relationship with Michael became more serious, Maria saw it as her ticket to happiness. It offered her a way out of her home and an opportunity to have the devoted family of her dreams. Although Michael was not feeling the same urgency to have a serious relationship, Maria quickly asserted herself in a position of control and shaped the relationship to meet her needs. Michael and Maria were married within a year, and less than a year later, their first child, David, was born. Maria and Michael's first years together were turbulent ones. Michael had an artistic career that often required him to be away for a week at a time. Maria became increasingly moody and sullen and began to accuse Michael of abandoning her, of leaving her to the task of raising their child by herself. In turn, Michael felt that Maria made unreasonable demands of him and that nothing he did for her was ever good enough.

When David was 4 years old, their daughter, Elise, was born. By this time the marital relationship was becoming more conflictual, and Maria was becoming increasingly depressed. She finally sought help for her depression and saw a psychiatrist for over a year. In addition to prescribing antidepressants, the psychiatrist helped Maria to understand how her early feelings of rejection from and anger for her father were being played out in her current relationship. Although she gained some symptomatic relief, Maria's depression became episodic over the next few years; therapy never seemed to be effective or long-lasting.

Like her mother, Maria began to devote more of her time to her children. The rewards of this devotion were offset, however, by the growing problems she began to have with her son David. Maria's major concern with David was his encopresis. She often appealed to Michael for help in dealing with this situation, but his efforts were never sufficient to effect a change. As David grew older, Maria became almost hysterical in her attempts to control his encopresis. She tried to shame him, cajole him, bribe him, and threaten him, but nothing seemed to work. Maria began to feel that David soiled his pants just to spite her. What frustrated her even more, however, was that there were periods (up to a month in duration) during which David would not have any "accidents." Although Maria did not recognize the pattern at the time, these periods tended to coincide with relatively peaceful times in the family. Unfortunately, these periods were always short-lived, and would be followed by even more intense struggles.

The pattern that existed (although not obvious to either Maria or Michael) was that Maria would begin to feel lonely and isolated, and would then turn to Michael for support and affection. Michael, however, perceived these behaviors from Maria as attempts to control and dominate him, and consequently, he would react by distancing himself from her. Maria would become very sensitive to Michael's aloof behavior and would react by attempting to get closer to David and Elise. In particular, she became more demanding of the children, and overreacted to their misbehavior, especially to what she perceived as David's noncompliance. The frequency of David's "accidents" would increase, and the battle between David and Maria would be refueled. At these times, Maria would also seek out her mother's companionship. Her mother was quite receptive to Maria's need for support and understanding, and enjoyed being able to take care of her daughter once again. The final element in this pattern was that Maria's depression would increase, and the level of stress in her home would escalate. Elise somehow seemed to escape being in the spotlight during these major episodes of tension and conflict, but she was often put in the role of comforting her mother. In fact, Maria often felt that Elise was the only one in the family who truly understood and cared about her. The family situation finally deteriorated to the point where Maria once again sought therapy. Maria's presenting problem was her depression, which she attributed both to her son's difficulty with encopresis and to the lack of support she felt from her husband in dealing with this problem.

This example is rich in details highlighting the notion that both individuals and their families can be vulnerable to stress and to one of its frequent consequences—the onset of depression. On the basis of the information provided in this description, the Richardson family would be viewed as rigid and unhealthy. The two primary presenting symptoms (Maria's depression and David's encopresis) play important roles in the family system. Specifically, Maria's depression is often a response to a lack of closeness and involvement between her and her husband, Michael. It is likely that these times of distance in her marriage activate memories for Maria of her early relationship with her father, triggering perceptions of men as cold and unapproachable and leading her to experience feelings of helplessness about her relationship with Michael. Indeed, this situation most often occurs when Michael is very busy at work; when their relationship is more intimate, Maria is less likely to be depressed. Unfortunately, Michael's strong self-sufficiency and needs for independence both increase the frequency of these periods of marital distance (and hence, of Maria's depressive episodes) and lead him to respond to Maria's depression and needs for intimacy by withdrawing even further. Finally, David's problem with encopresis (an example of "detouring") also plays a major role in the family system by preventing his parents from engaging in what would likely be relationship-threatening battles. As we mentioned earlier, we will make extensive use of this example in subsequent chapters in formulating more specific hypotheses about the relationship between depressive symptomatology and family functioning, in terms of both the assessment stage and the planning of intervention strategies.

Chapter 3

General Treatment Principles and Strategies Characteristic of Interpersonal Systems Therapy for Depression

Before the specifics of the therapy sessions in Chapters 4, 5, and 6 are detailed, we will outline in this chapter eight principles of therapy that will provide the clinician with an overview of some fundamental guidelines in treating depressed individuals from an interpersonal systems perspective. The identification and description of specific therapist tasks and strategies will alert and sensitize the therapist to activities necessary for the organization and planning of therapy sessions. Finally, the presentation of specific therapy techniques will provide the clinician with the appropriate tools to treat depressed individuals. Although it is clearly recognized that each case of depression will have its own unique features, circumstances, and complexities, the following information should nonetheless be relevant and valuable in the majority of cases.

As we noted earlier, there are numerous systems of interpersonally oriented therapy, each with its own theoretical concepts and treatment applications. Nevertheless, several important characteristics also exist that are common to most of these treatment approaches. We will present these features and, in addition, describe their relevance to the treatment of depression.

1. *Therapy is action-oriented rather than interpretation-oriented.* Unlike psychoanalysis, for example, interpersonal systems therapy maintains a strong focus on immediate change. The primary goal of many systems therapists is to stimulate patterns of communication and behavioral sequences that interrupt the depression-exacerbating interactions that brought the couple or family into therapy. There is a strong emphasis on producing more adaptive functional fam-

ily relationships in the therapy sessions themselves. When interpretations are used, they are generally descriptive. For example, the therapist might say:

> Did you notice, Mr. Jones, that when your wife was speaking just now, you were looking at her, and reached over and stroked her arm when she was talking about feeling alienated in the family? The children seemed to follow your lead and also appeared attentive and supportive. Compare this to previous occasions when you would become upset and frustrated, and would look out the window or at the floor when your wife spoke about these same feelings. At these times your children also became fidgety and started quarreling with each other, and your wife would begin to look even more distraught.

2. *The focus of therapy is on the here and now rather than on historical events.* Consistent with an interactional conceptualization of the family as an organizational system is the focus on the "here and now." Again, in contrast to psychoanalytic theory and its emphasis on historical antecedents in the development of depression, systems theory largely ignores distant historical events in understanding the basis for dysfunctional behavior. Rather, systems theory maintains that all behavior (whether functional or dysfunctional) can be understood by attending solely to the recent interactional patterns that exist among family members and to the rules that govern the family. Although the assessment phase may involve obtaining some historical information about the family, this is done primarily to gain a more comprehensive understanding of how the family system operates, and how it came to "need" or use the current depressive symptoms. Following the initial assessment period, however, the focus of the therapy is on what is happening currently in the family and on how the depression is currently being maintained.

3. *The systems therapist is an active contributor and participant in the therapeutic process.* The therapist not only is instrumental in helping the couple or family to generate treatment goals, but also assumes considerable responsibility in undertaking the work to accomplish these goals. If progress is not being made, the therapist evaluates what he is doing in the therapy sessions and may consult with another therapist in devising alternative treatment strategies. The systems therapist accepts responsibility for planning the strategies and implementing the treatment techniques that are most likely to produce change in a given family. Although the therapist's level of activity may vary depending on whether he is working within the family system or has stepped outside of it to more clearly observe a transaction, the therapist is constantly involved in moving the family toward their stated goals.

4. *The therapist adopts a problem-solving approach which attaches considerable importance to the alleviation of depression.* Indeed, therapy is typically not viewed as successful unless the presenting depressive symptoms have disappeared (or at least have diminished significantly) by the end of therapy. The therapist is generally concerned with helping the family with their stated problems, rather than with "higher level" or "loftier" issues toward which the thera-

pist might prefer the family to work. Although the therapist will determine *how* the family needs to change, it is ultimately the family who will determine *what* they want to change. Finally, because the therapist focuses on clearly defined problems, the therapy sessions are generally very structured and closely follow a consistent theme.

5. *The therapist explores family interaction patterns that are involved in maintaining depressive behavior.* This task represents a crucial aspect of the therapist's job. Unless the therapist is able to clearly discern problematic family interaction patterns, it will be virtually impossible to help the family give up these behaviors and adopt more adaptive behaviors that will permit the dissolution or relinquishment of the depressive symptoms. Many techniques are available to aid the family therapist in this assessment task. The therapist can stimulate the family in the therapy session to act and react in the same way they do at home. Alternatively, the therapist can observe the spontaneous transactions that occur among family members. The therapist might also use the technique of enactment (to be discussed in greater detail) wherein the family is asked to recreate the sequence of interactions that occurred at home, and then the elicited transactions are observed.

6. *Therapy is generally short-term.* Although systems-oriented family therapy can vary from 5 weeks to 1 year, it generally occurs within a 3-month time frame. This duration is clearly consistent with the problem-focused, here-and-now approach aimed at the alleviation of the depressive symptomatic behavior. Long-term therapy is often considered by family therapists to be the result of an unfocused treatment process that lacks clearly defined goals. This emphasis on short-term treatment also follows from a belief that the therapist's job is not to remake or reconstruct the individual, couple, or family, but rather to help them develop ways of relating to each other that are more conducive to nondepressive, healthy, adaptive interactions.

7. *The therapist removes the focus from the identified depressed patient and draws the marital dyad or the entire family into treatment.* This principle has particular importance for the assessment phase of treatment. In the description of depression presented in Chapter 2, we emphasized the importance of considering the role of both the individual and the family in maintaining depression. General systems theorists often take a more dramatic stance and view the identified depressed patient as the representation of a breakdown in the family system. In both of these frameworks, the therapist must look beyond the depressed individual, encompassing a broader focus to understand more completely the nature of the depression and its reciprocal relationship to dysfunctional interactional patterns in the family. To accomplish this goal, the depressed patient must be removed from the spotlight and placed in a more appropriate and therapeutically useful context within the family system.

8. *The emphasis in the therapy sessions is on process rather than content.* Although content is clearly important and, indeed, provides one major means

by which the therapist comes to understand how the family views the depression, the process of a transaction may negate the content of what is being said. For example, if parents repeatedly tell their depressed daughter that she is allowed to freely express her feelings, and yet become angry and rejecting whenever she says something to which they object, then that process is far more revealing than is the content of what is being said. Thus, the therapist is as interested in how information is communicated and in how individuals respond to each other, as in what is actually being said.

As a related point, the therapist is not often concerned with the issue of why something has happened; "why" questions tend to be unproductive and frequently lead to feelings of guilt and blame. Instead, the therapist attends to the sequence of interactions stimulated by an event. This principle maintains that one reason a family gets "stuck" is that they become overly concerned with the content of their conflict, which often takes them down a dead-end road or into an inescapable maze. A therapist who becomes too involved with the content of the family's arguments, to the neglect of the process of their interactions, may become absorbed into the family's pathology. The occurrence of this process of absorption may be indicated when a therapist finds herself or himself in alliance with one family member or experiences a particular situation with the same degree of emotional intensity as does the family.

TASKS OF THERAPY

In addition to these general principles and strategies, the therapist also engages in specific tasks during the course of his or her involvement with a depressed patient and family. As detailed in the following chapter, the first task of the therapist is to conduct a complete assessment with the family. This process involves diagnosing the depression and assessing its functional role in the family. In addition to specific therapeutic tasks, the therapist also uses particular techniques and intervention strategies consistent with the orientation described earlier. We will outline the more important of these strategies beginning first with therapy tasks and then continuing with specific techniques. In the following chapters, these tasks and techniques will be highlighted and discussed as they occur in the presentation of the therapy transcripts of the case presented in Chapter 2.

Determining Whom to See in Therapy

An important initial task of therapy involves determining exactly who should attend the therapy sessions. In Chapter 4 we present detailed procedures to guide the therapist in conducting a comprehensive assessment of the depression and its role in the family. On completion of this assessment, the therapist should be able to begin to conceptualize the role of the depression within the family system and to identify, at least tentatively, the depression-maintaining sequences of behaviors among family members. Next, the therapist must determine which family members should be involved in the subsequent therapy sessions. Although the general systems concepts will always apply, the results of the assessment data and the family interactional patterns will determine who should be included in the sessions. The therapist may decide to include the entire family, the marital couple, a parent-child dyad, one individual, or a combination of the above.

For example, if on the basis of the assessment results it is believed that the depression is actually the result of marital conflict being detoured through the child, the therapist may decide that the marital dyad should receive separate treatment. If, however, the family is characterized by marital turmoil and is rigid and resistant, with a corresponding commitment to seeing a depressed child exclusively as the source of the problem, the entire family might be seen until the system is more flexible and the parents better able to examine their problematic relationship. As another example, if a family member (e.g., the depressed person) has low self-esteem and is viewed by the therapist as fragile, that person may need individual support in addition to the marital or family sessions. In this latter situation, therapy can frequently include more than one combination of family members. Moreover, as therapy progresses, the therapist may determine that it is appropriate to change the constellation of who is being seen because of either new information or a modification of interpersonal interactions. As a general rule, however, it is beneficial to include the whole family during the last few sessions to ensure that the members are indeed functioning well together and to work out any residual problems the family wishes to address.

Structuring the Sessions

Following the assessment phase and the decision of who will be seen in therapy (described in greater detail in the next chapter), the therapist must establish with the family members the specific therapy ground rules and should negotiate a contract for a specified number of sessions. It is imperative that the ground rules be agreed upon by both the family members and the therapist. One ground rule might be that following the decision regarding who will be involved in therapy, a session will be held only if everyone is present. Therefore, if it is decided that the whole family will be involved, and the wife calls to say that her husband cannot attend a particular session but the rest of the family can, the therapist will reschedule the session to a time when everyone can be present. Another ground rule might be that a family will be seen at certain intervals (e.g., once per week); if a crisis occurs, the family must deal with it as best they can until their next scheduled appointment.

Two final areas of ground rules involve the length of each session and the conditions for leaving the therapy room before the end of the session. Both of these rules are important to reduce the family's anxiety level by informing them of what is expected. With regard to the former expectation (duration), the length of the sessions is generally determined as a function of who will be seen in treatment and the clinician's own preference. If the entire family is being seen, $1^1/_2$ hours may be required to accomplish what might take only one hour with an individual or a couple. With respect to leaving the room during therapy, if the clinician does not make this rule explicit, it often happens that when interactions become too heated or intense, one member will leave the room. Not only is this behavior generally disruptive to the therapy process, but also often interrupts important interactional patterns by preventing a complete understanding of the issues or a resolution of the conflict.

A similar issue involves the number of sessions during which a family is seen. The therapist has several options in this regard. First, a set number of sessions can be agreed upon (e.g., 15) and after 10 sessions the issue of termination may be raised. The family can then either continue for five more sessions to consolidate their gains or can elect to save these remaining sessions for future use. Taking a somewhat different tack, the therapist and family might agree to meet for a specified number of sessions, after which they will assess their progress and determine the need for future involvement. Yet another option is for the therapist to specify the number of sessions he offers, and then to terminate at the end of that period regardless of how much or how little progress has been made. The rationale for this somewhat unorthodox approach is that clearly limiting the number of sessions serves to provide the participants with a definite time period during which they must attain their treatment goals. The intention here is that when working under a time limit, family members will be more focused and will introduce less extraneous material.

Educating the Family

The fundamental objectives of this therapist task are twofold. First, the therapist must help the family to appreciate the importance of working together as a system to both understand the depression and alleviate it. In essence, the therapist must teach the family about systems and how they work. This aspect of therapy is particularly important given most people's tendency to conceptualize depression in linear and intrapsychic terms. If the therapist is to work effectively with a family, that family must be helped to expand its perception of the depression.

Educating the family is important: If the therapist is to persuade the appropriate family members to become involved in treatment, they will need an acceptable rationale for doing so. A common reaction encountered by many family therapists is, "I'm not the one with the problem, and I don't see why I need to come here." A good way for the therapist to respond to such remarks is to stress the importance of that person's help in adequately understanding the problem and effecting a positive change. The following excerpt, taken from a case in which the wife was depressed and the husband was resistant to becoming involved in therapy, illustrates this strategy:

> I can understand your concern about becoming involved in therapy, Mr. Holbert. After all, as you have stated, it is your wife who is depressed. I have found, how- ever, that having the spouse's perspective on the problem is most valuable. Usually the person who is depressed sees their situation in pretty bleak terms, which gener- ally isn't altogether accurate. Not only that, but to be of any help I need to know what it is that people in the family have already done in an attempt to make things better. Most important, I have discovered that without the spouse's help it is pretty hard to get rid of the depression. So I really hope, Mr. Holbert, that you could find the time in your busy schedule to become involved in this difficult job.

The second aspect of this task involves educating the family about each fam- ily member's role in the treatment process. It is helpful for the therapist to outline in detail what the family can expect from therapy, and what is expected from each of them. Clients frequently approach therapy with the implicit assumption that all they have to do is to tell the therapist what the problem is and the thera- pist will implement the appropriate corrective measures. Although this assump- tion may be more or less accurate in some individual approaches to treatment, it is particularly inaccurate in most schools of family therapy. Certainly, most family therapists are active contributors to the content of the therapy sessions; their goal, however, is to help the family utilize its own resources and strengths to make and maintain its desired changes. Moreover, the therapist communi- cates this information to the family in a variety of ways. For example, the clini- cian may accomplish this task early in therapy by telling the family that they will be able to find solutions to their problems more readily than she or he can, because they know themselves so much better than he or she does. The therapist might further explain that his or her role in the partnership will involve helping the family to find or develop the skills necessary to implement its selected solu- tions. During the course of therapy, the therapist continues to reinforce this posi- tion by generally refusing to offer advice, and by quickly pointing out and praising the family's healthy reactions to a variety of situations. In sum, the ther- apist informs the family members that they will be doing most of the work in the sessions and that his or her involvement will consist primarily of helping them find the tools to do this work effectively.

Formulating Treatment Goals

As we have already stated, it is essential that the therapist and family agree on the specific goals they will pursue. Therapy would be chaotic and unfocused if the therapist was working toward one set of goals and the family another. It is important to realize, however, that these goals may nevertheless be flexible; it is made clear to the family that if the situation warrants, a new set of goals can be negotiated at any time during the therapy process. For example, in the situation described earlier in which the family had a strong commitment to dealing only with the depressed child, the parents after a few sessions may begin to recognize their underlying hostility for each other and decide that improving their own marital relationship is an important new goal of therapy. This could then be negotiated as a separate treatment goal. Although each family will generate its own specific goals for therapy, Minuchin and Fisman (1981) describe three goals that most families have in common: (1) to free the identified patient of symptoms; (2) to reduce the family's overall levels of stress and conflict; and (3) to help the family learn more effective ways of coping. Finally, all treatment goals are generally made as specific and concrete as possible.

THERAPY TECHNIQUES

The value of using well-defined intervention techniques in family therapy has gained such widespread acceptance in the field that Minuchin and Fisman (1981) have devoted an entire book to these strategies. Although the list to be presented is not intended to be exhaustive, it does represent those strategies that we consider to be most useful in effecting change in families with a depressed member. These techniques are designed to provide the therapist with a repertoire of skills necessary to proceed from the opening moves of therapy to the final session, when the family is ready for termination. Both the general tasks already outlined and the following intervention strategies will be highlighted in the therapy transcripts presented in Chapters 5 and 6. The use of a particular technique and the rationale for its use at that particular point in the session also will be discussed.

1. *Joining with the family.* This process is one of the first activities undertaken by the therapist when seeing a new family. Joining, conceptually similar to the "therapeutic alliance," is the process by which the therapist lets the family members know that he or she understands them and can truly appreciate their predicament. It is the means by which the therapist communicates to the family that they are important and can work together. By joining with the family, the therapist is able to gain important information about family functioning, because once joining has occurred, the family is much more likely to openly reveal themselves to the therapist. Moreover, when the therapist successfully joins with the family, the family achieves the feelings of security and protection necessary to attempt a change. As Minuchin and Fisman (1981) state, joining is the glue that holds the therapeutic system together. It involves supporting the family in such a way that a congruence between therapist and family is established, and a common ground between therapist and family is found. Without being pretentious or insincere, the therapist finds a way to meld with the family.

Joining can be accomplished in a variety of ways, some quite direct and others so imperceptible that they seem more perceptions than observable behavior. For example, the therapist can begin to express himself in a manner similar to that used by the family members, making use of the same phrases, intonations, sentence structure, etc. The therapist's body language and posture can also mirror that of the family; depending on the characteristics of the family, the therapist's personality can even become more boisterous or more timid. Finally, joining can also be accomplished by tracking the family (i.e., attentively listening to each family member tell their story). The following case illustrates the therapist's attempts at joining that occurred during an initial interview.

> The Pearson family consisted of a depressed husband, a timid wife, and their three rather vocal rough-and-tumble children. Mr. Pearson was a truck driver and provided a modest income for his family. Neither Mr. nor Mrs. Pearson was well educated, and Mr. Pearson's speech was unpolished and riddled with slang. The Pearson family appeared for their first session in tattered and dirty clothes. Mr. Pearson immediately gave the impression that he did not expect the young, clean-cut therapist to understand him at all. The therapist immediately recognized his disadvantage and embarked on a course to overcome his "handicap." He began to mirror some of Mr. Pearson's vocabulary in his questions regarding Mr. Pearson's job and showed a genuine interest in the type of truck Mr. Pearson drove. The therapist was able to draw on his own experience of having worked for two summers for his uncle, who was also a truck driver. His display of knowledge related to the trucking business quickly put Mr. Pearson at ease. After less than 10 minutes of "trucking" talk, Mr. Pearson was ready to participate in therapy with a new, energized outlook.

The value of joining cannot be overemphasized. Indeed, some therapists contend that without successful joining, therapy will be ineffective in promoting change.

   2. *Reframing the problem.* When a family enters therapy, members come armed with their own assessment of the depression, a "reality" to which they often feel a strong commitment and one that is generally negative. Indeed, the manner in which the family has framed or conceptualized the depression often contributes to its maintenance and exacerbation. The therapist's task, then, is to reframe the depression in such a way that the family members relinquish their previous entrenched conceptualizations of the depression and, in doing so, become free to change. The therapist must persuade the family that the reality they have constructed can be modified. This new reality would challenge the role of the symptom-bearer within the family.

> Bob and Betty Duncan and their children were once a close-knit family. They began to experience difficulties because their adolescent daughter Samantha was becoming increasingly withdrawn and isolated from her parents. The Duncans could not understand how Samantha, who was once so considerate, cheerful, and devoted to her family, could have undergone such a complete personality transformation. She no longer eagerly volunteered her help. She avoided contact with her family and shared very little of her daily life with them. The Duncans viewed this behavior as unacceptable and disrespectful. Moreover, they began to regard

Samantha's behavior as deliberately rude, rejecting, and antagonistic. Despite the Duncans' repeated efforts to "help" Samantha return to her previous pleasant self, she remained determined to follow her newly established path. The more pressure the Duncans applied, the more withdrawn Samantha became. Finally, following an episode in which Samantha took an overdose of medication, Mr. and Mrs. Duncan sought treatment. They came to therapy with a view of reality that included a daughter whose level of functioning had deteriorated, who was rejecting them and their value system, and who was impervious to their efforts to help her.

The Duncans were trapped in their efforts to solve their problem by their construction of the realities of the situation. As long as they viewed their daughter's change and depression as fundamentally negative and as a threat to their perception of their role as giving, providing parents, their primary goal could only be the return of their "old" Samantha. Moreover, as long as Samantha felt that her parents were trying to hold her back, she would have to counter that pressure with an equal or greater amount of resistance. Unfortunately, because of the rejection and lack of support she was perceiving from her parents, Samantha was becoming depressed. Conversely, the Duncans were interpreting Samantha's withdrawal as rejection. This family was trapped in an escalating interactional pattern that was reinforcing and maintaining the problem behaviors.

In this example, the therapist might reframe the situation by encouraging the Duncans to see Samantha's recent changes as positive. After all, she was trying to become more autonomous and independent, a change she felt would please her parents. However, Samantha is not quite sure she is ready for this new independence and responsibility and so is attempting to execute the change in such a way (i.e., ineptly) that she is also signaling to her parents that she still needs their help. The therapist might point out that the parents were indeed trying to help their daughter, but perhaps in the wrong direction. Rather than trying to help Samantha return to her previous stage, they might consider trying to help her master this new stage more successfully. Thus, the therapist has reframed the family's problem from one in which the daughter is rejecting her parents, to one in which she is trying to please them, but is not doing a very good job of it. Once the "problem" has been successfully reframed, and this conceptualization becomes the new reality, the parents are in the position of providing more constructive help that is consistent with this new framework.

3. *Enactment.* This technique is designed to facilitate a clearer, more accurate understanding of the family by encouraging them to interact in the therapy sessions as they do at home. Enactment is necessary to allow the therapist to conduct a more accurate assessment of the family, while avoiding the limitations inherent in the family's subjective recall of events. Enactment also largely prevents family members from selectively providing information, as they typically do when presenting a verbal account of a particular situation. The therapist instructs the family to repeat the performance in his or her presence. The assumption underlying the utility of enactment is that once a family becomes

absorbed in enacting a problem, the rules that govern the family system will be activated with a level of intensity similar to that of their routine or habitual behavior. Once the therapist facilitates this transaction, she or he is in a position to observe the multiple levels of communication that are occurring and thereby to gain a better understanding of the sequences of behavior maintaining the presenting problem.

> Claire and Brian Avery sought therapy for their 16-year-old son, Mike, who had become first withdrawn and then depressed following a breakup with his girlfriend. The Averys also had a 15-year-old daughter and a 10-year-old son. During the second session the therapist was trying to elicit information from the family as to how each member was reacting to Mike's new habit of coming directly home from school, going straight to his room, and locking the door. There was so much disagreement and so many interruptions that after 20 minutes the therapist realized she had only a vague idea of how this adolescent's depression was being handled by the family. The therapist called a "time out" and explained to the family that her visual memory was far superior to her verbal memory and that she simply could not formulate a picture of what was happening in this situation. She requested that the family arrange themselves as if the therapy office was their family room at home. She then asked Mike to designate one corner of the office as his bedroom, and then to go out of the office and enter again as if it were his home, and to do what he does when he comes home from school. The therapist then encouraged the family to do and say what they would when this happened at home. After a few attempts to explain to the therapist what they would say and being redirected by the therapist to act it out, the family was able to become as absorbed in the enactment as if it were actually occurring in the home.

In addition to providing valuable assessment information, enactment also affords an opportunity for therapeutic intervention aimed at interrupting dysfunctional interactions and stimulating their replacement by more adaptive behaviors.

4. *Restructuring.* Family structure refers to the pattern of relating that has developed among family members and that through frequent repetition has become part of the ongoing family choreography. At one point in a family's development, an action may have been initiated as a solution to a problem. In the development of depression in a family member, the action taken is often one of other members coming to the aid of the depressed person and trying to be cheerful and supportive. That initial solution may subsequently become absorbed into the family structure, and continue to be used even though it is no longer adaptive. Thus, a family may continue to react in a specific way through habit rather than through utility. Moreover, as we noted earlier, some types of families have general dysfunctional structures (e.g., chaotic, rigid, disengaged, and enmeshed) that will be exacerbated by the development of depression. Despite the difficulty of the task in such cases, these maladaptive structures must be altered in order for the family to become asymptomatic. The therapist must challenge this family structure by questioning the necessity and value of the way things are being done.

Mr. and Mrs. Williams brought their epileptic son Tommy to therapy because of his teacher's concern that his lethargic, passive behavior and his tendency to cry easily might be indications of depression. Mr. and Mrs. Williams could not understand how Tommy could possibly be depressed; after all, they did so much for him and were both devoted to ensuring his happiness. However, they did acknowledge that the symptoms reported by Tommy's teacher were also being exhibited at home, with perhaps even greater intensity and frequency.

In utilizing the strategy of restructuring, the therapist might challenge the Williams' tendency to be overprotective of Tommy, noting that their behavior might be inadvertently reinforcing an image of their son as an inadequate, incapable child. Although their manner of behaving with Tommy may have been a reasonable one in the early stages of his epilepsy, before it was adequately controlled by medication, their behaviors are no longer appropriate. Once the therapist has successfully challenged a family's dysfunctional structure, he or she must help its members find a new structure that is more adaptive and responsive to their current demands and requirements.

5. *Altering boundaries.* Family boundaries refer to the pattern of interaction that separates members of one subgrouping or subsystem within a family from those of another. Family systems are composed of several subsystems, which typically include at a minimum the parental relationship, the marital relationship, the sibling relationship, and the individual. In addition, each family may also have its own particular set of subsystems, alliances defined by close bonds between (or among) particular family members. A mother and daughter in a family, for example, may feel a closer bond than do the mother and son.

Boundaries can be concrete, as exemplified by the closed door separating the parents' bedroom from the rest of the house, or they can be intangible, as depicted by the daughter who feels that she cannot talk with her father. In large part, boundaries define the membership of subsystems and their relationships to each other. Another example of boundaries is represented by a family hierarchy that differentiates those members of the family who hold executive, decision-making positions (parents) from those who are expected to respond to and respect these members (children). It is generally acknowledged that healthy, functional families have clear boundaries, with the parents effectively established as heads of the family. Disturbances in family boundaries can result in the enmeshed, disengaged, chaotic, or rigid families described earlier, in which the family members experience difficulties in understanding or enacting their roles in the family. Family dysfunction or depression often develops when stress on the family results in a violation or change in the hierarchy, the family members' roles, and the subsystem boundaries. One of the therapist's tasks in these cases is to help the family restore its previous hierarchy, roles, and homeostatic state.

A family responded to the pressures imposed by temporary job demands requiring the father to be absent from home for prolonged periods of time by becoming increasingly stressed. Under the weight of growing responsibilities, the mother began to become depressed. The oldest son responded to his mother's depression by elevating himself to the position of "man of the family." In this new position, the son proved himself to be a capable and worthy "mate." Indeed, in some ways his attention and support appeared to reinforce his mother's depression. In this new role, the son assumed many executive functions that previously were performed by his father, and he was removed from his sibling subsystem and placed in the parental subsystem. Although this shift in position required that the son sacrifice numerous activities, it produced only minimal dysfunction (e.g., sibling jealousy) until the father's job situation returned to normal; then, more severe family dysfunction and depression began to develop, as the mother failed to support her husband's return to his parental position.

The therapist's task with this family is to delineate boundaries that remove the son from the parental subsystem and return him to the sibling subsystem. The therapist can effect this change by speaking frequently to the parents, asking their opinions of the children of the family, requesting that they sit together, separate from their children, and in general supporting them as the parents in the family. Once the therapist has successfully altered the family boundaries, she or he must immediately move into the issue of the marital relationship and explore with the couple what changes they both need to see occur in the relationship to prevent discouragement or unhappiness. This direction must be pursued immediately to prevent the mother from falling back into a depressive episode and must continue until the risk of a relapse is minimized.

6. *Constructing alternate realities.* A family coming to therapy brings with it a world view that has been constructed through experiences and values that have both historical and current meaning for the family. These world views generally have a history of validation within the family, the community, or the culture. Thus, people have beliefs and rituals that have meaning within their family or culture, but may seem unusual, unacceptable, or even bizarre to an observer. When a family system ceases to function adequately, it may be that their world view has imposed unhealthy limitations on them, resulting in depression in one or more family members. This world view must be altered or expanded to restore healthy functioning. There are several different ways to view the same event, but the family has elected a particular preferred one. The goal for the therapist is to construct a different world view — one that does not require the presence of the depressive symptoms.

As an example, a family reality may involve the belief that men hold a position of greater importance than women. This belief may further involve a corresponding set of expectations and responsibilities, such as that men must not show weakness or emotion. This world view may be functional until a son in the family is not able to meet these expectations.

Because of intense academic pressure, a son in such a family found himself becoming increasingly unable to complete his school requirements. As a result of his inability to cope with these pressures, he became depressed. His father's resulting anger only served to exacerbate the depression.

One of the therapist's initial tasks when this family presented for therapy was to initiate a new construction of reality, one that allowed men to express difficulty during times when they had problems coping with situations. The therapist can accomplish this task by appealing to family truths, but in so doing, expand on them. He might say, "Because you are parents with high expectations and good intentions for your children, you will want to help your son overcome his current difficulties." The therapist can utilize universal statements such as, "All people, whether male or female, young or old, will have times in their lives during which the demands placed upon them are excessive, and they will have trouble coping until they are able to find a way to deal adequately with these problems." The therapist can also supply expert advice that presents a different account of the family reality: "I think your son is so devoted to being a success, that even when the situation indicates that it is time for him to take a break, he is very reluctant to do so." For those families who hold tenaciously to their world view, the therapist may have to employ all of the foregoing techniques a number of times before he is successful at helping the family alter its belief system.

7. *Dealing with resistance.* In some families, the depression has been maintained through covert, long-standing patterns of interactions. In such cases the family has accumulated a lengthy history of reacting in predictable and consistent ways; any attempt to detour the family from this familiar course is bound to be difficult. In general, the more chronic the depression, the more likely the family will be to resist change, no matter how dysfunctional they have become.

As we have noted, another type of family in which the therapist is likely to encounter resistance is one in which the parents have diverted their conflict through a child. In these cases there is typically a strong commitment to maintaining the depressive symptomatic behavior, because alleviating the child's depression may expose the parents' unresolved conflict. The anxiety created by this possibility activates the family members to cling tenaciously to the depressive symptoms. The therapist's confirmation that a family is resistant to change is strengthened when repeated efforts to intervene (e.g., interpretations of family interactional patterns, suggestions, individual treatment, and promotion of open communication) are ineffective.

The use of certain paradoxical techniques can be helpful in these two situations. As Papp (1981) explains, a paradoxical intervention is one that is intended to accomplish the opposite of what is being implied. Papp cautions that there are certain situations in which paradoxical techniques should not be used. For example, crisis situations such as attempted suicide, violence, unwanted pregnancy, and sudden grief represent contraindications to the use of paradoxical procedures. Paradoxical techniques generally require considerable knowledge and skill on the part of the therapist to be implemented appropriately and effectively. With this caveat in mind, we will illustrate two paradoxical strategies that are relatively easy to use: redefining and restraining.

Redefining bears some similarity to reframing, a technique described earlier. The goal of redefining is to change the family's perception of the depression from a negative to a positive one. The depression is interpreted to the family so that it appears to serve the function of preserving the family's stability. Thus, depression in a child may be interpreted as the child's attempt to help the mother feel important and needed. Similarly, depression in a husband may be interpreted as an attempt to feel loved by and special to his family, and depression in a wife may be redefined by the therapist as a way of distracting the husband from pressures and stresses. Such intervention by the therapist supports the family interaction, rather than challenging or attempting to change it directly. The rationale behind this strategy is that once the pattern that produced the depression has been openly expressed, it loses its explanatory power, forcing the family to take direct responsibility for its behavior. Understandably, the effectiveness of this technique is largely dependent on accurate knowledge of the relationship between the depressive symptoms and their function within the family system.

The second paradoxical strategy, *restraining*, involves a warning from the therapist that since the depression is essential in maintaining family stability, the family must not try to change quickly. Indeed, whenever the family displays signs of changing, the therapist expresses concern and worry for the family that this change might produce undesirable consequences. The therapist actively portrays difficulties the family may encounter in making the changes. However, the family is allowed to change slowly despite all the therapist's cautions.

> Mr. and Mrs. Devereau came for therapy because their 10-year-old son Mark was periodically depressed. The therapist interpreted Mark's depression as serving to keep Mrs. Devereau from having to face her own unhappiness and dissatisfaction with her life. Mark's symptoms first surfaced shortly after he began school, an event Mrs. Devereau had greatly anticipated. She was eager to pursue her career after a 10-year interruption. However, after 6 months, numerous unsuccessful interviews, and aborted attempts to get her career back on track, Mrs. Devereau became withdrawn and depressed. Rather than confronting her growing feelings of inadequacy and self-doubt, she began to search for reasons she might still be needed at home. She found them when Mark began to exhibit signs of depression.

With confidence in the assessment of the function of the depressive symptomatology in this family, the therapist told Mark that it probably was very important for him to get depressed now and then, because it made his mother feel really needed. The therapist warned the Devereaus that if Mark did not get depressed, his mother might, and she might not be able to handle it as well as Mark. Mark was told that he was doing a very good job of protecting his mother by keeping her from facing her own disappointments and was encouraged to keep this "job" until he was sure his mom was strong enough to face her own unhappiness. Mrs. Devereau reacted strongly to this interpretation. The therapist cautioned the family not to try and change until Mrs. Devereau was sure that she was ready to make a second attempt at her career. She added that many women go through a difficult time when they attempt to reenter the work force after a long stay at home. Despite Mrs. Devereau's protestations that she was not that fragile, the therapist continued to discourage her from attempting to initiate changes too quickly. Indeed, every time Mrs. Devereau indicated steps that she was taking, the therapist pointed out pitfalls that other women had encountered. Mrs. Devereau slowly found the courage and strength to pursue her career, and with equal deliberation, Mark's depression lifted.

8. *Finding and emphasizing the family's strengths.* All families and individuals within families have aspects that, if noticed and understood, could be activated and honed and ultimately become beneficial to the family's growth and change. The therapist's task is to sift through individual and family characteristics until their strengths are unearthed. This process of exploration might require the therapist to work against previous training, which probably taught that gains in therapy were achieved by detecting and eradicating the pathology. In some cases the strengths will appear small and insignificant in comparison with more salient disturbing traits. Consequently, the therapist will require considerable skill to elevate these positive characteristics to prominent levels in the family system. The family's own capacity for healing and nurturing must be stimulated through the therapist's ongoing comments indicating considerable confidence in the family's ability to find its own solutions. The therapist must also quickly reinforce any actions displayed by a family member that resemble family support, nurturance, caring, competence, and the like. In addition, the therapist can actively construct tasks at which the family is likely to succeed, and then express pride in the family's ability to master them.

The Beeker family had been relocated to a factory town because of rising unemployment in their own small community. Their previous village was located in an isolated area and consequently had fostered overinvolvement among its citizens, including a suspected high incidence of incest. Although the Beeker family was referred for therapy because their daughter Linda had threatened to kill herself, the whole family presented in a depressed state. It appeared in all respects to be low-functioning. Neither parent was well educated. Mr. Beeker had recently been fired from his job, Mrs. Beeker was in and out of the hospital with various medical problems, and all three children were doing poorly in school. Moreover, during their third session, Linda broke into sobs and accused her father of having had sexual relations with her. At this point the therapist became discouraged about finding strengths to highlight. The therapist persisted in exploring every avenue in quest of this family's resources. Not only did each attempt fail to produce a positive dynamic, but it also had the unintended effect of making the family more despondent. In a moment of despair, the therapist had a flash of creativity. She asked the family what they were like before they moved. Mrs. Beeker, the first to respond, gave an account of all her community work helping the other less fortunate villagers. Her support included everything from baking to being a lay therapist. Her enthusiasm slowly ignited the whole family, and one by one, they voiced pleasure over their previous circumstances and accomplishments. By the end of the therapy hour the therapist felt she was working with a different family from the one with which she had begun. The therapist was now armed with an assortment of strengths on which to draw, to help the family deal more effectively with their current distressing situation.

The therapist may often have to exhibit high levels of ingenuity and creativity to uncover the strengths in some families. Moreover, once uncovered, the therapist must be adept at highlighting these strengths and helping the family mobilize to solve their problems.

INDIVIDUAL THERAPY TECHNIQUES

In the previous chapter, we presented a description of depression that ascribed importance to the role of the depressed individual's cognitive functioning in maintaining both the problematic interpersonal interactions and the depressive symptomatology. Specifically, we postulated that when depressed, individuals demonstrate greater attention and sensitivity to negative stimuli in their environment. Therefore, when others respond to the individual's depression with both positive and negative reactions, the depressed person is more likely to attend to the negative behaviors and, moreover, will find these reactions more aversive than they would in the absence of the depressed mood. In response to these reactions and perhaps in an effort to elicit more positive behaviors and support, the depressed individual becomes even more symptomatic, and the cycle worsens.

There are two major goals in working individually with the depressed person from an interpersonal systems perspective. First, the individual must understand the effects of his depression on those around him. In our experience, a brief and simple discussion of how depression can affect others is often sufficient to increase the individual's awareness and to make him more cognizant of his own behavior and more sensitive to its impact on others.

Second, the therapist must try to attenuate the depressed person's increased accessibility to negative stimuli. A number of procedures are available to accomplish this objective, and interestingly, several of these techniques are already used routinely by cognitive and behavioral therapists in the treatment of depression, albeit with different underlying rationales. As a first step toward this goal, the therapist should simply educate the patient, making him aware of the cognitive functioning engaged in by individuals when they are depressed, and how this manner of information processing affects their perceptions of their interactions with others. (This can be done in the context of the explanation described in the previous paragraph.) In addition, several procedures will be described that are aimed either at making the depressed individual more aware of positive behaviors or events in his or her environment or at providing the individual with a greater number of positive experiences.

To increase the depressed individual's awareness of the negative cognitive style and the positive aspects of his or her environment, a number of strategies are available to the clinician. The general goal is to help the individual monitor more accurately his or her thoughts and perceptions, both of her or his own and of other people's behaviors. To accomplish this goal, the depressed person should first be instructed to record all thoughts and behaviors surrounding "critical incidents," which are defined generally as events that evoke an affective reaction. Typically, these incidents will be interpersonal in nature, such as, "I got reprimanded by my employer," "My wife was dissatisfied with my behavior," "My mother made me feel guilty," and "My friend saw me coming and turned away." The therapist should be prepared to help the depressed individual keep such a diary and to discuss the recorded thoughts and events in subsequent sessions. This homework task is intended to make the patient more aware of both thought patterns and the environment and to prepare the patient for the second step in this procedure.

In the second stage, the depressed individual is required to continue to keep this daily record, but is also requested in addition to record positive events and the behaviors and reactions of others, both positive and negative. The patient may require assistance and encouragement from the therapist in completing this task. The patient might protest, for example, that nothing positive happens to him or her, and that people's reactions are solely negative. Here the therapist can take advantage of the fact that the depressed patient is being seen not only in individual sessions, but also in sessions with the family. The therapist can integrate these two sessions by pointing out to the depressed person, during the family sessions, instances when family members are responding positively to him. In doing this, the therapist must ensure that this information is not communicated to the depressed patient in an "I told you so" manner. Rather, a skillful and tactful therapist will couch these messages in terms of the caring behaviors of the family members, and how easy it is for the depressed person to overlook these positive behaviors when sometimes accompanied by other negative behavior or affect.

To reiterate, we are not implying that the depressed individual is distorting his or her perceptions of the environment or that the family members are in fact paragons of positive reinforcement who are mistakenly perceived as negative by the depressed person. We are simply suggesting that people respond to depressed individuals with both positive and negative reactions, and that depressed persons, like everyone else, experience both positive and negative events. While depressed, however, individuals focus more readily on negative rather than positive reactions and events, and the goal of this stage of therapy is to help them regain a more balanced perception of their environment. In fact, the results of several recent studies suggest that simply monitoring positive events is beneficial in alleviating depressive symptomatology (e.g., Dobson & Joffe, 1986).

In addition to helping depressed individuals become more aware of positive aspects of their environment, the therapist should encourage them to increase the number of their pleasurable activities (Lewinsohn, Biglan, & Zeiss, 1976). Several questionnaires are available to help the therapist and patient identify potentially pleasant or positive activities. Cautela (1977) has developed the Reinforcement Survey Schedule, and Arkowitz (1986, personal communication) is developing the Sources of Self-Esteem Inventory. The most frequently used questionnaire for this purpose, however, is MacPhillamy and Lewinsohn's (1982) Pleasant Events Schedule (PES). The PES is a psychometrically sound, 320-item inventory or menu of events often found enjoyable by adults. Any of these questionnaires, used in conjunction with discussions with the individual about what was enjoyable before depression occurred, will facilitate the task of identifying positive events and activities.

After potentially reinforcing activities have been identified, the therapist should encourage the depressed individual to engage in some of these activities. In undertaking this task, both Beck et al. (1979) and Lewinsohn et al. (1976) recommend that the therapist work with the patient to organize a daily schedule in which these activities are explicitly included. Guidelines for the therapist to follow in setting up this schedule are available, all of which are intended to maximize the probability of the patient's successful performance in following the schedule:

1. As Beck and Lewinsohn suggest, the schedule should be organized on an hourly basis. Having to account for hourly slots forces the schedule to be very explicit.
2. It is important to ensure that the focus of the schedule is on the execution of specific, observable, goal-oriented activities, rather than on the experience of certain affects (e.g., "riding my bicycle," or "reading the first chapter of my novel," rather than "feeling good" or "not being sad").
3. The scheduled activities should begin with small steps that require minimal effort by the patient to assure success. Using the principle of shaping, graded steps should be used in scheduling the activities in subsequent weeks.
4. The depressed patient must be instructed to reinforce or reward himself or herself for engaging in the activity, rather than for the outcome of the event. Thus, the individual should allow himself to feel good about going out to buy a gardening tool, rather than chastise himself because the store he went to did not have the tool in stock.

Generalization

Not only may engaging in an increased number of positive activities reduce the individual's level of depression, but also, as Beck et al. (1979) note, the accompanying experience of mastery increases self-esteem. To ensure the maintenance of this higher self-esteem following the termination of therapy, it is important to enhance the "transfer of training," or generalization, from the therapy sessions to extra-therapy (i.e., real-life) situations.

In discussing this concept, Gottman and Lieblum (1973) describe three techniques for strengthening transfer of training. In training behavioral skills, the therapist must teach the patient the general principle underlying the training before the training itself, so that the patient may apply the principle to extratherapy situations. Therefore, in teaching more effective communication skills to a married couple in which one spouse is depressed, it is important with respect to increasing generalization that the therapist educate the couple about general principles of communication before training them in specific behavioral skills.

The second way to increase transfer of training is to ensure that during therapy the patient has sampled extensively from the population of situations to which the responses and behaviors are to be generalized. Thus, to the extent that the therapy situation can simulate the patient's real-life environment, transfer of training will occur. The interpersonal systems approach to intervention described in this guidebook includes procedures designed to increase generalization. For example, the identified depressed patient is treated in the context of his or her "natural environment," that is, within the marital or family system in which the depression is occurring. Moreover, several of the procedures described in this chapter also increase generalization. The use of enactment of various situations, for example, and of encouraging the depressed patient to identify and engage in pleasant events or activities outside the therapy situation should result in increased transfer.

In a final procedure designed to maximize generalization, Gottman and Lieblum (1973) recommend that as therapy draws to a close, the therapist should minimize intervention; furthermore, an increasing proportion of the therapy tasks should be assigned as homework. Gottman and Lieblum (1973) also suggest, in an interesting use of reframing, that the therapist should prepare the patient, family, or both, for the possibility of relapse, but should help the patient view it as a learning experience. Thus, the therapist can reframe the possible recurrence of the depression as an opportunity for the patient and spouse or family to handle the depression differently, to observe their responses to the depression from a different perspective, and to use the coping techniques learned in therapy.

At this point, the reader should have an overview of the treatment goals, techniques, and intervention strategies that can be utilized in both family and individual sessions in an interpersonal systems treatment of depression. These principles, strategies, and techniques will be illustrated in detail in the following chapters, in which the reader will be taken in a step-by-step fashion from the assessment session, through termination of therapy to the follow-up session.

Chapter 4
Assessment of Depression: A Systems Perspective

In this chapter an interpersonal systems approach to the assessment of depression will be described. With respect to assessing the depressed individual, we will briefly review the criteria necessary for a DSM-III diagnosis of depression, and will outline specific structured interviewing procedures that can be used to make a reliable diagnosis. In addition, we will review frequently used self-report measures of depression. In describing the assessment of the depressed person, we will try to point out those specific symptoms and aspects of depression with particular implications for the type of treatment that should be offered to the client.

Consistent with the description of depression presented in Chapter 2, it is our position that assessment of the depressed individual and assessment of the marital dyad or family are of equal importance, and that both are necessary precursors to an interpersonal systems approach to treatment. Therefore, in this chapter the typical individual assessment procedure for depression will be extended to include an evaluation of the immediate social environment of the depressed person. In this context, techniques used in interviewing families with a depressed member will be described, and measures to assess the quality of the marital and family relationships of the depressed individual will be presented. Assessment techniques that have grown out of the behavioral observation literature also will be discussed, with an illustration of their relevance for the clinician.

Intelligent use of these diverse assessment instruments and techniques will result in a more comprehensive formulation of the depressed individual's condition and circumstances, and should help the therapist in providing the direction for the selection and implementation of specific treatment strategies. Moreover, these measures will permit the therapist to conduct an ongoing assessment of the individual and family's responses to intervention, so that the treatment strategies may be modified as necessary. Finally, these measures will allow the clinician to evaluate both the efficacy of treatment and the maintenance of gains made during therapy. In closing this chapter, procedures that can be used by the clinician to conduct such an evaluation will be described.

ASSESSING THE CONTEXT
OF THE DEPRESSION

Who to See in the Assessment Session

In organizing the assessment session or sessions, we recommend that the therapist start by seeing either the marital dyad or the entire family, depending on the nature of the referral and the impact of the depression on the family. The assessment and therapeutic process begins from the family member's first telephone contact with the therapist, during which the therapist should make explicit the ground rules for an interpersonal approach to therapy. In all probability, the single rule with the greatest initial impact on the contacting family member involves the decision regarding who is to be seen in therapy. Most often, the family member initiating the first contact with the therapist will define the problem as involving only one family member (most frequently a child or the member him- or herself, but often the spouse) or only one part of the family (typically the marital dyad). At this point, the therapist must decide which family members are to be seen in the subsequent assessment session.

In contrast to most individually oriented therapies, our position is that the marital dyad is generally the smallest unit that is profitably seen in therapy. There are exceptions to this principle, such as individuals who are depressed but not involved in a significant relationship with another person, and recent widows or widowers who have no other family and are mourning the death of their spouse. These individuals may best be treated with an individual therapy approach for depression that maintains a focus on interpersonal dynamics, such as Interpersonal Psychotherapy (Klerman et al., 1984) and Social Skills Training (Hersen, Bellack, Himmelhoch, & Thase, 1984).

Another exception to seeing at least the marital dyad in therapy involves cases in which an individual from an intact family contacts a therapist requesting intervention for personal depression, and despite the therapist's request, refuses to involve the spouse or children in the treatment process. The therapist must then make a decision regarding his or her willingness to work with this person alone. Certainly it is important to respect people's wishes concerning their preferences for the type of treatment they receive. The decision to treat a depressed person in individual therapy, however, should not be made without careful consideration. It is clear from the literature reviewed in Chapter 1 that significant interpersonal factors are associated with depression. Depressed individuals are often characterized by marital difficulties, and both spouses and children of depressed persons have exhibited elevated levels of psychopathology; it is likely, therefore, that these factors will also be relevant in the case of the depressed individual just described. Indeed, the fact that this person explicitly refuses to involve a spouse or children in the treatment process increases this possibility. Furthermore, as we also noted in Chapter 1, Weissman (1979; Bothwell & Weissman, 1977) found that although individual treatment for depressed women was successful in alleviating their depressive symptomatology, their roles as wives and mothers continued to be impaired following treatment. Thus, a therapist who sees a depressed individual alone may begin therapy at a disadvantage. The depressive symptoms may be alleviated through individual therapy, but broader aspects of the individual's impaired social functioning and interpersonal environment may remain unchanged.

The decision to refrain from working with individuals in therapy because they refuse to involve their spouses or families in treatment is difficult for a therapist to make. It can be argued that it is better to see the individual and effect at least symptomatic improvement in the depression than to refuse the person altogether. We have considerable sympathy for this position, and there are many marital and family therapists who, if pressed, would see the individual, at least for an initial assessment, under these conditions. Indeed, the therapist may form a sufficiently strong alliance with the patient in the initial assessment session that the person agrees to involve the family in subsequent sessions.

It has been our experience, however, that if treated alone these depressed persons do not do as well in therapy in the longer term as do similar depressed individuals seen in treatment with their families. They do not improve symptomatically as quickly, their gains are typically more limited, and they often do not maintain these gains over as long a period of time. Consequently, we strongly recommend that, whenever possible, therapists decide to see either the marital dyad or the entire family, at least for the initial assessment interview, rather than the depressed individual alone. Moreover, for reasons to be discussed, it is important that the couple or family be involved right from the first session. Although it is possible to introduce other family members into therapy later in the process, marital and family therapists generally agree that this practice has serious drawbacks.

The Marital Dyad or the Family?

As a general principle, we believe that it is important to see all members of a depressed person's family or, at a minimum, both spouses, at least for the initial assessment session. Given this belief and, indeed, the interpersonal framework described in this guidebook, the question arises as to when it is appropriate to work with only the marital dyad and under what conditions the therapist should require that the entire family attend the sessions.

Generally, the decision concerning the appropriateness of assessing only the couple, versus the entire family, rests on the nature of the presenting problem and the therapist's perception of the functioning of the children. Assuming that the "identified patient" (i.e., the individual who is exhibiting symptoms of depression) is an adult, there are essentially two situations in which only the couple need attend the initial assessment session (in addition to the case in which the couple has no children). First, if from the information provided during the initial contact the therapist is reasonably certain that the children are not seriously affected by the depression, it may be best not to involve them in therapy, at least in the beginning. Results of studies suggest that if there is any bias in the perceptions of depressed mothers, it is to report more disturbance in their children than is actually there. Therefore, if the contact person is a depressed parent who reports that the children generally seem unaffected by the depression, it is usually best to assume that this report is veridical and to see only the marital dyad in the first session.

The second situation in which the therapist may prefer to see the couple alone concerns the ages of the children. Although family therapists disagree on this issue, our experience is that even if the children appear to be adversely affected by their parent's depression, the therapist may forego seeing them in therapy if they are too young to derive direct benefit from a family therapy approach or to participate actively in the sessions. If, after contact with the parents, concern remains about a particular child in a family, the therapist may suggest that the child be seen by a child therapist. The exact age younger than which family therapy may be of little benefit to children is largely a matter of opinion, but as a general rule we believe that children younger than 6 years of age belong in this category.

Finally, therapy with the entire family is also warranted when the child is the identified patient. It is interesting to note that a depressed mother often will contact a therapist with concerns about her children. The children are frequently described as conduct disordered, or as exhibiting behavioral disturbances; less often, they are portrayed as withdrawn and depressed. As we noted earlier, a depressed mother may overestimate the deviant behavior of her children. We also know, however, that children of depressed mothers demonstrate a higher incidence of deviant behavior and, therefore, may in fact be disturbed. Consequently, it is important in either case that the therapist engage the entire family in therapy.

During the assessment interview with the family, the spouse plays an important role in corroborating (or not corroborating) the referring parent's perceptions of the children. It is likely that the identified child does exhibit conduct disorder or behavioral disturbances. It is also possible, however, that the referring parent (typically the mother) is depressed, and that her depression is both affecting and being affected by the behavior and functioning of the child. Although therapy with these families initially may focus on the child's behavior within the family context, in many cases it ultimately will center on the mother and her depression.

Finally, we should emphasize that while the decision of who to see in the assessment sessions is important, it is not set in stone. For example, if after seeing both spouses in an assessment session the therapist decides that the children should be involved in the therapeutic process, they can be included in subsequent sessions. Similarly, if the therapist decides that the children should not be involved, a recommendation that they be excluded from subsequent sessions can be made.

The clinician should be aware, however, that these "post-hoc" decisions are not without their disadvantages. Bringing into therapy a family member who was not asked to attend the initial sessions has important implications. It could mean to the rest of the family that they, but not the new member, are absolved of responsibility for the situation that brought them to therapy. By the same token, the newly involved member may feel that the rest of the family has decided that he or she is to blame for the family's difficulty and, consequently, may demonstrate significant resistance to attending therapy. Excusing from subsequent sessions a family member who has been seen for the assessment interview can also be problematic. The individual may believe that she or he is not responsible in any way for the situation that brought the family to seek treatment. Similarly, and perhaps more importantly, those family members who are asked to remain in therapy may feel that the therapist believes that they, and not the other individuals, have caused or contributed to the problem and may demonstrate resistance to the treatment process.

The therapist cannot circumvent all of these situations. As a general rule, it is less problematic for family members to perceive absolution than blame, that is, for the therapist to exempt individuals from therapy than to ask to see members who were initially absent from the sessions. Thus, the therapist who asks to see the entire family for the initial session is in a better position of not having to request that an absent family member attend subsequent sessions. Moreover, even if the therapist later chooses to work with only some of the family members, the opportunity to obtain first-hand information by observing the family's interactions may later prove invaluable. Therefore, we strongly recommend that in the initial contact with the referring family member, the therapist clearly explain the ground rules for conducting therapy and, if appropriate according to the guidelines just presented, request that the entire family be present at least for the assessment session. In explaining this rule to the family member, it is usually sufficient simply to state that because the goal of the initial session is to gather as much information as possible about the depression, the presence of the entire family allows everyone who is close to or who cares about the identified patient to offer their perceptions and observations.

The Initial Assessment Interview

In the initial telephone contact with the referring family member, the therapist should determine the membership of the family system. In general, the "family" is usually defined as those members living in the household at the time of the interview, although there are exceptions to this definition. Occasionally the therapist may decide to include other family members who do not live within the family's household but who still retain close emotional ties with the family. Similarly, the therapist may wish to see unrelated people who do live in the household and will define the "family" as such.

We have already noted that most family therapists agree that one ground rule of therapy should be that all relevant family members must attend at least the assessment sessions. Although it is often less problematic logistically to deal with only part of a family, we believe that the unwillingness of family members to attend therapy often reflects the presence of isolation, distrust, anger, or rejection in the family, and because it may also indicate a resistance to treatment or to giving up the problem, it is generally a poor prognostic indicator. As a final, more pragmatic consideration, it is difficult to assess accurately the functioning of the family and its psychopathology in the absence of one or more family members.

In the initial contacts with the couple or family, the therapist must establish a relationship that is positive, yet separate from the dysfunctional marital or family system. To as great an extent as possible, the therapist should attempt to formulate an explanation of the depression which allows all family members to receive some benefit from the symptomatic improvement of the depressed individual, and which requires the spouses or family as a unit to take responsibility for finding solutions to the problematic depressive behavior.

Haley (1976) outlined a straightforward procedure for conducting an initial interview with a family. Because Haley's suggestions are aimed at clinicians engaged in the practice of general family therapy, we have adapted them here to make them more relevant and specific to the problem of depression in a family member. The initial interview proceeds essentially through four stages: (a) social, (b) problem, (c) interaction, and (d) goal formulation.

The Social Stage. In the social stage, the family is greeted, and the therapist attempts to make the family members feel relaxed and at ease. It is important at this stage that all family members be involved in the interview. Asking the name of each family member and the ages of the children, and gathering some relatively innocuous demographic information are useful techniques in accomplishing this goal. The therapist can inquire about the parents' jobs, the length of their marriage, the name of the children, what grades they are in, their favorite subjects, and so forth. In beginning this stage of the interview, the therapist should avoid beginning with the identified depressed individual, communicating instead to the family that he is interested in the family as a whole rather than in the identified individual.

The social stage also provides the therapist with the first opportunity to observe the family interacting. The family's seating arrangement should be recorded, noting who sits beside the depressed member and who sits away from him or her. The therapist should begin to form hypotheses concerning possible alliances and schisms within the family and their relationship to the depression, but as Haley (1976) cautions, the therapist should regard these formulations as preliminary and not share them with the family at this point.

The therapist should also attend carefully to the demeanor and behavior of the depressed family member. We described in detail in Chapter 1 the symptoms required for a DSM-III diagnosis of depression, and although the therapist will later conduct an individual diagnostic assessment of the depressed person, he or she must nevertheless remain cognizant of these characteristics and criteria while interacting with the family. The therapist should attend to the level of involvement of the depressed individual and to the context of any displays of depressive symptoms. Observing the differential responses of family members to these depressive behaviors is crucial for the therapist both to understand the processes by which the depression may be maintained and, more importantly, to plan an appropriate intervention strategy.

The Problem Stage. Following this relatively brief introductory period is the problem stage, which has two aspects. First, the therapist attempts to put the interview in context for the family, and second, he or she obtains information from the family members concerning their perceptions of the problem or problems that brought them to seek therapy. In providing a context to the assessment interview, the therapist should attempt to clarify for the family her or his perception of the problem and to share with the family his or her understanding of the purpose of the session. In undertaking this task, the therapist might say something like, "On the phone, Mrs. Clarke, you mentioned that you were concerned about your daughter Jennifer feeling depressed, and that you had run out of ideas about ways that you could try and help her. Perhaps we can begin by asking everyone why they think you have all come here today." Or, "I know a bit about the circumstances that bring you here. I would like to know more about them, and would like the help of all of you in order to give me a better understanding of the situation." In addition, any contact with a referring agent should also be described, and the family should be informed of the presence of any recording equipment or of any personnel who might be observing the session from behind a one-way mirror. The therapist should check to see whether the family members understand and agree with the statement of the purpose of the interview. Any disagreements should be discussed and resolved at this point.

In the second phase of the problem stage, the therapist obtains information from the family concerning their perceptions of the reason they came for therapy. Because the nature of the referral likely involved the depression of one of the family members, it is reasonable that this depression will be the focus of each participant's response, at least initially. Despite the possibility of redundancy, the therapist must elicit a statement from each family member, in turn, of his or her view of the presenting (or other) problems. The therapist might inquire of each member, "How would you describe the problem that brings you to see me?" Coyne and Segal (1982) note that four separate questions are really being asked here: (a) What is the specific problem that has led the family member or members to seek treatment? (b) How is the problem expressed in their daily lives? (c) Why did they seek therapy now, as opposed to weeks or months ago? and (d) How was this particular agency or therapist chosen? Certainly, some family members will have more information than others about some of these areas. Nevertheless, the therapist should obtain as complete a statement as possible from each family member.

In this, the first real task of therapy, it is imperative that each family member receive an equal chance to speak without interruption. By involving all members in the session, the therapist challenges their probable assumption that the depressed family member is both the cause and the expression of all the family's difficulties. Moreover, the initial complaints about the depressed person and his or her behavior are gradually replaced by a more cohesive family process, with each member playing a role. The therapist must control this aspect of the session, however, and be clear and direct in all statements. Complicated or awkward questions should be avoided and at this point, any highly charged exchanges or confrontations between family members should not be allowed. If an interaction between two or more family members begins to escalate, the therapist should note this covertly and then intervene. A couple or family who experiences an initial session that is too stressful is likely to discontinue therapy.

While the order in which the clinician addresses the participants is obviously of some importance, therapists disagree as to what this order should be. In our experience, it is usually best to ask the parent or parents first and then proceed chronologically with the children. If both parents are present, the therapist might simply address them both and leave it to them to decide who will respond. In fact, the process by which the parents determine which of them will respond may be of interest to the therapist. Alternatively, some therapists prefer to begin with the parent who seems more withdrawn, hesitant, or passive, to involve that parent in the assessment and treatment process. Still other clinicians prefer to begin with the most powerful parent, thereby increasing the probability of the family returning for therapy. As the bottom line, it seems important to begin with one parent, as opposed to the children, but beyond this, it is more critical to ensure that by the end of this information-gathering process, the therapist has sought each family members' perspective on the present difficulty and has a clear understanding of their perceptions of the depression.

The therapist must also obtain information in this stage concerning the procedures that the couple or family members have already implemented in unsuccessful attempts to ameliorate the depression. Was the depression ignored or confronted and by which family members? What were the effects of each attempt? The therapist should ensure that descriptions of these attempted solutions are elicited in concrete, behavioral terms. Determining what the family has already done to deal with the depression will aid the therapist, in devising alternate treatment strategies and gaining a more comprehensive understanding of the maintenance of the depression, the structure of the family system, and the nature of the relationships among family members.

The Interaction Stage. In the next stage of the assessment interview, the interaction stage, the therapist essentially drops out of the conversation. In the previous stage the therapist elicited each family member's comments about the depression and acted as a "hub" through which all statements were directed. In this interaction stage, the therapist encourages the family members to talk to each other directly about the depression, to interact among themselves. As Haley (1976) notes, if they continue to talk to the therapist or involve him in their interaction, he must maneuver them back to talking with each other.

It is helpful to divide this interaction stage into two segments. In the first segment, the therapist simply observes the quality and pattern of interactions among the family members. Later in this chapter we will describe a coding scheme that can be used to help the therapist systematize and record these observations. While the therapist still avoids being drawn into the couple or family interactions, in this segment he does not try to affect the conversations in any other way. That is, the therapist does not try to draw inactive family members into the interaction, or to keep overly talkative members from monopolizing the conversation. Information on who speaks to whom, and who does not speak, is important for the therapist in understanding the family's day-to-day functioning around the depression.

This first segment can continue for 5 or 6 minutes, with the therapist monitoring the pattern of interactions. In the second segment, the therapist takes a more active role in directing the interaction. When any two family members are interacting, the therapist should be prepared to introduce a third member into the conversation, if that member has not yet participated. By being directive, the therapist ensures that by the end of the interaction stage, he or she will have observed the manner and frequency with which all family members interact with each other in the absence of an actively involved and participating therapist. More importantly, the therapist will have a better sense of the couple or family and the nature of the relationships among the family members. On the basis of the manner in which the family members deal with the depressed individual, the therapist should now be able to formulate at least preliminary hypotheses concerning the maintenance and role of the depression in the couple or family.

ASSESSMENT OF THE
INDIVIDUAL SUBSYSTEMS

After the second segment of the interaction stage, the therapist should tell the family that she or he would like to meet with some of the family members separately, and would also like them all to complete a number of forms. If the therapist is seeing only the marital dyad in this session, the couple should be informed that he or she would like to meet with both spouses individually, and would like them both to complete a number of questionnaires. Although this formal assessment process requires some orchestration or synchronization, in order to assess the depressed individual and all of the relevant subsystems, in our experience any inconvenience incurred in this enterprise has been more than compensated by the additional information obtained from the family members. As an alternative procedure, the family members could be given the questionnaires in packets and requested either to mail them to the therapist or bring them to their next session. Although this is a workable arrangement, it has been less satisfactory than the procedure to be described. The information from these measures is not immediately available to the therapist for use in the second session, and as a result the therapist will lose time in understanding the family's situation and in implementing appropriate intervention strategies. Furthermore, and perhaps of greater consequence when it occurs, one or more family members may "forget" to return the questionnaires. Although this information may itself be important concerning the motivation or resistance of particular family members to treatment, potentially useful data from the questionnaires is lost or, at best, delayed even further. For these reasons, we strongly recommend that the therapist have the family members complete the measures during the assessment session.

Before the final, goal-definition stage of the assessment interview is discussed, we will describe in the following sections various diagnostic interviews and self-report measures that can be used to assess depression in adults and children, and to evaluate diverse aspects of marital and/or family relationships. The choice of which measures to use depends upon the therapist's preliminary hypotheses, formulated on the basis of information gleaned during the initial part of the assessment interview. One goal of this phase of the assessment process is to supplement the therapist's knowledge of the identified depressed patient and the other family members and, in particular, to gain a more comprehensive understanding of the functional relationship between the individual's depression and the family's functioning. Specific depression-associated and marital/family-associated criteria also will be presented, to serve as indications and cautions in using the interpersonal systems-oriented therapy approach described in this guidebook. The therapist should bear these criteria in mind while assessing the depressed individual and family and deciding on the appropriate treatment.

In terms of logistics, while the therapist is interviewing the depressed individual alone, the spouse (and children, if present) are requested to complete a number of questionnaires in another room. When this interview is completed, the "teams" trade places: the depressed individual fills out the questionnaires, while one or more of the other family members meet with the therapist. This choreography continues until the therapist has collected the necessary information from the appropriate subsystems (usually about 30 to 45 minutes). When children are present, the therapist may see the depressed parent alone and then with the spouse. In addition, if one of the children demonstrates depressive symptoms or evidence of other behavioral disturbance, or if the children appear to be inhibited by their parents' presence, the therapist may also spend some time alone with the children. With a couple in which one spouse is depressed, the therapist should arrange to spend individual time with both spouses. Following these subsystem assessments, the therapist meets again with the family or marital dyad for the final part of the session.

Assessment of Depression

In accord with our clinical research strategy, we recommend that both interview and self-report measures be used to assess both depressive symptomatology and changes in response to treatment. Thus, in the following section we present information about commonly-used interview and self-report measures of depression for adults, and for children and adolescents.

Interview Measures for Depression: Adult Measures

Schedule for Affective Disorders and Schizophrenia. The Schedule for Affective Disorders and Schizophrenia (SADS) was developed by Endicott and Spitzer (1978) to increase the reliability of interviewer-derived psychiatric diagnoses. The SADS covers not only depression, but also such diagnostic categories as schizophrenia, anxiety disorders, and personality disorders. There are three different versions of the SADS: the regular, the lifetime, and the change version. Of these three, the regular version will likely be of most use to the practising clinician, although we suggest that the change version be administered at least once following therapy. The regular version of the SADS has two parts. In Part I, the severity of the patient's current symptoms is assessed, both in the past week and during the patient's worst recent level of functioning. Part II of the SADS provides a psychiatric and social history-taking format. If the clinician has used the regular version of the SADS in conducting the initial diagnostic interview, we suggest that the final interview at the end of treatment use the SADS change version, which includes only those questions from Part I of the regular version that assess severity. By comparing the severity of symptoms before and after treatment, the clinician will have an objective measure of change.

Hamilton Rating Scale for Depression. Although the recent advent of structured diagnostic interview schedules has altered the situation somewhat, the Hamilton Rating Scale for Depression (HRSD; Hamilton, 1960) remains the most frequently used interviewer-rated measure of depression. Hamilton originally intended the HRSD to be used as an index of severity in patients who had already been diagnosed as depressed. It is important to note, therefore, that this measure was designed to yield not a diagnosis, but rather a depressive severity score in patients already diagnosed as depressed.

The HRSD contains 21 items covering mood, behavioral, somatic, and cognitive symptoms. By convention, only 17 of Hamilton's original 21 items are typically scored. The HRSD is most commonly administered by experienced clinicians, although investigators have demonstrated that laypersons can be trained, in a relatively short time, to reach acceptable levels of administration. Furthermore, Endicott, Cohen, Nee, Fleiss, and Sarantakos (1981) demonstrated that HRSD scores can be reliably derived from a SADS interview, so that the clinician may obtain information for both of these measures through a single, comprehensive interview. The HRSD has been shown to be sensitive to change in the severity of depressive symptomatology over time and, consequently, is useful as a measure of the efficacy of therapy. Finally, we should note that Carroll, Feinberg, Smouse, Rawson, and Greden (1981) have developed a self-report version of the HRSD, the Carroll Rating Scale for Depression.

Interview Measures for Depression: Child and Adolescent Measures

The Child Assessment Schedule. The Child Assessment Schedule (CAS; Hodges, Kline, Stern, Cytryn, & McKnew, 1982) is a structured psychological interview for the clinical assessment of children between the ages of 7 and 12 years. The CAS was designed to provide systematic and comprehensive information about a child's psychological and psychiatric functioning. Furthermore, in designing the interview, Hodges et al. (1982) chose questions and response items that inquired specifically about each of the diagnostic criteria for the major childhood disorders presented in DSM-III. This matching procedure is an invaluable aid to the therapist in making a differential diagnosis.

The CAS consists of two parts and is modeled after adult diagnostic interviews. In the first part of the interview the child responds yes or no to approximately 75 questions. In the second part of the CAS, the clinician records observations about the child after the interview has been completed. The CAS has demonstrated adequate interrater reliability and discrimination among groups of child inpatients, outpatients, and normal controls. Interestingly, the CAS also discriminated between children of affectively disturbed mothers and those of normal mothers.

The Interview Schedule for Children. The Interview Schedule for Children (ISC; Kovacs, 1983) is a structured interview that yields a DSM-III diagnosis for the child. Two forms of the ISC are available, permitting its use for both intake and follow-up assessment. The ISC focuses on the current phenomenology of the child's difficulties, encompassing major symptoms of psychopathol-

ogy and severity of current condition, mental status, behavioral observations
during the interview, and clinicians' impressions. Kovacs (1983) has reported
high interrater reliability for the ISC.

Self-Report Measures of Depression: Adult Measures

Beck Depression Inventory. The Beck Depression Inventory (BDI) is probably
the most frequently used self-report method of assessing depressive symptomatology. It was originally developed by Beck, Ward, Mendelson, Mock, and
Erbaugh (1961) as an interviewer-assisted procedure, and consists of 84 self-
evaluative statements grouped into 21 categories,* chosen to assess the affective, cognitive, motivational, and physiological symptoms of depression. It is
important to note that the BDI was not designed to yield a discrete diagnosis of
depression; rather, it was constructed to measure depression as one single dimension of psychopathology that cuts across a wide variety of diagnostic categories.
Its major focus, therefore, is on the depth or severity of depressive symptomatology.

The BDI has high internal consistency, with split-half reliability coefficients
averaging 0.86. Although there have been some problems in this respect, the
BDI does correlate reasonably well with clinicians' ratings of severity of depression and with other self-report measures of depression. It is considered effective
as a screening device; Hammen (1981) has suggested that the BDI is the most
satisfactory self-rating instrument for assessing severity of depression. The BDI
has been used successfully both as a criterion for patient identification and as an
indicator of change in depressive symptomatology as a function of treatment
(e.g., McLean & Hakstian, 1979).

Center for Epidemiological Studies Depression Scale. The Center for Epidemiological Studies Depression Scale (CES-D) is a 20-item scale designed to measure the current level of depressive symptomatology in individuals from the
general population. For each item, respondents indicate on a 4-point scale how
frequently they have experienced that symptom in the past week. The items
assess depressed mood, feelings of guilt and worthlessness, feelings of hopelessness, psychomotor retardation, appetite loss, and sleep disturbance, although
there is a particular emphasis on affective symptoms. Like the BDI, the CES-D
was designed to measure depression as one dimension of psychopathology that
might cut across various diagnostic categories. In fact, there is sufficient
research suggesting that the CES-D should not be used as a clinical diagnostic
instrument (Lewinsohn & Teri, 1982). It is considered a useful screening device,

---

* There is also a shorter, 13-category version of the BDI, which correlates very highly with the
original longer version.

however, to identify those persons in the general population who may be at risk for depression (Radloff, 1977), and in this context, it may be appropriate for the spouse and family members of the depressed individual.

Zung Self-Rating Depression Scale. The Zung Self-Rating Depression Scale (SDS; Zung, 1965) consists of 20 items assessing symptoms of depression identified in previous factor analytic studies of the syndrome of depression. These 20 items assess "pervasive affect," "physiological equivalents or concomitants," and "psychological concomitants." Although the Zung SDS correlates moderately well with other self-report measures of depression, there is some question regarding its ability to differentiate levels of severity within depressed populations, and as Rehm (1976, p. 239) states, "The SDS is psychometrically unsophisticated . . . (and its) . . . use in behavioral practice and research is questionable pending stronger psychometric support."

MMPI-D Scale. The MMPI-D scale, 1 of the 10 clinical scales of the MMPI, was originally developed to identify severely depressed patients. It consists of 60 empirically-derived true-false items. Certainly the MMPI is one of the most familiar psychological assessment instruments. The MMPI-D scale, however, has been repeatedly criticized for both the heterogeneity of its items and its complex factor structure. To address these drawbacks of the scale, Dempsey (1964) constructed the MMPI-D-30, a 30-item version of the MMPI-D scale. Although the MMPI-D-30 is a more nearly unidimensional depression scale than is the MMPI-D scale, it still has limitations. It shares with the MMPI-D scale the problem of heterogeneity of item pool, and as Hammen (1981) notes, the MMPI-D-30 does not sample from the entire range of depressive symptomatology.

Self-Report Measures of Depression: Child and Adolescent Measures

The Childhood Depression Inventory. Although there are a few other self-report child depression scales (e.g., Children's Depression Scale; Tisher & Lang, 1983), the Childhood Depression Inventory (CDI; Kovacs, 1983) was the first and is probably the most widely used self-report measure of depression in children. Consequently, it will be the only self-report child measure of depression discussed herein. The CDI, developed from the Beck Depression Inventory, was designed for use with school-age children and adolescents. It consists of 27 items assessing the presence and severity of an array of "overt" symptoms of childhood depression, such as sadness, anhedonia, suicidal ideation, and sleep and appetite disturbances. The CDI has demonstrated acceptable test-retest reliability, internal consistency, and concurrent validity, correlating with clinicians' global ratings of depression in children. Furthermore, the CDI discriminates among depressed children, patients in other diagnostic groups, and nonselected normal school-age children (Kovacs, 1983).

We have not been exhaustive in the presentation of these assessment instruments, but rather have intended this to be an overview of representative measures of depression in children and adults. In our own work with depressed patients, we utilize a particular subset of these measures. For adults, we administer the SADS interview and derive a Hamilton Rating Scale score from that interview. In addition, the adults complete the Beck Depression Inventory. For children, we administer the Child Assessment Schedule and ask the child to complete the Children's Depression Inventory (CDI). We also ask the parents to complete the CDI as they predict their child will, to assess their perceptions of their child's functioning.

INTERVIEWING THE DEPRESSED PATIENT

Diagnostic interviews with depressed patients are one of the most difficult interviews to conduct. We commented in Chapter 1 on the results of investigations of the interpersonal behavior of depressed individuals and the responses of other people to the depressed person. In general, depressed individuals are characterized by negative verbalizations, dysphoric mood, and a lack of interest in activities. In addition, they may demonstrate slowed and monotonous speech, weepiness, and in some cases overt hostility. Individuals interacting with depressed persons respond negatively to these behaviors, experiencing frustration, anxiety, and hostility, and eventually avoiding or rejecting the depressed person.

The therapist interviewing the depressed patient must be sensitive to this body of research. The therapist is not immune to experiences of the same responses and affect exhibited by others interacting with the depressed person. Consequently, it is imperative that the therapist continually monitor his or her feelings and behavior to avoid demonstrating the frustration, impatience, or irritability that she or he may be experiencing during the interview. Moreover, the therapist must be sensitive to both verbal and nonverbal aspects of depression. In addition to the content of the interview, the therapist should pay particular attention to the patient's rate and quality of speech, overt motor behavior, and posture.

The interview with the depressed patient will require active participation by the therapist. The discouragement associated with the depression will likely cause the patient to be pessimistic about the outcome of treatment, and consequently, he or she is likely to take a relatively passive role in the interview. Depressed patients generally lack spontaneity, and often wait for the therapist to speak, while staring down at the floor. Depressed patients often feel more comfortable when the therapist leads the interview; for this reason, it is important that the therapist be organized in his interviewing. In fact, if the therapist adopts a strategy of being more passive, with the goal of forcing the patient to become a more active participant, the unintended result may be a patient who feels even more incompetent, frustrated, and depressed.

The therapist might begin the assessment interview by commenting on the depressed person's retardation and lowering of mood, rather than with more threatening or anxiety-inducing content-related aspects of the patient's functioning. The therapist's general manner with the depressed individual should be one of concern and empathy, rather than a cheerful or humorous facade meant to offset the patient's depression. Although the therapist may prefer the interview to flow more quickly than it probably will, the pace of the interview should reflect the patient's depression to a greater extent than it does the therapist's preference. The interview, then, is likely to be slow and deliberate, with frequent periods of silence. Again, it is important that the therapist be organized so that these periods of silence, which can be interpreted by the patient as disinterest or dissatisfaction by the therapist, can be kept to a minimum.

Information to be Collected

There are a number of areas of the patient's history and current functioning about which the therapist should inquire. With respect to historical information, the therapist should determine the patient's family history of depression, that is, is there a history of depression in the patient's first-degree relatives (parents and siblings)? Bipolar and endogenous depressions are often associated with a positive family history. The therapist should also inquire about the patient's personal history of depression. Is this the first episode the patient has experienced, or have there been previous episodes? This area of inquiry will be particularly important in making a decision regarding the use of antidepressant medication (see below). Any significant medical history should be explored to determine the primary or secondary nature of the current depressive episode.

It is also imperative that the therapist determine the patient's potential for suicidal behavior, and consequently, if the patient does not do so, the therapist must introduce the subject of suicide into the interview. It is best for the therapist's questioning in this area to be direct. Questions such as, "Have you had thoughts of committing suicide?" or "Have you felt that you want to kill yourself?" are important to ask, even if the answer is no. The question communicates caring on the part of the therapist and lets the patient know that this is not a "taboo" subject. If the patient has thought of suicide, the therapist must probe further. Has the patient formulated a specific plan? Has she or he taken any specific action on his or her suicidal thoughts? Many clinicians have suggested that this direct questioning itself is of therapeutic value.

Assessment of Symptoms

The therapist must carefully assess the depressive symptoms of the patient. In conducting this assessment, the clinician may find it helpful to rely on the DSM-III criteria presented in Chapter 1, and to utilize structured interview schedules for depression, such as the SADS or the HRSD, as well as such self-report measures as the BDI. The therapist should obtain information about the history of the patient's current episode and about any concomitant physical symptoms. In conducting this interview, the therapist also must probe beyond the patient's current symptomatology, to inquire about symptoms experienced during the worst part of the current episode. For example, patients with moderately severe depression may have intermittent periods of up to a full day during which a number of symptoms may remit.

In outlining the following areas of inquiry for the therapist, we have used as a guide the Hamilton Rating Scale for Depression (see also Klerman et al., 1984, and Miller, Bishop, Norman, & Maddever, 1985). These areas and specific questions are not meant to represent a complete diagnostic interview with a depressed individual, but rather they should provide guidelines for the therapist to follow in conducting the interview.

Areas of Inquiry

Depressed Mood

How have you been feeling over the past week?
Have you felt low in spirits, down in the dumps, gloomy, or depressed?
How bad has it been?
What percentage of time over the past week have you felt this way?

Lack of Reactivity

Do you find it difficult to turn your attention away from your depression?
Have there been times over the past week when your mood has changed?
Can you think of anything that has happened over the past week (other than taking medication) that has made you feel better? How long did this feeling last?

Feelings of Guilt

Are you critical of yourself for your weaknesses or mistakes?
Have you blamed yourself for things that go wrong around you?
Do you think that your depression represents a punishment for something you did?
What was that, or in what way?
Do you hear voices threatening or accusing you?

Feelings of Worthlessness

What is your opinion of yourself compared to other people?
Do you feel inferior, or even worthless, compared to others?
Are there things about yourself that you like?

Hopelessness

How do you see the future?
Do you feel hopeless, that things won't get better?

Are these thoughts fleeting, that is, do they seem to occur for a while and then go away, or are they continuous, so that you can't seem to get them out of your mind?

When you talk about these feelings with others, does it help?

Can you be reassured?

Suicidal Tendencies
Have you felt that life is not worth living?

Have you wished you were dead?

Have you had thoughts of committing suicide?

Have you thought of a specific plan for committing suicide?

Have you started to do things according to that plan?

Have you actually made an attempt on your life?

Early Insomnia
(Be careful to take into consideration shift work, medication, or physical illness effects.)

When you go to bed, do you have trouble falling asleep?

How often?

How long does it take you to fall asleep?

Middle Insomnia
Once you fall asleep, do you wake up during the night?

What do you do when you wake up?

Do you get out of bed?

Can you get back to sleep?

Late Insomnia
Do you wake up earlier than your usual time, that is, earlier than the time you used to wake up before you became depressed?

Do you get out of bed?

Can you fall back asleep?

Fatigue
Have you had less energy than usual, been getting tired more easily?

Has this affected your work or other activities?

Loss of Interest
Have you lost interest in, or do you get less pleasure from, things that you used to enjoy?

Have you wanted to stay away from other people?

Have you stopped seeking out others for company, or do you avoid others when they seek you out?

Have you lost interest in work, hobbies, or recreational activities?

Do you find that you have trouble doing things you really need to do?

Have you stopped working because of your depression?

Have you let your appearance go?

Psychic Anxiety (tenseness, nervousness, apprehension, fright, and irritability)
Have there been times lately when you have felt very anxious or frightened?
Are these feelings fleeting, or are they continuous?
What percentage of the time over the past weeks would you say that you have
felt this way?
Do you find yourself worrying over little things?

Somatic Anxiety (complaints about gastrointestinal, abdominal, cardiovascu-
lar, respiratory, and urinary problems, bowel movements, and neuromuscular
functioning)
When you felt anxious, what was it like?
Did you notice your heart beating faster?
(Inquire similarly about other areas.)

Loss of Libido
Over the past month has there been any change in your interest in sex?
Does this represent a change from the way you usually feel about sex?

Hypochondriasis
How is your physical health?
Do you tend to worry about your health?
Are you so concerned with your physical health that you find it difficult to
think about other things?

Loss of or Increase in Appetite
How is your appetite compared to the way it usually is?
Do you have trouble with constipation or other problems with your stomach
or bowels?

Weight Gain or Loss
Since the trouble started, when not dieting, have you gained or lost any
weight?
Assess the patient's maximum weight loss since the start of the illness.

Diminished Concentration
Do you find it more difficult now to make everyday decisions?
To concentrate?

Diurnal Mood Variation
Is your depression regularly worse at any particular time of day?
In the morning?
In the afternoon?
In the evening?
At what time of day do you feel best?

Insight
Do you think there is anything the matter with you?
Do you regard yourself as being emotionally or physically ill?

What do you think is the matter?
What caused this?

Retardation (direct observation)
Retardation is assessed on the basis of the therapist's observations during the interview, rather than the patient's subjective complaints. Note slowness of thought, speech, and impaired concentration, decreased motor activity, and stupor.

Agitation (direct observation)
Agitation, restlessness associated with anxiety, is also rated on the basis of the interview. Note playing with hands or hair, nail biting, hand wringing, and the like.

DEPRESSION-ASSOCIATED CAUTIONS IN THE USE OF AN INTERPERSONAL SYSTEMS APPROACH TO TREATMENT

In assessing the depressed individual, the therapist must pay particular attention to three major aspects of the patient's depression. First, the therapist must determine where the patient's depression falls on the endogenous-reactive dimension described in Chapter 1. Spitzer, Endicott, and Robins' (1980) criteria for endogenous depression, presented in Table 4.1, should be used to assess the patient. Second, on the basis of the assessment, the therapist should be able to determine if suicide is an immediate risk. Finally, the therapist should obtain a history, if any, of the patient's alcohol or drug abuse. Each of these three areas have implications in the therapist's decision regarding whether or not to proceed with the interpersonal systems approach to treatment described in this guidebook.

Endogenous Features

Although it is beyond the scope of this text to provide guidelines concerning the use of medication, studies suggest that individuals exhibiting endogenous depressive symptoms (Table 4.1) may respond well to tricyclic antidepressant medication and that individuals exhibiting bipolar symptoms (Chapter 1) respond well to lithium carbonate. The therapist should be cognizant of these considerations. In a study of the efficacy of Interpersonal Psychotherapy for Depression (IPT), Prusoff, Weissman, Klerman, and Rounsaville (1980) reported that patients who exhibit severe sleep disturbance (especially middle and late insomnia), weight and appetite loss, psychomotor agitation or retardation, and loss of interest or reactivity responded poorly to both tricyclic antidepressants and IPT alone, but responded well to combined psychotherapy and

TOD-G

Table 4.1. Criteria for Endogenous Major Depressive Disorder

This category is considered for all subjects with a current episode that meets the criteria for probable or definite Major Depressive Disorder. It is applied to those subjects who show a particular symptom picture that many research studies indicate is associated with good response to somatic therapy. Ignore the presence or absence of precipitating events even though this feature is often associated with the term "endogenous."

From groups A and B a total of at least four symptoms for probable, six for definite, including at least one symptom from group A.

Group A

1. Distinct quality to depressed mood, i.e., depressed mood is perceived as distinctly different from the kind of feeling he would have or has had following the death of a loved one.
2. Lack of reactivity to environmental changes (once depressed doesn't feel better, even temporarily, when something good happens).
3. Mood is regularly worse in the morning.
4. *Pervasive loss* of interest or pleasure (some loss in *all* areas).

Group B

1. Feelings of self-reproach or excessive or inappropriate guilt.
2. Early morning awakening or middle insomnia.
3. Psychomotor retardation or agitation more than mere subjective feeling of being slowed down or restless).
4. Poor appetite.
5. Weight loss (two lbs. a week over several weeks or 20 lbs. in a year when not dieting).
6. Loss of interest or pleasure (may or may not be pervasive) in usual activities or decreased sexual drive.

Source: Spitzer, Endicott, & Robins (1980). Research Diagnostic Criteria (RDC). Used with permission.

medication. In contrast, nonendogenous depressed patients responded best to IPT and did not benefit from the addition of amitriptyline.

Haas, Clarkin, and Glick (1985) suggest that the depressive symptoms of dysphoria, anhedonia, anergia, and reduced motivation can have deleterious effects on marital and family relationships and, further, can prevent interpersonal behavior change. Consequently, they recommend a biphasic program of marital/family intervention for individuals exhibiting endogenous features. In the first phase the patient is treated with antidepressants early in therapy. Haas et al. (1985) suggest that the therapist also educate the patient and family about the disorder of depression and about strategies used to cope with residual symptoms and possible relapse. The therapist should also make it clear to the couple or family that the medication will affect only the depressed individual's insomnia, lack of libido, decreased concentration, and depressed mood. Communications- or family-oriented problems and patterns will not be altered by the use of medication, but must be dealt with actively by the couple or family. This information is congruent with Weissman and Friedman's work, which suggests that whereas medication reduces the patient's depressive symptoms, interpersonal and marital psychotherapy affects the patient's social functioning. Haas et al. (1985) recommend that the second stage of therapy, essentially a marital/family approach which includes a number of the therapeutic strategies described in Chapter 3, be initiated only after the symptoms of endogenous depression have cleared or remitted.

Potential for Suicide

The therapist must assess the possibility that the patient will attempt suicide, particularly if the patient meets diagnostic criteria for depression. Boyer and Guthrie (1985) present a comprehensive review of risk factors for suicide in depressed patients and describe a number of suicide assessment instruments. Positive risk factors include older men and postmenopausal women, a history of previous attempts, a personal and family history of psychiatric illness, early parental loss (recall the literature reviewed in Chapter 1), suicidal ideation, plan, or both, environmental stressors, and a current medical illness.

If the therapist has reason to believe that the patient presents a risk of suicide, appropriate action must be taken. Hospitalization is one possibility, but this should be considered only in severe cases. The therapist should also initiate a contract with the patient, stating that the patient will call the therapist or present him/herself at a hospital emergency room rather than act on suicidal impulses. If the client will not agree to a contract, hospitalization should be considered. Note that the possibility of suicide in a depressed individual does not preclude the use of the interpersonal systems approach to therapy described in this guidebook. A number of writers (e.g., Braverman, 1980; Richman, 1979) have discussed the use of marital or family therapy in treating suicidal clients and suggest that interpersonal systems therapy can be used in cases in which one depressed family member is suicidal. Clearly, however, the therapist must exercise caution in this endeavor.

Alcohol/Drug Abuse

The therapist should also assess the patient's history and current functioning with respect to substance abuse. Writers state that depression is the most common psychiatric condition found associated with alcoholism. Lehmann (1985) notes that the coexistence of depression in alcohol abusers is a poor prognostic sign, associated with a higher rate of relapse and a greater risk of suicide. Although several therapeutic techniques and strategies outlined in this guidebook are also used in these treatment programs for substance abuse, some specific therapeutic techniques, which differ from those described herein, have proven to be particularly useful in working with alcoholic addicts. Consequently, the family with an alcoholic member might be better treated with a specifically designed intervention program, and the determination of substance abuse, particularly given its strong association with depression, is an important assessment task for the clinician.

MARITAL AND FAMILY
ASSESSMENT

While the depressed individual is being interviewed, the spouse (and children) should be in another room completing selected questionnaires assessing various aspects of marital and family functioning. Although instruments are available for this purpose, most systems diagnosis is based more on clinical impressions and case descriptions than on psychometrically sound data and widely accepted conceptual schemes. Contributing to and compounding this situation is the fact that most current assessment techniques and diagnostic categories, because they are designed for use with individuals, are largely unsuitable for marital and family assessment. This lack of formal marital and family diagnostic assessment instruments and frameworks does not lessen the importance of the enterprise of diagnosis with couples and families. Ackerman's (1958) observation almost three decades ago is still valid today: " . . . without adequate diagnosis there can hardly be adequate therapy" (p. 9).

Although we can recognize the value of assessment, we do not yet have a great deal of information about the mapping of different marital and family systems to therapeutic strategies. Nevertheless, the assessment instruments to be described offer the therapist a relatively quick and comprehensive overview of the couple or family's relationship, information that might take far longer to elicit through interviews. These measures provide information concerning the couple or family's satisfaction with their relationships, specific significant areas of conflict, and the structure of the family and roles of the family members; they can also highlight important potential targets for intervention. Again, the choice of which of these measures to use depends on the information obtained during the first part of the assessment interview and on the hypotheses formulated by the clinician. If there is concern about the quality of the marital relationship, the Dyadic Adjustment Scale, the Areas of Change Questionnaire, and the Impact Message Inventory might prove useful. Similarly, if family concerns exist, the therapist might administer the Family Environment Scale or the Family Adaptability and Cohesion Evaluation Scales to all family members. In addition, we suggest that the direct observation techniques to be described be used in all cases.

Through the administration of these measures, the therapist should be able to test hypotheses generated throughout the initial part of the assessment interview, and to formulate new hypotheses: about the couple or family's rules and myths, their interpersonal style and behaviors, the structure of power and influence, the alliances that exist within the family, and the interpersonal strengths of the system. In combination with the assessment of depression, these measures should also give the therapist greater insight into the role or function of the depression within the marital or family system. Most importantly, on the basis of the results of all of these measures, the therapist should be able to set appropriate priorities for treatment and to develop more effective intervention strategies.

Self-Report Measures: Marital Assessment

The Locke-Wallace Marital Adjustment Test. The Locke-Wallace Marital Adjustment Test (MAT; Locke & Wallace, 1959) is the most frequently used measure of general marital satisfaction. It is a 15-item questionnaire requiring only 10 minutes to complete and less than 10 minutes to score for both spouses. The MAT assesses various aspects of marriage, such as communication, affection, sexual compatibility, social activities, and value differences. Because of the relatively low reliability of the MAT in measuring these more specific areas, however, it is best used as a rough measure of overall satisfaction with and attraction to the current marriage. A score of 100 is typically used on the MAT to differentiate distressed from nondistressed marriages.

The Dyadic Adjustment Scale. The Dyadic Adjustment Scale (DAS; Spanier, 1976) is a 32-item measure of marital satisfaction. It is composed of four factors: dyadic satisfaction (the degree to which the couple is satisfied with the present state of the relationship), dyadic cohesion (the degree to which the couple engages in activities together), dyadic consensus (the degree to which the couple agrees on matters of importance to the relationship), and affectionate expression (the degree to which the couple is satisfied with the expression of affection and sex in the relationship). Spanier has suggested that a cutoff score of 100 in one partner may indicate the presence of marital distress.

The Areas of Change Questionnaire. The Areas of Change Questionnaire (AOC; Weiss, Hops, & Patterson, 1973) focuses on the spouses' perceptions of strengths and weaknesses in their relationship. Couples are required to indicate which of 34 specific relationship behaviors they would like to see changed (e.g., spending money, sexual needs). Discrepancies between the partners can be calculated and the areas of agreement and disagreement identified. The AOC Questionnaire correlates highly with the level of marital satisfaction, and Weiss et al. (1973) suggest that it be used in providing a starting ground for one spouse to pinpoint instances of conflict about changing the behavior of the other.

The Impact Message Inventory. The Impact Message Inventory (IMI; Kiesler, 1975/1984) is a self-report measure of the impact of one person's interpersonal style as experienced by another person (e.g., a spouse). It is composed of 15 subscales (e.g., Dominant, Hostile, Agreeable, Nurturant) that fall on the two dimensions of Friendly-Hostile and Dominant-Submissive. Wiggins (1982, p.

200) concluded that "the Impact Message Inventory . . . provides a valuable source of clinical information that could not be derived from previous assessment devices." Kahn, Coyne, and Margolin (1985) and Gotlib (1986) reported that the IMI differentiated the interpersonal impact of depressed patients from that of nondepressed persons and, interestingly, the impact of spouses of depressed patients from that of spouses of nondepressed subjects.

Self-Report Measures: Family Assessment

Family Environment Scale. The Family Environment Scale (FES; Moos & Moos, 1981) was designed to measure the interpersonal relationships among family members and the social-environmental characteristics of families. The FES is a 90-item inventory (with a 40-item short form and a children's version) composed of 10 subscales assessing three underlying domains or dimensions of family functioning: Relationship, Personal Growth, and System Maintenance. The Relationship subscales assess the degree of help and support family members provide for one another, the openness of the family, and the degree of conflict among family members. The Personal Growth subscales measure the self-sufficiency of family members, their involvement in activities outside the family, and the degreee of emphasis on religious issues and values. Finally, the System Maintenance subscales assess the degree of organization and structure in planning family activities and the extent to which explicit rules and procedure are used to run family life. The FES also yields Family Incongruence scores for members of the family, which reflect the extent of disagreement among family members with respect to their perceptions of their family's functioning.

The FES can be used to describe or compare the social environments of different families, to compare parents' perceptions of their family environments with each other or with those of their children, or to assess, monitor, and facilitate change in family environments through therapeutic interventions. Several studies have used the FES to examine the family environments of depressed individuals. Mitchell, Cronkite, and Moos (1983) found that depressed patients reported less family support than did nondepressed controls. In assessing the family environment of a depressed adolescent girl, Moos and Fuhr (1982) found that her depression was in part a function of her parents' involvement in their careers and their resultant neglect of her needs. Finally, Wetzel and Redmond (1980) found that family support was the most important variable that discriminated between depressed and nondepressed men and women.

Family Adaptability and Cohesion Evaluation Scales. The Family Adaptability and Cohesion Evaluation Scales (FACES) was developed by Olson, Bell, and Portner (1978-1983) and recently revised by Olson, Russell, and Sprenkle (1983). The most recent version, FACES II, is a 30-item self-report measure based on the Circumplex Model of family systems (Olson et al., 1979). As mentioned in Chapter 2, the circumplex model describes styles of family functioning along the two independent dimensions of cohesion and adaptability. Olson and his colleagues postulate that a moderate balancing of both cohesion and adaptability is necessary for optimal family functioning.

FACES II assesses individual family members' perceptions of the family's cohesion and adaptability. Furthermore, FACES II was designed to be administered twice—once to assess how family members currently see their family (*perceived*) and once for how they would like it to be (*ideal*). A comparison of the perceived and ideal ratings yields a measure of satisfaction with the current family system. Each respondent receives a score for cohesion and adaptability dimensions. Thus, a Family Composite score may be obtained by summing like scores across different family members, and a Family Discrepancy score may be obtained by comparing responses of different family members.

Family Assessment Device. The McMaster Family Assessment Device (FAD; Miller, Epstein, Bishop, & Keitner, 1985) is a 53-item self-report measure based on the McMaster Model of Family Functioning (Epstein, Bishop, & Levin, 1978). The FAD was designed as a screening instrument to identify family problem areas simply and efficiently. The McMaster model considers six structural and organizational aspects of the current level of family functioning: problem solving, communication, roles, affective responsiveness, affective involvement, and behavior control. Because it is based on this model, the FAD similarly yields information from each family member on these six dimensions as well as on an additional General Functioning scale. The FAD has discriminated psychiatric (largely depressed) from nonclinical families, and appears to be a valid and economical self-report measure of family functioning.

Direct Observation Measures

Direct observations of behaviors may be conducted by trained observers, the therapist, significant others, or the clients themselves. Furthermore, they may be obtained in either controlled or naturalistic settings. Having spouses or other family members observe critical incidents in their everyday interactions is essential in understanding the environmental and social context of the family's behavior and in modifying the quality of the interactions in the system.

Spouse Observation Checklist. Weiss et al. (1973) developed the Spouse Observation Checklist (SOC) as an aid for couples to collect direct-observation data in their home environments. The SOC was designed to provide a behavioral accounting of the types of activities engaged in by spouses that have a positive or negative impact on their relationship. The SOC consists of approximately 400 items of spouse behavior, each of which the spouses can categorize as pleasing or displeasing. The SOC requires each spouse to act as a participant-observer, checking each item that occurs during a 24-hour period, and indicating how pleasing or displeasing each behavior is. In addition, both spouses rate their satisfaction with the relationship for that day on a 9-point scale. Thus, the SOC allows for identification of those specific behaviors that seem to be most important to the satisfaction of each spouse. Moreover, by having spouses make daily ratings throughout therapy, the SOC can monitor the ongoing progress and efficacy of the treatment. For example, Birchler, Weiss, and Vincent (1975) reported a pleasing-displeasing ratio of 30:1 for nondistressed couples, but only 4:1 for distressed couples.

The Marital Interaction Coding System. The Marital Interaction Coding System (MICS) is probably the most widely used coding system for marital interaction. It was developed by Hops, Wills, Patterson, and Weiss (1972) in an attempt to quantify the problem-solving interactions of spouses. The MICS currently contains 32 individual codes encompassing both verbal (e.g., agree and criticize) and nonverbal (e.g., smile/laugh and attention) behavior. In actual practice, these codes are typically collapsed to a much smaller number of summary codes (e.g., positive and negative verbal and nonverbal, problem-solving, and problem-description). In using the MICS, a couple is typically given 10 minutes to discuss a problem in their relationship, and their interaction is taped for later scoring. Studies utilizing the MICS have found that distressed couples use more negative and fewer positive behaviors and fewer problem-solving statements. Partners in distressed couples also tend to respond to their spouses' negative behaviors with negative behaviors of their own, thereby escalating the discussion into cycles of negative interaction.

The Couples Interaction Scoring System. The Couples Interaction Scoring System (CISS; Gottman, 1979) provides an objective, detailed, observational record of the interaction of married partners. The CISS differs from the MICS primarily in its more explicit separation of verbal and nonverbal aspects of communication among couples. Thus, the CISS really is composed of two independent coding systems: a content analysis system for the coding of verbal behaviors and an affect analysis system for the coding of nonverbal behaviors. Each codable unit of interaction receives both a content code and a nonverbal behavior code; in addition, the listener's nonverbal behavior can also be coded. By combining the eight content and three affect codes, the CISS assigns 1 of 24 unique codes to each codable unit. The CISS has been found to differentiate between distressed and nondistressed couples. For example, compared with nondistressed couples, distressed couples have a higher ratio of disagreement-agreement + disagreement and are more often characterized by negative reciprocity.

The Living in Familial Environments Coding System. This coding system (the LIFE system) was developed by Arthur, Hops, and Biglan (1982) expressly to study the interactions of depressed women and their families. It was adapted from the MICS, with the addition of depression-relevant content codes and seven codes for scoring affective behavior. The content codes cover such behaviors as elicit self-disclosure and worry, whereas the affective codes are used to score concomitant neutral, happy, caring, irritated, depressed, sarcastic, and whiny affect. Biglan et al. (1985) report that the LIFE coding system possesses high reliability and, as described in Chapter 1, discriminates the interactions of couples with a depressed partner from those without a depressed spouse.

In our own work with depressed couples and families, we have utilized a modified form of these coding systems, more specifically focused on behaviors that are associated with depression. Thus, in interactions between a depressed adult and the spouse, we attend to and code the occurrence of such behaviors as agreement, disagreement, problem-solving, negative self-statements, and offering help. When observing interactions between a depressed parent and a child, we code commands, positive and negative verbal and nonverbal behaviors, and time spent in joint versus solitary activity. Finally, when observing the interaction of an entire family with a depressed member, we pay particular attention to ignoring, interrupting, complaining, commands, and positive and negative statements. We have found that these behaviors consistently differentiate between interactions with and without a depressed participant, and between family interactions before and after treatment.

These direct-observation procedures and coding systems have contributed immeasurably to our understanding of the relationships among members of families undergoing various types of stress, and hold considerable promise in allowing a more comprehensive understanding of interpersonal aspects of depression. Unfortunately, because most clinicians view these coding systems as complicated and "unlearnable," their use has been relegated largely to the academic/research community. This is unfortunate. Not only are these systems appropriate for clinical use, but they help the clinician remain sensitive to and focus on conceptually important aspects of both the content and the process of the marital dyad or family's interactions.

We have found that clinicians are able to effectively use modified versions of these coding systems with a minimal amount of training. Furthermore, because most clinicians have neither the resources nor the time to record and then painstakingly score a couple or family's interactions, we have taught therapists to use these modified systems with clients *in vivo*. For example, these coding systems can be collapsed into the general codes of "positive," "neutral," and "negative" (more ambitious clinicians may wish to add "problem-solving" to this list). With some practice, the therapist will be able to code each statement by the family members, as they are interacting, into one of these categories, taking into con-

Spouse	Code	Spouse	Code	Spouse	Code	Spouse	Code
Husb		Husb		Husb		Husb	
Wife		Wife		Wife		Wife	
Husb		Husb		Husb		Husb	
Wife		Wife		Wife		Wife	
Husb		Husb		Husb		Husb	
Wife		Wife		Wife		Wife	
Husb		Husb		Husb		Husb	
Wife		Wife		Wife		Wife	
Husb		Husb		Husb		Husb	
Wife		Wife		Wife		Wife	
Husb		Husb		Husb		Husb	
Wife		Wife		Wife		Wife	
Husb		Husb		Husb		Husb	
Wife		Wife		Wife		Wife	

FIGURE 4.1. Response Scoring Sheet for Coding Interactions.

sideration both the verbal and nonverbal components of the statements. An example of a simple response record sheet for a couple's interaction is presented in Figure 4.1. By coding a 5- to 10-minute sample of the conversation during the *interaction stage* of the initial interview, patterns of positive and negative behavior (e.g., the negative reciprocity characteristic of distressed couples and the negative self-statements exhibited by depressed persons) will become readily apparent.

The therapist should pay particular attention to the behavior of the depressed person and the responses emitted by other family members to this individual; the patterns of these behaviors can be used both to gain a better understanding of the nature and maintenance of the depression and to suggest potential targets for intervention. A husband's responses to his wife's depressive behavior, for example, can provide important information about how the couple is dealing with the depression. Certainly, this task becomes more difficult as the number of family members present in a session increases. Nevertheless, it is still possible to conduct this systematic observation, and the information it yields for the clinician *and for the couple or family* concerning the quality of their interactions can be invaluable.

MARITAL/FAMILY-ASSOCIATED
CAUTIONS IN THE USE OF AN
INTERPERSONAL SYSTEMS
APPROACH TO TREATMENT

Because of the relative immaturity of marital and family therapy, and in particular, systems treatment for depression, it is difficult to turn to the therapy outcome literature for guidelines in deciding when and when not to use interpersonal systems therapy. For some therapists, this issue simply does not arise; these therapists maintain that marital/family therapy is the treatment of choice in all cases in which psychotherapy is indicated. In our view this is an extreme position. Not all couples and families will benefit from a systems-oriented therapy, and there are specific indications and contraindications for the effective use of this therapy.

Systems therapy may be indicated when symptoms are viewed by the clinician to be embedded in dysfunctional family relationships, or are conceptualized as an expression of the family's pain. Systems therapy is also commonly suggested as the treatment of choice when a child or adolescent is the presenting patient, and when the couple or family itself perceives the difficulties as caused by or affecting their relationships with one another. Finally, systems therapy should be considered if depression in one family member seems to be related to recent symptomatic improvement in another member or, more generally, to the behavior of another family member (e.g., a wife's depression worsens when her husband becomes busier at work).

With respect to contraindications for systems-oriented therapy, there may be practical limitations, such as the unavailability of key family members, which will prevent the formation of an effective therapeutic relationship. One or more family members may also indicate a strong preference to work with the therapist on an individual basis, and it is unlikely that systems therapy, implemented under duress, would be effective. An interpersonal systems approach may also be contraindicated if the family presents too late in the course of the disorder to bring about constructive change, or if the clinician's feeling is that the process of fragmentation cannot at this point be reversed. Therapy may still be of value in these cases to minimize the damage caused by the breakup.

Waldron-Skinner (1978) contends that it may be dangerous to conduct this form of therapy in cases in which "the emotional equilibrium is so precariously maintained that attempts at changing the relationship system may precipitate a severe decompensation on the part of one or more family members" (p. 61). As much as representing a cautionary note, this statement highlights a similarity between systems therapy and individual therapy: the therapist must always exercise mature clinical judgment in assessing a client for therapy. Change may be as dangerous to effect in particular individuals as it is in certain families.

Finally, several therapists have voiced concerns about working with a family in which one member is so grossly disturbed as to dominate the family with destructive affect or behavior, such as that characteristic of schizoid or paranoid individuals.

The Goal-Definition Stage. Following the diagnostic interview with the identified patient and the individual meetings with the spouse and appropriate family members, the family is brought together for the final segment of the session. The therapist's task in this goal-definition stage is twofold: first, to obtain from the family members a clear statement of their desired changes, and second, if possible at this point to devise and communicate to the family a preliminary treatment plan. Having interviewed the family members, and even more so after scoring the family's questionnaires, the therapist is in a better position to ensure that the goals proposed by the family members are both appropriate and attainable and the treatment plan viable. If the therapist cannot score the self-report instruments while the family waits during this session, the formulation of a treatment plan will have to wait until the next session.

In developing a statement of goals, the therapist should review for the couple or family his or her perceptions and understanding of their situation and should elicit from the family members a statement of their desired changes. It is not essential that the therapist's review or formulation be comprehensive at this point; indeed, the therapist likely has not yet had an opportunity to score and interpret the assessment instruments administered during the separate interviews with the family members. What is important is that the clinician communicate enough of his or her perceptions to help the family members think positively about their desired changes and to allow them to understand the rationale for a subsequent treatment plan.

Both the goals and the treatment plan, when proposed, should be stated clearly and in behavioral terms. Most patients will immediately respond that they would like to feel less depressed or anxious, or to communicate better; family members will often offer these as goals for the identified patient. While these are valid and, from the family's perspective, understandable targets for change, they are nevertheless vague and ill-defined. The goals eventually agreed upon by the therapist and couple or family must be stated in observable, measurable terms. Therefore, rather than citing "changes in levels of anxiety and depression," the therapist should work with the family members to help them focus on exactly how the anxiety or depression is manifested in the family, and on how they respond behaviorally to these manifestations. For example, "being less depressed" might become operationalized in part as "becoming more involved in pleasurable hobbies" or as "spending more time together in family activities." As Haley (1976) observed, one important reason for specifying the problem clearly is that the therapist can know when therapy has been successful. If the goals of intervention are specified in vague or general terms, the evaluation of treatment outcome will be unclear.

In addition to defining the treatment objectives in clear, behavioral terms, Coyne and Segal (1982) recommend that the therapist also try to phrase the goals in terms of increasing positive behaviors rather than decreasing negative behaviors. Thus, instead of the patient wanting to spend less time in bed, the therapist can rephrase the goal to spending more time in positive activities with the family. In outlining goals for change, the therapist is essentially making a contract with the family. Ideally, on the basis of the goals that are elicited, the therapist attempts to formulate a treatment plan leading to a reasonable change, one that all family members agree is desirable.

Once the goals are identified, the therapist should ask the couple or family to consider exactly how they will know that they are making progress toward reaching the goal. A goal elicited during the initial sessions rarely is attained by the next meeting; indeed, goals are rarely met on an all-or-none basis from one session to the next. Thus, there will likely be a process of "shaping" that occurs during therapy, in which the family members make progress toward a goal, even though they may not actually attain it as stated until some time later. Therefore, the therapist must alert the couple or family to this process. Some therapists make sure that the goals are so stated that they can be met by the next session. We have found that permitting families to "keep" their stated broader goals, while adding smaller goals throughout therapy, allows them to feel as though the broader goals are still the ones towards which they are working.

Ending the Interview. The therapist must attend to a number of details to ensure that the interview is ended appropriately. Ending the interview well maximizes the probability that the couple or family will return for treatment. The family should leave the initial interview knowing, at least generally, what is going to happen in the next sessions. The therapist must address the issue of which family members are to attend future sessions. Perhaps on the basis of the results of the assessment session, someone who attended this session is not needed in subsequent meetings. For example, if the therapist believes that the marital relationship is the focal point of the depression, and that the children will not benefit by being seen directly in therapy, he or she may request that only the couple attend subsequent sessions. Similarly, the therapist may ask the couple or family to bring to the next session a particular individual who did not attend the assessment interview, but who appears to play an important role in the family. In any case, at the end of the assessment, the family should know exactly who will be attending the subsequent sessions.

The therapist should set the time for the next session, and the ground rules for therapy should be agreed upon here. The family will likely want to know for how many sessions they can expect to be in treatment. Haley (1976) suggests that the therapist respond that treatment will be as brief as possible. If possible, the therapist should enter into a written contract with the family which states a specified number of sessions, each of a given length, over a specified period. If the goals change during therapy, the contract can be renegotiated. It is also useful to include in the contract the therapist's policy with respect both to payment for missed sessions and to sessions in which not everyone is present. An explicit written contract also has the added advantage of increasing the participants' commitment to therapy.

There will be times that the therapist is unable to score and integrate all of the assessment and questionnaire data during the first session. If the assessment continues for a second session, it is usually sufficient that the couple or family be aware of the issues just described and that decisions regarding these issues will be made during the next session.

Finally, the therapist might assign the family a simple task at the end of this initial session, so that they can immediately begin working toward their goals. This procedure maintains the involvement of the family members between this session and the next, and gives them the perception that they are now doing something constructive to deal with their situation. The task should be very simple, and should build upon work that has already been done by the couple or family during the session. For example, the family members will have described aspects of the identified patient's depression during the problem identification stage. The therapist can extend these descriptions by requesting that the family members each keep a log of the patient's depression over the next week and bring it to the subsequent session.

THE ASSESSMENT DATA

In closing this chapter, a few words about the nature and purpose of the data derived from the questionnaires that are completed by the family members are in order. We recognize that it may be overwhelming, at least initially, for the clinician to be confronted with what seems a mass of information. However, in our experience, these initial feelings of inundation dissipate rapidly with repeated use of these measures. There are many advantages to the therapist of utilizing standardized assessment instruments instead of (or in addition to) relying only on hunches or intuition. First, the clinician can build her or his own data base and will soon get a sense of how a particular patient or family compares with previous clients in various domains of functioning. Second, important information is obtained in a significantly shorter period and in a more standardized manner than would be the case without these measures. Third, these measures can identify specific targets for intervention (e.g., marital dysfunction, family cohesion) that might have taken far longer to recognize had these instruments not been used. Fourth, the results of these assessment instruments can facilitate the therapist's decision regarding which family members should be seen in treatment. For example, in assessing a family in which the couple referred their child for therapy, the assessment measures indicated a high level of marital distress. This pattern of results quickly led the therapist to consider the possibility that the spouses were "detouring" their marital difficulties through their child and it influenced the therapist's decision to continue treatment by seeing the entire family.

The final advantage to be discussed concerning the use of psychometrically sound assessment instruments is that they permit the therapist to evaluate objectively both the efficacy of the intervention procedures and the maintenance of gains in treatment. Treatment evaluation is an important issue, and space does not permit an extended discussion. We would like to comment briefly, however, on how the therapist might use repeated administrations of the assessment measures to evaluate the efficacy of therapy.

We suggest that at the termination of therapy, the clinician should make arrangements for a follow-up session with the individual, couple, or family in 3 to 6 months. We also suggest that the therapist require family members to complete the full assessment package at three points in time: the initial interview session, the termination session, and a 3- to 6-month follow-up session. By following this procedure, the therapist will be able to compare objectively the individual, couple, or family's level of functioning in a particular area before beginning treatment with that demonstrated at termination. Maintenance of treatment gains can be assessed similarly by comparing the postintervention levels with data obtained in a follow-up session. Finally, for specific target areas, we recommend that the participants complete brief measures at the beginning of each session. Thus, a measure of depression can be administered, as can a brief measure of marital adjustment.

Using this procedure, the therapist will be able to monitor and plot each session's depression and marital adjustment levels and, working together with the patient or family, will be able both to assess the impact of treatment on a weekly basis and to identify factors that appear to be affecting the patient's depression. Perhaps most importantly, both the therapist and the patient will have objective information concerning the patient's progress in treatment, and this information may be used as concrete and relatively immediate feedback in determining the effectiveness of the therapist's intervention strategies (which can then be altered accordingly).*

In the following two chapters, we will present an extended version of the transcript from the Richardson family's therapy. In Chapter 5 we will indicate how the procedures and measures described are implemented in the initial session with this family, and in Chapter 6 we will demonstrate how the principles and techniques presented in Chapter 3 are utilized in actual practice, from the second therapy session through to a 6-month follow-up.

---

* The interested reader is referred to Gottman and Lieblum (1973) and Jacobson, Follette, and Revenstorf (1984) for comprehensive discussions of the statistical treatment of these data.

Chapter 5
Stages of Treatment
I. The Assessment Stage

In the following two chapters we will utilize the procedures outlined thus far in this guidebook, and in a step-by-step fashion will describe the process of therapy from the beginning assessment phase (described in detail in the previous chapter) through termination of treatment. To provide the clinician with a meaningful and understandable guide, we will make this process as clear and concrete as possible. Therefore, we will begin with a brief description of the tasks that need to be accomplished and then present relevant case transcripts and, where appropriate, a discussion of the use of and rationale for the particular assessment and intervention procedures described. This presentation will be conducted in the context of a single, continuous case example.

INTRODUCTION AND ASSESSMENT

As noted in the previous chapter, the introduction stage begins with the first telephone contact requesting an appointment. The therapist's first task is to gather sufficient information to determine who in the family needs to come for the first session. Whether it is an intake worker or the therapist who is obtaining the information from the potential client, the principle is the same: either the marital couple or the entire family will be requested to attend the initial interview, depending on the information provided. Again, the general rule is that if the information provided indicates that only a parent is depressed and none of the children appear to be adversely affected or involved, the couple alone are instructed to come for the appointment. In contrast, if a child is identified as depressed, is described as the source of the depression, or is otherwise implicated in the problem, the entire family is requested to be present. A frequent reaction to such a request is the response, "Why should I be involved? It is my husband who is depressed," or "I don't see why my other children have to be there, since they don't have any problems," or, "My husband cannot take time from work, and besides, he says that looking after the children is my job." These are but a few examples of the many faces of resistance sometimes encountered by marital and family therapists.

The therapist can offer a number of responses that might help the person who is initiating the contact to see the value and importance of having other family members involved in the treatment process. The message given by the therapist at this point must contain the essential ingredients of respect and value for other family members, rather than blame. The preliminary telephone contact with Mrs. Maria Richardson, the woman in the case described in Chapter 2, is to be presented. We begin the conversation after Maria has already provided demographic information about her family and has discussed her reasons for seeking therapy. In addition, the therapist has already garnered sufficient information about Maria's depression to rule out the likelihood of suicide.

> *Therapist:* What is your idea right now, Maria, as to why you're becoming depressed again?
>
> *Maria:* Well, um, it seems like a lot of things, but maybe the biggest thing is the problem I've been having with my son. As I told you, David is 11 years old and he still soils himself. I've tried everything I can think of, but nothing seems to work . . . he still has accidents in his pants. I'm just worn out from trying to help him get rid of this disgusting habit. My husband accuses me of making such a big deal about it . . . in fact, he once even suggested that maybe if I left David alone, the problem would go away. Of course, that's easy for him to say . . . he's not there when it happens, and he's never had to clean up the mess.
>
> *Therapist:* It sounds like you feel pretty much that the burden of your son's problem has rested entirely on your shoulders, and that there hasn't been much support for you from your husband.
>
> *Maria:* Yeah, he just seems so laid back, and doesn't worry about things. He drives me nuts sometimes . . . I think if I left things up to him, the whole family would fall apart in nothing flat.

By this point in the conversation, the therapist has obtained sufficient information to indicate the need for the whole family to be involved in therapy, at least initially. Furthermore, the indication that one of the Richardson's two children appears to be entangled in Maria's depression is a major factor contributing to this decision.

> *Therapist:* Well Maria, it does seem from what you've been saying to me that making an appointment right now would be a good idea. What I'm going to recommend is probably a little different from what you've likely done in the past when you've been depressed. I'd like you and your husband and your two children to come for the first session. You see . . .
>
> *Maria:* (Interrupts with surprise) You mean you want my whole family to come and talk about my depression? Michael always gets fed up with me when I try to explain to him what's wrong. I was hoping that I could talk to someone who would understand how tough things are for me. You know, my family doesn't really know what I feel.

Therapist: I realize that this seems a little unusual, Maria, but I can already see that for too long you've been the one in the family who has been expected to keep things together, run the household, and solve all the problems that anyone in the family runs into. It sounds to me like you would be much happier if everyone in the family worked together to make the family closer.

Maria: Well, when you put it that way, I would be happier if the rest of my family did do a little bit more . . . they are part of the family, after all. But Michael really wouldn't come because of his work. His work comes first, you know . . . we do need the money, and besides, he's so independent, he thinks everyone should be able to solve their own problems.

Therapist: Michael is your husband, Maria, and if you're upset and depressed, I think in Michael's own way he is probably feeling upset, too. In fact, it's quite likely that your children are also distressed when they see you feeling so miserable. I would even bet that in some way everyone in your family has tried to do something to cheer you up. Maybe what they've tried hasn't worked, but if you really want things in your family to be different, and for everyone to work more like a team, we are going to need all their help. I've found that the best way to help people is to get to know their spouse, and whenever possible, the children too. I would like you to try to convince Michael that he and your children should come. Do you think you could do that?

Maria: Well, I know Elise will come—she's my little helper—but I'll have to work a little bit on Michael and David. But, um, I think I can probably convince them.

Therapist: Good. I'll look forward to meeting you and your family, Maria. Now I'll pass you over to my secretary so that she can work out an appointment time with you that will be convenient for both you and your husband. I would really prefer to see your whole family, so if something comes up that you all cannot make the appointment, please call ahead of time and we'll arrange another time.

This excerpt outlines the therapist's first contact with the client. She has introduced the idea of the family as a system by talking about the entire family being affected when one person is not functioning well, and that if the situation (i.e., Maria's depression) is to improve, the whole family must work together. Furthermore, the therapist has presented this framework to Maria in a benevolent rather than in an accusatory or blaming manner. This transcript also highlights one specific way of dealing with resistance to the idea of having other family members involved in "the client's" therapy. This first contact is instrumental in setting the stage for what is to follow in the actual therapy proper. Moreover, if the therapist has not been successfully persuasive in convincing the caller to include other family members, he or she may lose the client. This therapist was successful, however, and the entire Richardson family arrived on the day of the assessment. We noted in the previous chapter that the initial interview can be conceptualized as comprising four stages: the social stage, the problem identification stage, the interaction stage, and the goal-definition stage. In the following section we present the dialogue and relevant discussion from the first interview with the Richardson family, organized according to these stages.

The Social Stage

This stage is important to ensure that all family members feel as comfortable as possible and to leave everyone with the impression that they will all be involved in the therapy process and have an important contribution to make. The therapist must realize that most families enter therapy feeling defensive and embarrassed, and attempts to ease these feelings must be initiated immediately. Any attempts by family members to launch right into the problem must be blocked by the therapist until everyone has been made to feel reasonably comfortable. The therapist begins the observational and assessment process on greeting the family.

> *Therapist:* Hello, Mr. and Mrs. Richardson. I'm Sarah Collins. Please come in. This must be David and Elise. I'm pleased to meet you. Just go ahead and sit wherever you would like. (She pauses until the family is seated.) Did you have any trouble finding your way here today?
>
> *Maria:* No, not really. My friend used to come here for a while, and she told me how to get here. Besides, I had a pretty good idea where this center was anyway.
>
> *Therapist:* (to Mr. Richardson) Thank you for taking time from your job to come today. I really appreciate your effort, especially since your wife told me on the phone how busy you are. What exactly do you do, uh . . . Do you mind if I call you Michael?
>
> *Michael:* No, Michael is fine. I'm an artistic designer for one of the larger firms in the area.
>
> *Therapist:* That sounds like an exciting career. Have you been doing that for long?
>
> *Michael:* Well actually, in one way or another I've been doing it for about 15 years. Even when I was a kid, I liked to paint, and design cars. I was always making things to help decorate the house. My parents used to say I was probably going to be some kind of artist when I grew up.
>
> *Therapist:* Well, Michael, it sounds like you're very talented. (Michael looks a little embarrassed, but quite pleased with the therapist's compliment.)
>
> *Maria:* Michael is very modest, and doesn't talk very much about his work. For that matter, Michael doesn't talk very much about most things. I usually find out things about him quite by accident.

Since Maria had indicated on the phone that her husband was likely to be resistant to coming to therapy, the therapist elected to begin the social stage with him. She also attempts to make him feel comfortable by talking about his work, an area the therapist had hypothesized as being a "safe" and interesting one for him. Moreover, by starting with a parent, the therapist is also supporting the hierarchical structure of the family. Consistent with this approach, the therapist was about to turn her attention to Maria, when Maria entered the conversation. Because Maria's statement sounded like a lead-in to a discussion of her problem (lack of communication between herself and Michael), however, the therapist steers her away from this comment, while acknowledging what Maria has said.

> *Therapist:* Hmm, I wonder if Michael is one of those "still waters run deep" individuals? Maria, I didn't ask you on the phone if you work outside the home.

Maria: Oh, I used to before we had children. But now I am so busy just taking care of the house and children that I hardly have time for anything else. (Hesitating) I have thought of it from time to time, though, but I don't know how I would find the time. Besides, my mother thinks it is really bad for the children to have a working mother.

Therapist: Well, Maria, you certainly impressed me on the phone as someone who is very dedicated and takes her responsibilities very seriously.

Michael: That's a true statement if I ever heard one. (The therapist thought she detected a hint of sarcasm in Michael's voice.)

Elise: (who has been sitting quietly and playing with her doll, interjects) I sometimes help my mommy clean the house. She calls me her little helper.

Therapist: Well, Elise, I wondered that the minute I saw you. I thought you might be a real helper to your mom. That's a very pretty doll. What's her name?

Elise: Tina Marie. I picked that name out all by myself. I have lots of dolls at home; they sit on my bed every day until I get home. If I come and visit you again, can I show you my favorite?

Therapist: Why, I think that would be just fine, Elise. (Pause) How do you happen to have so many dolls?

Elise: My mommy and daddy gave most of them to me. Santa Claus gave me some more, and David gave me a Cabbage Patch doll for my birthday.

Therapist: What a lucky girl you are to get so many nice toys. David, your sister sounds happy about the present you bought her.

David: (just shrugs his shoulders)

Maria: David, answer Dr. Collins! And look at her when she speaks to you.

The therapist begins to get a sense of Maria's anger at her son, and David's separation from the rest of the family. The seating positions selected by the family also support this hypothesis. Maria and Elise chose to sit on the couch, while Michael selected the chair next to the couch, and David picked the chair near the door, which was also somewhat removed from the other chairs. Although the rest of the family seem comfortable at this point, the therapist wants to draw David in before she leaves the social stage and moves into the problem description stage.

Therapist: (to David) I noticed that you are wearing a Toronto Maple Leaf sweater, David. Are you a fan of theirs?

David: (looking down) Yeah. Sometimes my dad takes me to a game, when he's not working. Just the two of us go together.

Therapist: You know what, David? One of their players used to live next door to me when I was younger.

David: (suddenly perking up) Really? Or are you just kidding me?

Therapist: No, I'm serious. It's Wendel Clark. Do you know him?

David: Really? Wow! He's one of my favorite players.

The therapist and David talked for another minute about hockey, until he too was feeling relatively comfortable about being in the office. It was largely a matter of luck that the therapist so quickly found an area of interest that she and David could share. By doing so, however, she has already begun the process of joining. The entire Richardson family is now feeling a little more relaxed, and the therapist can move onto the next stage.

Problem Identification Stage

During this stage the therapist elicits from each family member what they see as the problem and why each feels they are at the session. It is important in this stage to begin to educate the family about what the therapist expects from them and what they can expect from her. The therapist will set the stage here for helping the family understand that they must work together to solve their difficulties. The therapist should try to make the transition from the previous social stage to the problem identification stage comfortable and nonthreatening.

> *Therapist:* Well, now that we have had a bit of a chance for me to get to know you, let me briefly tell you my understanding of why you are here. Maria indicated to me on the telephone that she has been feeling quite depressed, and that she has felt that way from time to time for many years. She called me to try and get help for her depression. I asked Maria to bring all of you with her today because I find the best way to understand someone's problem is to have help from the whole family, both in trying to understand the problem and in trying to find some solutions to make things better. So far, all I know is a little bit about what brings you here. I would like to know more about that, and I would like everybody's help in understanding the situation better. To begin with, I would like each of you to tell me why you think you are here today.
>
> *Elise:* (before either parent has a chance to respond, Elise blurts out) We're here so that you can make my mommy happy again.

The therapist must make a quick decision here regarding whether to let Elise be the first to talk about the problem, or whether to encourage one of her parents to begin. As noted in Chapter 4, Haley (1976) generally recommends beginning with the adult who is less involved with the problem (in this case, Michael) or with the adult who holds the most power in the family (likely Maria). Another crucial concern in establishing an order for obtaining information about the problem is to minimize the likelihood that one family member will feel singled out and blamed. Yet at the same time, the therapist wants to obtain everyone's perceptions of the problems, and makes a decision to let Elise proceed. She seems genuinely concerned about her mother's well-being, and because she spoke first, she may also be the one member of the family most affected by Maria's depression. Elise, being a child, is also likely to provide a relatively "honest" description of Maria's depression. Again, if the initial description of a problem is overly intense or critical, it may create too much defensiveness or anxiety in the family members, thereby discouraging openness and a willingness to discuss the problem and perhaps increasing their reluctance to continue therapy.

> *Therapist:* Elise, how can you tell your mom is unhappy?
>
> *Elise:* Well, I see her crying sometimes, and she gets very mad at David when he . . . (She looks at David to see if she dare describe his problem. Her inquiring look is met with an angry glare from David) . . . when he . . . does things to upset mommy.

Therapist: So sometimes David does things that make your mom unhappy. Does anything else make your mom sad?

Elise: Well, sometimes if we leave the house really messy, mommy gets pretty mad at all of us.

The therapist decides to broaden the focus by inquiring whether or not other people in the family are unhappy. This move is consistent with the therapist's goal of drawing the whole family into the therapeutic process and removing the focus from one individual. This tactic requires a delicate balance, however, between preventing one person from being singled out, and obtaining a clear and specific account of the presenting problem or problems. The therapist intentionally directs this question to Michael, the adult less involved in the problem, to include him more directly in the therapy process.

Therapist: Michael, do you think anyone else in your family is unhappy?

Michael: I think Elise is right about my wife—she does get depressed often. And, well, maybe sometimes David does, too. He and his mother get into a lot of battles, and then he clams up for a while, but he doesn't talk to anybody about what's bothering him. I guess he's kind of like me when it comes to talking about feelings.

Maria: (with tears in her eyes) Sometimes they both frustrate me so much. I try to talk to them and get them to tell me what's bothering them, but Michael is right—they both keep everything inside them. Michael thinks I get too emotional about most things, but I think it's important to get your feelings out into the open. Those two are like stones. Nothing seems to bother either of them.

Therapist: (to Maria) It seems like some of your family is feeling that one problem in the family is that you are unhappy. What do you think makes this family not as happy as it could be?

Again, the therapist is removing the focus from Maria, and looking more broadly at the family system.

Maria: I'm not really sure . . . maybe one thing is that I try very hard to make things nice and pleasant for my family, but they don't seem to appreciate everything I do for them. (begins to cry) If only everyone would try a little harder and cooperate more, then I wouldn't have to get after them all the time.

The therapist waits to see whether anyone is going to try and comfort Maria. Elise reaches over and gives Maria a kleenex and a big hug. Michael and David, however, appear to be very uncomfortable. Both are shifting in their seats and looking away.

Therapist: (to Michael) Is this typically what happens at home when your wife shows her feelings this way?

Michael: (looking somewhat embarrassed) Well, I guess so. I never know what to do. I try to tell her that things aren't that bad, and that she really doesn't need to cry. Sometimes I even try and tell her how lucky we are compared to some of our friends and family. But everything I try to do to cheer her up just seems to upset her more. I guess I've just given up trying.

Maria: (to Michael) You always make me feel so rotten, like I'm stupid to let little things upset me. But they're not little things. You just seem so impatient with me, that I . . . I can't control my feelings the way you do.

Therapist: Does anyone else in this family cry?

Elise: I do sometimes, when my friends at school run away on me and won't play with me. And sometimes I cry when David won't let me play with him.

Therapist: (to David) Do you ever cry, David?

David: No, I don't cry. Crying is for girls or for sissies. And I'm not a sissy for sure!

Maria: Michael hardly shows any of his feelings, either. I can't tell when he's angry or sad or frustrated or anything. He always looks so cool, calm, and collected.

Michael: (somewhat defensively) I just think that life's too short to let things bother you. I think I just have more patience than Maria. She expects more of people than I do. People are always disappointing her. She's always worrying about someone or something. I guess I've just learned to take things as they come. Worrying doesn't get you anywhere.

A family rule or reality is clearly beginning to emerge: Only the female members of this family are allowed to express feelings of sadness. This rule will put particular pressure on David to maintain his composure. Furthermore, this information is significant because the therapist is beginning to question whether David might at times also feel depressed. So far in the session, he has remained withdrawn and detached, with his eyes downcast. It is also quite likely that crying is viewed negatively in this family. Consequently, as long as emotion has this negative connotation, Maria will be labeled the disturbed family member. At this point, then, the therapist is formulating two hypotheses: (a) Maria is the person in this family who expresses both her own and the family's emotion, but this behavior is viewed negatively, especially by Michael; and (b) David might also be experiencing emotional turmoil, but because the male members of this family are not allowed to be emotional, he is under pressure to control his feelings. Both of these hypotheses will need further exploration. The therapist also must continue to explore with each family member their view of the problem to ultimately generate clearly defined problem areas and related treatment goals.

Therapist: (to Michael) Do you think you could tell me, as specifically as you can, what you see as the problem in this family?

Michael: Well I guess the main problem is Maria's depression. She has been this way on and off for a long time. It is really hard on the family when she feels this way.

Therapist: In what way is it hard on the family . . . I mean specifically.

Michael: I don't think Maria realizes what kind of force she has in this family, but when she is depressed, everybody feels it.

Therapist: How in particular do you feel it, Michael?

Michael: It's like, well, at those times I can't do anything right. She seems to always be mad at me for something, and I don't usually even know what I did wrong. She is pretty hard to be around at those times.

Therapist: Do you have any of your own ideas, Michael, as to why Maria starts to feel this way?

Michael: No, not really. It seems to be a lot of little things, but nothing that seems big enough to me to make her get depressed.

Maria: That's not true, Michael. I've told you lots of times that if you helped me out more with the kids, and if you were home more, things would be easier. Or even if you listened to me when I tried to tell you some of the hassles I've had during the day. . . . But you just seem really disinterested all the time, like I'm boring you or something. Sometimes I think you don't want to be a part of this family. You always seem to want to be doing something away from home. You know, just when things are pleasant at home and everyone seems to be getting along, something happens to send us flying back to square one.

Following this exchange between Maria and Michael, the therapist has a glimpse of some potential marital dissatisfaction in this couple. This is not the appropriate time to explore this issue further, however, and the therapist decides it would be more beneficial to keep the family focused on identifying major problems. This marital dissatisfaction issue will be pursued further both in the following interaction stage and in a separate interview with Maria and Michael. It is essential to point out that during this problem identification stage, the therapist's primary task is to gather information. Consequently, interpretations and advice or directives should be eschewed. The therapist must be careful not to start shaping the family here. Rather, the whole family should be drawn into the treatment process by encouraging every member to talk and give an opinion on issues. Some family members (e.g., Maria and Elise) will be better at this task than others (e.g., Michael and David). These latter members will have to be handled more gently to draw them out.

During this entire exploration phase the therapist is observing everyone's behavior and reactions. It is particularly important, when one person is talking, for the therapist to observe the reactions of the other family members. The therapist not only listens carefully to what is being said, but also observes the non-verbal messages that are being communicated. Thus, even at this stage in which the value of the content of what is being said is at its peak, the therapist must also attend to the process of the interactions. Although it may be difficult for the therapist to keep some families focused on delineating the problems, it is crucial during this stage to prevent the family from digressing to other topics. This digression is especially likely to occur with verbal families who are experiencing a high level of emotional intensity.

Therapist: Maria, we have heard one concern that your family has, that you are depressed. You have also indicated that you would like Michael to be more involved with the family. Is there anything else that is a problem in your family?

Maria: Well . . . (looking at David) I know David gets very upset with me when I talk about this, and I know Michael and I don't see eye-to-eye on this, but . . . (as David's eyes start to water, Maria hesitates) (to David) You know this is a problem, and I told you we would probably talk about it today. (At this point Maria also has tears trickling down her cheeks.)

Therapist: (to David) Is this a problem you would like to tell me about, David, or would you prefer that someone else in the family tell me?

David: (with eyes very red and fighting back the tears) No, no one! (in a very angry tone).

Elise: (coming to David's rescue) David is very embarrassed about . . . it . . . and he doesn't like us to tell anybody about it, but you know what . . . he dirties his pants.

David: (yelling at Elise) You shut up, you little tattle tale! It's not true!

Maria: David, you know it is true.

Therapist: (Gently) Can you tell me in your own words, David, what you think are the problems in this family?

David: (reluctantly, after a few minutes of glum silence) Just my mom being miserable all the time. She's always getting after everyone, mostly me.

Therapist: What besides your mom's unhappiness is a problem in this family? Do you ever feel down in the dumps like your mom does?

David: No! I'd be fine if everyone just left me alone. That's the only problem I know of.

Therapist: What about the soiling that your mom and sister mentioned? Do you think that is a problem?

David: (looking dejected and fighting back his tears, refuses to answer the question)

Therapist: Well David, we don't have to talk more about that problem right now, if it is making you feel so unhappy. I'll just mark down that it is one of the problems this family has, and we can talk about it more later. (addressing no one in particular) Now, are there any other problems in this family that people would like to change?

David: (blurting out angrily) Yeah, someone should tell Elise to leave my things alone and stay out of my room. She thinks she can just use my things whenever she wants. (he is getting even with Elise)

Elise: (to David) Well, you never play with me. You're always too busy with your friends or all your toys and computer games. You're mean to me.

Maria: Elise tries so hard with David . . . she just worships him and he's always pushing her away.

The therapist wonders at this point if Elise and David's relationship might be a metaphor for the marital relationship. This is noted as another tentative hypothesis, but not one to be pursued at this time. At this stage in the interview, the therapist has asked everyone to comment on what they think is the problem in the family and now has a good idea of the family's views of their various concerns. On the basis of the information gathered so far, the therapist has begun to formulate hypotheses about the family problems, the interactional patterns that maintain these problems, and the interventions required to bring about the desired changes. The therapist, however, still has much to learn about the family, and these hypotheses are regarded as preliminary and tentative. Briefly, the therapist has learned that everyone in the family has identified Maria's depression as a significant problem. Although Maria accepts this "problem" position, she also views Michael's unavailability to the family and David's encopresis as major areas of concern. These three problem areas are identified as the main presenting problems.

In addition to this factual information, however, the therapist has formed several other hypotheses or interpretations about this family based on observations during this problem identification stage. For example, the therapist has detected considerable anger in Maria's tone when talking to or about her son. David has some awareness of his mother's feelings, as evidenced by his reluctance to participate in the session and by his display of tears while Maria was describing her concerns about him. A more subtle source of conflict was detected between Maria and Michael. This observation led the therapist to speculate that Maria and Michael are having marital difficulties that are being detoured through David. The therapist was also careful to note the behaviors of other family members while one person was speaking, and this procedure yielded interesting information. Specifically, Elise paid close attention to how her mother was feeling, and was the only one to display support for her. Michael and David, however, both appeared uncomfortable with Maria's expression of her feelings, and tended to look down or away from her when she became visibly upset. Similarly, David appeared to be embarrassed when he himself became upset, obviously struggling to hold back his tears. He also aimed several surreptitious glances at his father to discern Michael's reaction to his display of feelings.

Regardless of how confident the therapist is of his or her interpretations regarding the family dynamics, it is important that they not be verbalized at this stage in therapy. To do so involves too much risk; the therapist could easily alienate the family by an incorrect interpretation or by a correct interpretation that is delivered prematurely (i.e., an interpretation that is too painful for a family to hear at this stage in the therapy process).

The next step in the problem identification stage is to elicit more specific information about the presenting concerns in terms of both the circumstances surrounding their occurrence and the measures each family member has taken to reduce the problem. In families in which there are problems in addition to the depression, this information must also be obtained on these secondary areas of concern. Following the family's report of what each person sees as the problems in the family, the therapist elicits detailed information concerning when these problems are most likely to occur, while paying close attention to family members' transactional patterns. This information will reveal who relates to whom, how, when, and with what kind of emotional reactions. During this process the therapist will also obtain further insight into the family boundaries and the various family subsystems, although more comprehensive information in these areas will be derived in the interaction stage. When the therapist has collected sufficient information from the family's verbal descriptions of the problem, the next stage can begin.

The Interaction Stage

Entry into this stage should be a gradual and natural extension of the previous stage. The therapist will slowly draw back from being the center of the discussion, as family members are encouraged to speak to each other directly regarding the opinions expressed previously. Initially, most families continue to talk to the therapist, but after consistent directions to speak directly to the family member concerned, most families will be able to comply with relative ease. For those families that have difficulty expressing themselves, however, the therapist may have to be more active in priming the family for this task, perhaps by giving the family a particular topic to discuss or requesting that they enact a recent sequence of events related to an area of concern. Once this is initiated, however, the therapist will be immediately struck by the amount of interaction in the family. Although some of the information revealed by these transactions will be explicit and direct, other information will be more subtle and based on the covert rules governing the family system. To unveil the structure, organization, and dynamics in a family, the therapist must establish a degree of trust and openness that permits a family to reveal itself at both a verbal and a nonverbal level. As this trust grows, the therapist is permitted to explore more painful and sensitive areas, beginning with areas that are less threatening to the family. By the time the family is ready for the interaction stage, the therapist will have identified potentially revealing and important areas to explore further through having the family members interact with each other.

> *Therapist:* Michael, could you talk directly with Maria about what makes her feel depressed?
> *Michael:* Well, I think she has told me often enough when she gets upset. And we usually end up having some kind of argument when we talk about that.
> *Therapist:* I know it may seem like talking about the same old issues, but I think it will help me to get a really good understanding about what your family is like.
> *Michael:* (he hesitates at first but then goes ahead) Honey, you know I worry about you when you get depressed. I want you to be happy, but sometimes I just don't know what to do to help.

The therapist prepares to observe the interaction between Michael and Maria, and to code the valence of their statements on the coding sheet presented in Figure 4.1. Michael's response suggests that he views Maria's depression as a reflection of his inability to make her happy. As long as he interprets her depression in this way he is likely to continue to get defensive when Maria starts to voice her concerns about a problem. The therapist should obtain a clear and precise account of the interactional pattern that has been established in this area of concern before applying an intervention strategy that allows a different path to be carved.

> *Maria:* Well, you always make me feel so guilty for getting upset about something. I don't even tell you half of what goes on because I am afraid of upsetting you. I just end up feeling like a failure or a disappointment to you if I can't handle everything on my own.
> *Michael:* That's not fair, Maria. I don't expect a lot from you; it's you who expects so much from yourself. In fact, you expect perfection from the whole family. You always get annoyed with the kids because they aren't doing exactly what you want them to.
> *Maria:* (begins to cry) I work very hard to make things good for the whole family, but it seems I have to do all the work myself.

As this conversation continues, it becomes more intense, with both Michael and Maria digressing quickly from the issue of Maria's depression. Considerable pent-up anger and disappointment is being expressed in their interchange. Indeed, as the therapist records the quality of the exchanges between Maria and Michael, the negative reciprocity characteristic of distressed couples becomes even more obvious. As the exchange of accusations continues, Elise and David become noticeably restless and begin to squabble. David in particular attempts to provoke Elise into a fight. Elise is torn between defending herself and trying to comfort her mother. Within 10 minutes, a clear pattern begins to emerge. First, Maria communicates some frustration or upset, and Michael then becomes defensive and annoyed. This transaction is followed by a mutual negatively toned exchange of disappointments and accusations. The children become upset and initiate their own strategies to deal with the conflict between their parents. Elise tries to comfort her mother by sitting closer to her and giving her hugs. David's strategy is more intrusive; he reacts to the tension by becoming loud and aggressive, trying to stimulate a fight between himself and his sister. Michael ultimately abandons the conflict with his wife and becomes increasingly quiet and withdrawn. Maria's frustration, agitation and helplessness escalate, and, probably because Michael is no longer emotionally available, she redirects her feelings of anger and disappointment onto David. David reacts to this attack by becoming uncooperative and noncompliant to his mother's requests to "settle down and behave." As Maria feels increasingly out of control and incompetent and fails to enlist Michael's aid, her feelings of depression swell. Finally, in addition to these direct observations, the therapist hypothesizes that David's next step in this sequence of transactions is to become encopretic, depressed, or both.

The foregoing discussion highlights the importance of the interaction stage of therapy. It is unlikely that the family members could have conveyed this transactional information verbally to the therapist. Moreover, they are probably unaware for the most part of the series of interactions that occurred. Only by observing the family choreography was the therapist able to discover the sequence of interactions that surrounded Maria's depression. This pattern of interactions is highly informative in that it contains the essential components of the major problems identified by the family. Although the therapist has uncovered extremely valuable information in understanding how Maria's depression is triggered (or maintained), considerably more information must still be obtained before intervention strategies can be planned. This material will be procured by continued observation of family interactions and by the results of the objective assessment instruments completed by the family members later in the interview. As the interactional process unfolds, the therapist makes ongoing notes about secondary interactions to be explored further. With this family, the therapist decides to pursue the interaction presented above to reveal the next sequence of behaviors. (It is worth reiterating that even though the therapist has begun to understand the nature of the family's transactions and their relationships both to the occurrence of Maria's depression and to the other problems identified by the family as areas of concern, interpretations should be withheld until additional corroborating information is obtained.)

The therapist continues with this stage, alternating between direct questioning of the family and encouraging family members to interact with each other until she acquires a clearer understanding of the dynamics of Maria's depression. Moreover, because the therapist wondered earlier if David might also become depressed at times, she made direct inquiries concerning this possibility. Although David denied feeling "down in the dumps" or sad, his parents (Maria in particular) felt that this might be a possibility, especially because David does not often share his feelings with them. The therapist has sufficient concerns about David to warrant spending time alone with him. Bringing together all of the information acquired so far, the therapist is now ready to plan the next stage of the assessment interview. Specifically, she has decided to spend individual time first with Maria and then with David to explore more fully the severity and circumstances related to their depressions. In addition, both Maria and David will complete self-report depression inventories (the BDI and CDI, respectively). The therapist wishes to test the hypothesis that Maria and Michael are experiencing marital difficulties and, consequently, will spend time alone with the two of them. In addition, both will be asked to complete the Dyadic Adjustment Scale. Finally, to provide data related to the overall family functioning which will complement the family assessment interview, the therapist decides to ask the family members to complete the Family Environment Scale.

The therapist has spent considerable time drawing the whole family into the therapeutic process. Consistent with our conceptualization of depression, however, which attaches considerable importance to both the systemic and the individual aspects of a person's functioning, the therapist also allows individual time for family members who she believes will benefit from this attention. As we will see, this practice is important in both the assessment and treatment phases of therapy.

In seeing Maria alone, the therapist conducted a SADS interview, assessing Maria on DSM-III criteria. Maria quite clearly demonstrated a prominent dysphoric mood, and told the therapist that she had lost interest in many of her usual activities. In addition to dysphoria, Maria complained of poor appetite (although she apparently had not lost a significant amount of weight) and loss of energy. She commented frequently during the interview on how worthless she felt, and her speech and motor functioning were clearly slowed. This symptom picture, combined with the lack of delusions, hallucinations, or evidence of brain dysfunction, led the therapist to apply a DSM-III diagnosis of Major Depressive Episode.

Once a diagnosis was reached, the therapist explored other areas of importance with Maria. After extensive questioning, the therapist was satisfied that

Maria was not suicidal. To help in deciding whether to refer Maria for evaluation for psychotropic medication, the therapist assessed Maria on the criteria for endogenous depression presented in Chapter 4. Because Maria did not meet criteria for probable endogenous depression, the therapist decided against making this referral. Consistent with her diagnosis, Maria obtained a score on the Beck Depression Inventory of 39.

The therapist also saw David in a brief individual session, and followed the Interview Schedule for Children. David did not meet formal criteria for depression; he did, however, obtain a score on the Child Depression Inventory of 17. Given the cutoff of 13 on this questionnaire to identify depression in children, however, the therapist made a note to monitor David's progress carefully.

The results of the marital interview and Maria and Michael's responses to the Dyadic Adjustment Scale supported the therapist's initial hypothesis of the presence of marital conflict. Although Maria demonstrated greater dissatisfaction with her marriage than did Michael (Maria's DAS score was 81; Michael's DAS score was 94), it was promising that both stated a strong commitment to the importance of a satisfactory marital relationship. Neither Maria nor Michael was able openly to label marital difficulties as an area of concern; however, they were able to recognize areas of disagreement and left open the possibility of exploring these issues at a later point.

The results of the family assessment were generally consistent with the information obtained for this family thus far and revealed several areas of discord. The Family Environment Scale profile for Maria and Michael is presented in Figure 5.1. The Richardsons perceive themselves as a strongly achievement-oriented, competitive family with very high standards. Although Maria indicated satisfaction with the strong importance of organization, structure, and set rules and procedures in the family, the other family members, and Michael in particular, felt that the family structure was unnecessarily rigid. All of the family members agreed on the significant amount of conflict in the family, but they disagreed as to the source of this stress. Maria indicated that she receives little support and help from the other family members, and that they frequently do not meet her expectations regarding self-sufficiency and independence. Michael, however, perceived the family's level of support for Maria as adequate and attributed the conflict to Maria's high expectations. Interestingly, although Elise's profile was very similar to Maria's, David's profile was most like Michael's, indicating the possible presence of a schism in the family.

Goal-Definition Stage

Having now met individually with Maria and David and having seen Maria and Michael together, the therapist has two options at this point in the therapy process, depending on time limitations. If there is sufficient time to allow her to

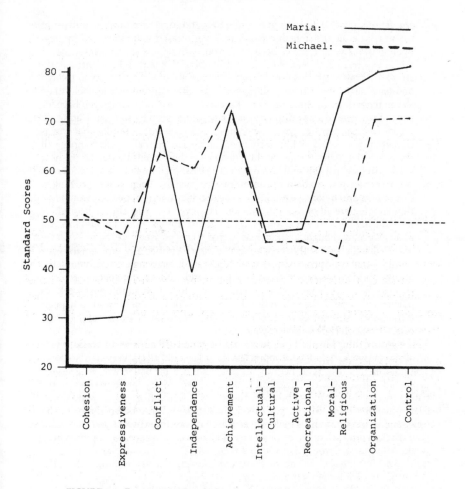

FIGURE 5.1. Pretreatment Family Environment Scale Profile.

score and integrate the information derived from the interview and the formal assessment instruments while the family waits, on regrouping the therapist can proceed with summarizing the initial formulation of this family and negotiating relevant treatment goals with them. If, however, the therapist cannot perform this task at this time, a brief summary statement should be offered to the family which contains both an element of feedback and direction for the subsequent session. This communication should also contain an understanding and concern for the family. The following excerpt conveys the essence of this message.

Therapist: Well, we've had an opportunity to spend some time together and get to know a little bit about each other. I am both pleased and impressed by how open with me you all were. Because of your willingness to share information with me, I feel I have learned a great deal about this family. I am particularly struck by how much this family seems to care about each other, even though you have difficulty at times finding ways to communicate that to each other. When these difficult times happen, it seems like the good feelings you have for each other seem to grow dimmer, and they get replaced by sad, frustrating, or angry feelings. I got a strong sense from everyone in the family that this is something you would all like to change. I appreciate your efforts to complete all those questionnaires for me, and I will go over them carefully during the next week. I'm sure that this will give me an even clearer picture of the specific areas of concern for you. So before I summarize for you what I believe is happening in this family, and before we establish some specific treatment goals, I would like time to integrate all of that information. However, it would also be helpful for me if during the next week you would all do two things. First, I would like you all to give more thought to the concerns that you expressed here today. What we will be doing is taking the three areas you have identified as a problem for your family—that is, Maria's depression, Michael's limited time available for the family, and David's problem with soiling—and working out specific goals to address them. And that is what I would like you to talk about this next week. In particular, I would like you to decide what specifically would need to happen differently in this family in order for us to be able to say "we are making progress." Is that all right with everyone? Good.

The second thing I would like you all to do is what I call a homework task. It will involve some work, but I would appreciate it if you would all try very hard to do it. The goal of this task is to help us all understand a bit better why Maria gets depressed. What I would like you all to do is to keep a diary for yourselves, without having to show it to anybody. In this diary, I would like you to write down every time you think Maria, your mommy, gets sad. Write down the date, the time, and what you think is making her feel that way. I don't want you to discuss your diaries with each other, because I would like everyone's separate opinion next week. And Maria, I would like you to do the same thing. I would like everyone to try and act just the way you normally would. Don't try to do anything differently.

I would like for all of us to meet again next week. In that meeting we'll decide who in the family I'll be meeting with in subsequent sessions, how long our sessions will be, and how often we'll meet. We'll also work out some specific goals and plans for what we will try to accomplish here during our time together. Now, does anybody have any questions about the homework task or anything else I just said? Good. It was nice to have met you. I'll look forward to seeing you all next week.

In offering this statement to the family, the therapist has communicated empathy and understanding and has emphasized the family's strengths of openness and their caring for each other. The therapist has also left the family with an assignment to be completed over the next week. Although relatively simple, the assignment of a homework task serves to bridge the two sessions and to keep the family involved in the therapeutic process. In this situation in which more time is required to score and interpret the test data, the therapist would begin the second session with a more thorough summary of how the family is functioning, including information derived from the formal assessment instruments. This feedback summary should meet the general criteria outlined below. The treatment goals would then be clearly formulated, the therapy plan devised, and a contract drawn up. For organizational simplicity, this information is essentially described in the succeeding section, for the situation in which the therapist has had an opportunity in the initial session to review and integrate the formal assessment data before the final meeting with the family. To avoid redundancy, the next chapter will begin as if all these activities were performed in the first session.

When the therapist is able to score, interpret, and synthesize the information on the family, she can proceed with the next stage of the therapy process. The therapist now faces the challenging task of developing a formulation of the case. As Karpel and Strauss (1983) suggest, the presenting problem or problems must be understood in all their degrees of complexity. The therapist must pull together all the information collected from a variety of sources and address the questions raised earlier in this guidebook. What has contributed to the development of the problem? What pattern of interactions within the family system serve to support or maintain the symptom or set of symptoms? What function or purpose does the symptom serve for both the individual and the family system? To accomplish this task, the therapist must draw on the information obtained regarding the family's structure, boundaries, and subsystems and the roles assumed by the individuals within these subsystems. In some cases the information provided will be either so complex or incomplete that the therapist may require more than one assessment session to develop a complete formulation. We believe that it is preferable to take the additional time to accomplish this task, rather than risk the setbacks potentially incurred by an inaccurate formulation. If the therapist's initial hypotheses are supported by subsequent observations and are continually refined and honed on the basis of additional information, the therapist will have growing confidence in the case formulation. If, however, the therapist was vacillating between competing hypotheses throughout the session, more information clearly is required.

The therapist's evaluative summary for the family, which precedes the negotiation of specific treatment goals and the therapy contract, is also a complex task. This feedback summary requires careful consideration regarding wording and presentation. Families, at least initially, are generally very defensive. Consequently, the therapist must present an account of the problem that is both meaningful and acceptable to the family. Although this task requires significant skill, the therapist generally should avoid confrontational and threatening accounts and should adhere as closely as possible to a formulation that is based on direct information provided by the family and that is congruent with the family's current needs and level of functioning. The summary must be clearly articulated and expressed in a language that is readily understandable by the family; the therapist should avoid technical terms and psychological jargon. Finally, the therapist is also cautioned against singling out any family member in a critical or judgmental manner. When delivering the summary, the therapist must continually monitor the family's reaction to what he or she is saying. If any adverse or hostile reactions are detected, the therapist should probably soften and modify the presentation.

With regard to our case example, the therapist has synthesized the information from the family interview, the individual sessions with Maria and David, the spousal interview, and the data obtained from the assessment inventories. Considered collectively, the information revealed a fairly consistent picture of the dynamics of this family. The individual sessions with both Maria and David, in conjunction with the results of the depression inventories (recall Maria's BDI score of 39 and David's CDI score of 17), indicated that, indeed, both mother and son were experiencing depressive symptomatology, although David's degree of depression was less severe than Maria's, who met DSM-III criteria for Major Depressive Episode. Maria also revealed herself to have very high standards for herself as well as her family. Her self-concept was strongly tied to her roles as a mother and a wife. As her responsibilities in these two areas diminished, so did her self-esteem. Maria also stated in her individual session that from time to time she had considered securing a position outside the home, but that at such times she was actively discouraged from doing so by her mother (who had rigid beliefs about the roles and responsibilities of women).

Although Maria was readily able to talk in detail about her concerns and seemed likely to benefit from some sessions of individual treatment, David's response was the opposite. He was very defensive throughout his individual contact and was afraid of being singled out in any way. Consequently, he was unlikely at this point to benefit from individual attention.

The results of the marital interview and assessment indicated the presence of marital conflict, but because of Maria and Michael's reluctance to deal with these concerns at this point, the therapist decided to leave open the possibility of seeing Maria and Michael together. Finally, the results of the family assessment yielded areas of conflict and concern and increased the therapist's confidence in the appropriateness of taking an interpersonal systems approach to treatment with this family.

In sum, the assessment measures yielded a profile of the Richardsons as a family system characterized by only moderate levels of cohesion and adaptability. Both Maria and David were experiencing significant levels of depression, and Maria and Michael were also experiencing a moderate degree of marital discord. Maria perceived little support from the rest of her family and, in particular, from Michael; moreover, this perception was exacerbated during her periods of depression. The results of these measures also indicated two potentially important areas for intervention with this family. First, the therapist felt that it was important to encourage a higher level of mutual support and understanding among the family members. Second, the family members needed to learn more adaptive and effective problem-solving and communication skills, thereby reducing both Maria's high need for structure and organization and the significant level of stress in the family. Although the therapist may choose not to articulate these areas to the family in the form of specific treatment goals, they nevertheless help to identify stress points in the family and to make her cognizant of these difficulties as she conducts the intervention.

Based on an integration of all this material, the therapist offered the following summary to the family:

> *Therapist:* We've had a fair bit of time today to talk and get to know each other. I'm very pleased with how open you have all been with me, and with your patience and cooperation in filling out those inventories. Your willingness to do such a good job today has certainly made my job easier. The first thing that struck me about this family is how close you are and how much care and concern you feel for each other. Each of you in your own way feels a strong devotion to the family. Michael, you clearly work very hard to support your family and provide as best you can for them, even though it sometimes means sacrificing your own free time and interests. And you, Maria, have impressed me very much with the amount of energy and effort you pour into your family. You clearly want the best for them, and have repeatedly shown your willingness to make personal sacrifices to ensure that everyone else's needs are being met. It is not at all surprising to me that sometimes the two of you get burned out and don't seem to have the energy to keep your heads above water. My guess is that at these times neither of you has the strength to keep the family on an even keel, and things then start to backslide. Since Maria sees keeping the family running as pretty much her "job," I think she feels more responsible when this backsliding occurs and, thus, gets pretty down about things. (pauses) Elise too tries very hard to make this family happy. I noticed that she is very sensitive to people's feelings, and when she sees someone upset, she tries to find ways to cheer them up. It looks to me like David is a little bit like both his parents, particularly his mother, in that he has very high standards. I think he tries to do things perfectly, and when he is not able to, he comes down pretty hard on himself. Overall, I think families such as this who have such high standards and a strong commitment to one another are bound to undergo periods of high stress. Usually, people have different ways of dealing with this stress. Some people, such as you, Michael, throw themselves even harder into their work. Other people, like you, Maria, get depressed or easily upset a lot. Even Elise and David have developed ways of dealing with this stress. Elise tries to be cheerful and make everyone feel better, and David clams up and holds a lot in. I think that because you are such a close family, it would be helpful if we set up a few sessions for everyone to come in. I think you can all be pretty helpful to one another, and I feel pretty sure that if you all work on things together, it won't take long to get this family back on track.

The family members were assigned the homework task just described. Even before the precise treatment goals are negotiated with the family members, the therapist has obtained sufficient information from the assessment session and the questionnaires to make a decision that the entire family should be seen for the initial sessions. The therapist will now proceed to work with the family members to elicit and decide upon specific treatment goals. As noted in the previous chapter, it is important that these goals be clearly stated, concrete, straightforward, and amenable to change. Moreover, they must accurately reflect the family's current level of needs and perception of the problem. Once established, these goals are expressed in an open-ended manner, allowing for the option of changing them as therapy progresses. This flexibility also applies to the issue of who will be seen in therapy.

After a relatively brief negotiation period with the Richardson family, the family and therapist decided to focus on Maria's depression, David's encopresis, and Michael's lack of involvement in the family. The therapist then worked with the family to operationalize these goals. The goals with respect to Maria's depression were operationalized and agreed upon as follows: Maria was to engage in more of her favorite hobbies (e.g., refinishing furniture, crocheting, taking piano lessons, and ceramics); the family was to spend 3 more hours together each week in pleasurable activities than they were currently doing; and Maria was to take one half day every week and spend it with a friend. With respect to his encopresis, David was to have more free days from soiling and was to spend less time worrying about the family. Finally, Michael was to plan one activity a week for his family, he and Maria were to spend one evening together as a couple, and Michael was to talk more to Maria about his work and hobbies; whenever Michael had difficulty planning an event for his family, Elise was to help him out and was also to think of an activity on her own. By carefully defining these treatment goals, it will be relatively easy for both the therapist and the family to assess the progress they are making in each of the three problem areas.

Direct attention to the marital conflict and to David's relatively mild depression was temporarily placed on hold, first because this couple was not yet ready to work on marital issues, and second because David had emitted strong signals that he did not want to be singled out in therapy. The therapist decided that it would be best to start with family sessions, interspersed with a few individual sessions with Maria. She also recommended that Michael and Maria have a few sessions together to deal with issues and concerns around Maria's depression that were best done in the absence of the children. The family agreed to this approach, with a noticeable sigh of relief from David at not having to be seen on his own.

The final activity to be accomplished in this session was to set the ground rules for therapy. The therapist and family contracted for 10 sessions, with a review to be conducted at that time aimed at evaluating the progress made, examining the treatment goals, and making any necessary revisions. The need to contract for further sessions would also be assessed at that time. Family sessions were designated as being $1^1/_2$ hours long, whereas individual sessions and meetings with the couple were set for 1 hour. The therapist instructed the Richardsons that at the end of each session she would inform them who she wished to be present at the next session. She further emphasized the importance of following through precisely with these recommendations. If any of the individuals who were expected to attend a particular session were unable to attend, they were to contact the therapist and arrange to be seen at an alternate time. The first set of sessions were scheduled on a once-a-week basis. With all this agreed upon, the therapist was to write this information up briefly as a contract to be given to the family and signed at the next session.

Chapter 6
Stages of Treatment
II. The Intervention Stage

In this chapter we will provide the highlights of the remainder of the 10 sessions contracted for with the Richardson family. Many of the therapy principles and techniques outlined in the previous chapters will be illustrated. Again, portions of the transcripts from the sessions will be interspersed with discussions of the relevant techniques and processes. Finally, because the therapist requested Maria to complete the Beck Depression Inventory at the beginning of each session, these data will also be presented.

In preparing for the second session, the therapist should review all of the information collected on the family both in the interview and from the assessment data. This information is critical to the successful outcome of treatment, as it provides the material for understanding the level of individual and family functioning, and for revealing patterns of interaction that may be maintaining the depressive behavior.

INTERVENTION
Session 2: The Family *(Maria's BDI = 35)*

This session represents the "action stage" of therapy. The therapist must utilize all the collected information to promote healthier functioning and produce the desired changes. The therapist begins the second session with the Richardson family by presenting them with the contract containing the terms outlined in the previous chapter. Presenting each family member with his or her own typed copy of the contract makes the goals of therapy and, indeed, the entire therapeutic process, more salient and important to the family. Moreover, a therapy contract helps to focus the family or individual on the relevant treatment objectives and may increase their motivation to change.

After formally greeting the family and engaging in a few moments of social conversation while Maria completed the BDI, the therapist gave each family member a copy of the contract. The family was asked to read the contract and determine whether any changes were needed. Because the therapist had encouraged the family to be concrete and specific regarding both the presenting problems and their desired treatment goals, no changes were required. After everyone signed the agreement, the therapist reminded the family that the contract was not written in stone and could be renegotiated at any point in the therapy process.

> *Therapist:* Before we talk about how you all did on your homework task, I would like to know if anyone has any questions or thoughts about our session last week.
>
> *Elise:* Well I was glad we came. Mommy seemed to be happier after we left last week. But David said he didn't want to come back to this . . . dumb place.
>
> *Maria:* Michael and I talked quite a bit about what was said last week, but he still isn't sure why we all need to come, since the biggest concern we have is my feeling depressed. And I guess I also feel the same way.
>
> *Therapist:* That is an important issue, Maria, and I admit that it is one that is sometimes hard to explain. I have often found that providing an example makes it easier to understand the reason that I think you should all attend. Perhaps reviewing the homework assignment will make this concept clearer. So, maybe we can go over the homework now. Everyone was supposed to write down every time they believed that Maria was depressed or sad. You were asked to write down the date, the time, and what you think it was made her feel that way. Did everyone do it?
>
> *Maria:* We talked about it just before we left home, and we all wrote down something except for David. He said he forgot, even though I reminded everyone several times during the week.
>
> *Therapist:* Well, we'll talk about that later too, but for now could the rest of you give me what you wrote and I'll look it over.

The therapist decided not to risk further alienating David by singling him out about his failure to complete the homework task, reasoning that it would be more effective to try to entice him to cooperate in future sessions. A review of the notes revealed that Maria clearly felt depressed more often than was perceived by her family. Maria indicated that she was depressed every day and listed such reasons as, "unable to complete all the jobs I wanted to today," "David's soiling," "fight with Michael," "no reason, just felt like crying all day," "feeling like a failure, like my life has no purpose," and "I can't seem to get through to Michael—he just doesn't seem to understand me." Elise had reported the next highest frequency, which included, "David and I were fighting over whose turn it was to use the computer," "David messed his pants again," "Daddy said he would be home for supper but then came home very late—he always works too much," "I tried to cheer mommy up but she got mad at me and told me to stop bugging her—I didn't mean to make her mad," and "Grandma called and mom was crying when she hung up the phone." Michael's list contained only three incidents: "David's accident," "the kids were getting on her nerves," and "I had to work late and couldn't make it home for dinner." With respect to time of day, Maria seemed to be more upset during the evenings.

> *Therapist:* Thank you for doing this task; it helps me to get a clearer picture of what you all think makes Maria feel depressed. I know you didn't write yours down, David, but can you remember any of them?
>
> *David:* Well just two times. One was when our dog pooped on the kitchen floor, mom just started to cry and went to her room and shut the door. I cleaned up the mess, but she didn't even say thank you. Then the other time was on Saturday: every time Elise and me did anything she was yelling at us, but I don't know if that was mad or sad—it seemed like both. And, oh yeah, I just remembered, one night daddy didn't come home for supper and she threw his dinner in the garbage, and she was crying too.
>
> *Therapist:* Thank you, David; that was very helpful. You even mentioned some things that nobody else did.

The therapist then shared with the family what was on the rest of the lists. This actually generated a fair bit of discussion and provided an excellent entry for the therapist to return to Maria and Michael's hesitation about the whole family becoming involved in treating Maria's depression.

> *Therapist:* You know, as I sat back and listened to you all talking about what you felt made Maria depressed and how you each tried to cheer her up, and saw how some things seemed to help and some seemed to backfire, it reminded me once again about how important it is to have you all come here and work together to make things better in your family. If you weren't all here, I wouldn't have any idea about what you all think and feel, and how each of you in your own way is trying to find ways to make Maria happier. So, Maria, to answer your earlier question about why the whole family needs to be involved in coming here, I think it is going to take the efforts of your family working together to make this family function better. If you weren't such a close family who are all so affected by each other it might not be as necessary. And looking at the examples you provided, all of you were in some way involved in or affected by Maria's depression. Does that answer your question, Maria? Michael?
>
> *Michael:* Yeah, I guess it does make a lot of sense. I think we are just a family who needs to really understand why we are doing something. But once something is clear to us, we all work very hard at it.
>
> *Maria:* Michael's right. We always think things through before we go ahead and do them.

The therapist has been acquiring more information about how the whole family might be involved in Maria's depression. She has encouraged the Richardsons to become more directly involved in discussing each person's perceptions of Maria's depression as well as the situations that seem to trigger it. For the first time, everyone is sharing and discussing their feelings about Maria's depression rather than simply reacting to it. As this process continues, Elise begins to look relieved that her mother's problems are not strongly related to her own behavior.

David, however, and to a somewhat lesser degree, Michael, feel they are somehow being blamed by Maria as "causing" her depression. Michael expressed strong feelings that all his attempts to bring Maria out of her depression were generally futile. David felt singled out and unfairly treated by his mother. As the therapy session continued, the therapist requested the family to enact several of the situations that had been included on their lists of Maria's depressed moods. (It is important to point out here that although Maria's depression is significant and ongoing, she, like most depressed persons, tended to have periods of greater and lesser depression, and these episodes are what are being considered here.)

The therapist's evaluation of these enactments provided further support for her earlier hypothesis that Maria's depression stemmed largely from her inability to elicit the kind of behavior she wished from her husband. This couple was trapped in a pattern of interactions that prevented either of them from having their needs met. Moreover, this pattern was repetitive and predictable. Maria's attempts to be close to Michael were interpreted by him as controlling and demanding. As Michael responded to his wife's "requests" by withdrawing and withholding even more from her, Maria became critical and rejecting. This conflict intensified to a certain level, and then a shift occurred. With "help" from David (provided in the form of his misbehavior), Maria redirected her anger and frustration toward her son. Reinforcing this redirection, Michael frequently responded to Maria's criticisms of David by supporting her in her frustrations and concerns regarding David's noncompliant and encopretic behavior.

As this session draws to a close, the therapist uses the technique of reframing, and reframes this interactional sequence in a positive way, with the purpose of providing the family with an alternative perspective for viewing David's problematic behavior. Families generally view symptoms in ways that do not promote change, and often attribute negative or insidious motives to the person exhibiting the problem behavior. Moreover, families often consider themselves to be "stuck" in their dysfunctional interactional patterns. Thus, a major objective of this reframing technique is to free the family from its prescribed style of responding, thereby creating the opportunity to consider other, more productive behaviors. The therapist must stimulate new interactional patterns that will both meet the goals of the family and eliminate the "need" for the symptoms.

Therapist: You know, the more I get to know this family, the more impressed I become at how close you all are, and how willing you are to take whatever measures you can to ensure that nothing breaks this family up. Just before we stop for today, I would like to share with you an idea about what I saw happening here as you acted out some of those situations that have been occurring at home. It has become even more obvious to me today how hard Maria works to ensure the best for her family. I think Michael realizes that as long as his wife is looking after family affairs so competently, he doesn't have to worry about the family and can concentrate more on his work. Michael, too, is attempting to provide as much as he possibly can for his family. Many other husbands and fathers are not nearly as devoted as Michael. Elise has a pretty important job in this family, too. She is very protective of her mother and tries to do whatever she can to ensure Maria's happiness. Now David's contribution to this family may not be as obvious as the others, but it is nevertheless just as important. As I watched what transpired among you today, it reminded me of bullfights I have seen in Spain. When Maria and Michael get into an argument, they seemed like the matador and the bull. When the encounter became too intense, out came David to distract the bull. Now, I'm not saying people in this family are like bulls, or anything like that. But when Maria and Michael argue, I think that David, probably without even realizing it, begins to act up in some way to distract his parents from arguing. This is his attempt to try and help out, even though we could probably all agree it doesn't make the family feel better. However, it does help Maria and Michael to get closer and be on the same side. At the same time, Maria often reacts to this situation with frustration and helplessness. This in turn seems to stimulate or exacerbate her feelings of depression.

Maria: You mean that you think David's acting up is his way of trying to be helpful. That seems like a pretty unusual way of looking at it.

Therapist: I agree; it does seem different. But maybe you could take a few minutes to think about the times David is most difficult at home and see if perhaps it has been at times when you and Michael are upset with each other.

Michael: Well I can think of a few occasions, but . . .

Michael and Maria were clearly hesitant to accept this interpretation of David's behavior. However, they did not present the therapist with the degree of resistance often manifested by families to reframing interventions. The more a family is locked into a particular view of the problem or the more they are threatened by an alternative conceptualization, or both, the more resistance they will present. This family's cautious willingness to consider the therapist's interpretation as viable allows her to have more confidence in her working hypotheses of the dynamics of this family. If she had encountered strong resistance from the family, the therapist would have modified her hypotheses and her approach in accord with the family's response.

As we indicated previously, an important feature of our therapeutic intervention is the assignment of directives. The importance of providing the family with alternative ways of interacting is strongly emphasized. Thus, not only must the family conceptualize the problem behavior or behaviors differently, but also they must be given opportunities to react to them in ways that promote healthier and more positive interactions. Furthermore, the therapist must draw on the strengths and resources of the family to produce these positive changes. Thus, the therapist issued the following directive to the family to be completed between this and the next session:

Therapist: I know I've presented you with a way of looking at David's behavior that right now feels foreign to you, but I would like you to try an assignment between now and our next session that should help to clarify this viewpoint. Therefore, as unusual as it may sound to you, I would like you to try to behave the way I just described things. Michael and Maria, when you get into an argument I would like you to allow David an opportunity to distract you. And David, I want you to make sure you create some kind of fuss if you think your parents are getting too serious in their argument. You can start an argument with your sister, become uncooperative with your parents, become moody, or do something else that you think might distract your parents. Don't get too carried away, though. Also, Michael and Maria, if you think David is not intervening soon enough, I would like you to give him a prearranged signal to do something to distract you from your quarrel. Your assignment, Elise, will be to do whatever you can to cheer up your mother whenever you think she is feeling sad or depressed. Does everybody think they can do this?

Maria: Well I guess so, if you think it is going to help, though I'm not sure how this is going to make things better at home.

David: (grumbling under his breath) Yeah, I can do it, but it sounds kind of dumb to me.

Elise: I'm sure I'll be pretty good at my job.

Michael: (smiling) Well, I just hope Maria and I can find something to argue about.

This assignment highlights another important aspect of a directive: It takes the interactional pattern from the covert level to the overt. In so doing, the interaction typically loses much of its power. Moreover, because the family has been instructed to act out a sequence they have already unknowingly been doing, they begin to assume greater control over their behavior. A final characteristic of this directive is that everyone has a role in it. This aspect reinforces the systemic or interactional conceptualization of the depression, and helps everyone in the family to feel that they will be a part of the solution to the problem. The therapist ends this second session with the instruction that the next session will also include the whole family.

Session 3: The Family *(Maria's BDI = 26)*

The therapist's primary goals during this session are to review the directive from the previous meeting and to explore each member's reactions to his or her specific role in the transaction. The therapist should be as explicit and specific as possible in gathering this information, because the data are crucial in planning both who to see in subsequent sessions and the appropriate interventions to produce the desired changes. To accomplish these objectives, the therapist must always acknowledge and accept the family or individual's views of the depression and then extend or alter those views in such a way that new options for responding are created. If the therapist begins at a point that is inconsistent with the family members' views of the problem, those individuals may feel that the therapist does not understand them, and consequently, they may feel compelled to convince the therapist of the veridicality of their position. Often, the therapist assumes that it is the family's unsuccessful attempted solution to a problem that becomes, or that is, the problem. Consequently, the therapist must interrupt the attempted solution and suggest an alternate course that is acceptable to the family.

The therapist immediately noted a difference in the Richardson family on their arrival for the third session. David, who had been sulky, withdrawn, and reluctant to cooperate in the previous two sessions, arrived in high spirits. He was the first (rather than the last) family member to enter the therapy room. He greeted the therapist with a cheerful "hello," and even brought a couple of his computer toys to show to the therapist. Again, after a few minutes of social conversation, the therapist began to explore the outcome of the directive given at the end of the last session. The family had been quite diligent in carrying out the homework, and everyone reported no difficulty in completing their part of the assignment. The family was, in fact, quite pleased with the outcome. They had made the task into somewhat of a game, and often found that in the middle of the production it would suddenly seem absurd, and they would break into laughter. This naturally eased the tension of the moment. David, in particular, had enjoyed his part. He was particularly pleased when, according to instructions, he could become disruptive and noncompliant with impunity. Michael and Maria, for their part, initially found it difficult not to react negatively to David's behavior, but reported that it got easier by about the third time. They also reported that David never went too far in his acting up. Elise, too, felt quite proud of how she had carried out her instructions. Maria admitted that she had been unaware of just how concerned her daughter had been about her and how much Elise had tried to comfort her.

Maria felt somewhat embarrassed on realizing how often during the week she had felt frustrated and annoyed with Michael. One clear outcome of the directive was that she could no longer displace her feelings of frustration and disappointment onto David. Because David's behavior had been reframed as an attempt to ease the tension between Michael and Maria, whenever he had acted up during the week, she had tried to perceive his behavior in that light (and on an occasion when she did not, David was quick to remind her). Consequently, Maria's old pattern of reacting to marital tension was blocked. In a sense, by implementing this directive the family was "forced" to look at the problem differently. David's good mood was attributed to a week of feeling helpful to his parents and not feeling singled out and rejected. Interestingly, there were no incidents of soiling during the week. It is likely that because of the directive, David did not have to resort to such extreme measures. Moreover, despite Maria's stated feelings of embarrassment, it was Michael who appeared to have been most affected by this assignment. He was initially detached and uncommunicative. After several unsuccessful attempts by the therapist to obtain Michael's account of how the assignment went, she decided that she would have to be more creative in drawing him out. On the basis of the information provided by the rest of the family, the therapist had a relatively good idea of what the week had been like for Michael, and she was able to use this information in approaching him.

> *Therapist:* I feel a little badly, Michael, for not warning you last week that your job in this assignment was likely going to be the most difficult and emotionally draining. In fact, I thought about it quite a bit after you left, but in the end decided that you had pretty broad shoulders, and would be able to weather the

situation relatively well. I hope I wasn't wrong. (By communicating this statement the therapist is conveying to Michael her understanding of how he must be feeling and, in addition, is appealing to his strength to be able to deal with a difficult situation.)

Michael: (looking somewhat relieved) Well, it is reassuring that at least you understand what a difficult time I had. I felt overwhelmed and bombarded every time I came home. To top it off, we are under deadline pressures at work, and I've just wanted to come home and unwind. I simply haven't had as much energy as I usually have to be helpful to Maria. It felt like every time I came home I was being assaulted. To be honest, by the end of the week I had to force myself to come home. (This was actually an unusual and revealing statement for Michael to make, as it intimated at his feelings of vulnerability.)

Maria responded to Michael's disclosure by becoming teary and reporting that she had always felt that he resented her expressing her feelings, although he had always denied this. This exchange between Maria and Michael began to expose some of the underlying marital conflict that the therapist had hypothesized was primarily responsible for maintaining Maria's depression. The therapist realized, however, that she was still on tenuous ground because of the couple's initial reluctance to acknowledge any marital disharmony. The therapist determined that the next session should be a "couple" session, but was searching for a way to present this decision in a nonthreatening way.

Therapist: I think I have a pretty good idea now from all of you what last week's experiment was like. Now that you have completed the role play and and we have had time to review all the details, I would like to know from you, Michael and Maria, whether the pattern you performed last week was familiar? Do you think that the way we talked about it last session and the way you role-played it during the week have some truth to them?

Maria: The more I think about it, the more reasonable it seems, although I must admit that when you first mentioned it, it did seem pretty silly. But even if that is what goes on naturally at home, what are we supposed to do about it?

Michael: I would probably agree with Maria that this is what goes on at home, but it is not usually that bad. I don't know whether this was just an unusually difficult week or whether your suggesting that we act it out that way actually made it worse.

Therapist: Well, it seems that you are both saying that it seemed pretty realistic. What about you two (to the children)? Did it seem like somebody else's family or did it feel like what sometimes happens in your family?

David: (eagerly) It sure seemed real to me.

Elise: Me too. I think we did a good job at being ourselves (an astute observation for this little girl).

Therapist: (to Michael and Maria) What do you think would be the outcome of that scenario if David and Elise did not have a part in it?

Maria: I'm not sure I understand what you mean.

Therapist: Well, let's say that we had an act in which David and Elise did not have any lines, David couldn't distract you and Michael, and Elise couldn't comfort you. What would be the outcome of an argument or heated discussion between you and Michael?

Maria: I honestly don't know. I guess it would depend a lot on my mood, Michael's mood, and what the argument was about. Besides (somewhat defensively), we don't fight that often anyway. It just seems to come in fits and starts. Wouldn't you agree, Michael?

Michael: Yes, we don't get into arguments very much at all, except maybe for this past week. And I agree with Maria that the outcome of our discussions would depend on the particular circumstances.

Therapist: (again, drawing on the resources of the couple) Well, you all did so well carrying out your assignment last week that rather than waiting a bit, I think we can move right into the next stage. First, I would agree with you, Michael and Maria. I, too, have no idea what the outcome would be if we asked Elise and David to stay "off the stage," so to speak, and be in the audience for the next week or two. From what I know of you two already, I feel confident that you do not need your children's help to resolve your differences of opinion. You are both strong, resourceful people with considerable common sense and good problem-solving abilities. Perhaps the children's attempts to be helpful result in sidetracking you both, such that you aren't able to get back to the real issue. If you weren't both so sensitive to the needs of your children, this may not happen.

The therapist has taken her earlier interpretation one step further and, in addition, has supported the parents in their ability to work out issues between them without the help of their children. The therapist should constantly be looking for ways to capitalize on the family's strengths in promoting positive change.

Therapist: The homework task that I'm going to give you this week is much like last week's, but a little harder. Michael and Maria, I would like you to do the same thing you did last week, but this time, David and Elise, I want you to just watch or ignore what your parents are doing. You are *not* to try and help them. That means, David, that you must work very hard at not creating any distractions for your parents, no matter how tempted you feel to create a disturbance of some sort. I know this is going to be hard for you because we have already seen how very good you are at helping out your parents. Do you think you can do this just for 2 weeks?

David: (bravely accepting the challenge) Yes, I'm positive I can do it.

Therapist: Your job, Elise, is going to be just about as hard as David's. Every time you see your mom looking unhappy or depressed, you are going to have to trust your mom that she knows how to cheer herself up. So what that means, Elise, is that for this next couple of weeks, you are going to have to be on "vacation" from your usual job of cheering up your mom.

Therapist: (to Maria) Do you think that would be OK with you? We wouldn't want Elise to worry about your feeling that she was ignoring you or that she didn't care about you anymore. She would just be doing this as part of our assignment.

Maria: Yes, that would be OK with me, and you wouldn't have to worry about me, honey (gives Elise a hug).

Elise: Well, if mommy says it's OK, then I know I can do it, but I think my job is going to be harder than David's.

Therapist: I think this will be an interesting week for your family, and I am anxious to find out what happens. (to Maria and Michael) Also, in keeping with the idea that David and Elise are on vacation for a couple of weeks, it might be very helpful if just the two of you came in next week, and the week after that, I'll either see both of you or just Maria alone. After that you can all come back, and Elise and David can tell me at that time how they did. Is that alright with everyone? (Everyone agrees to this plan.)

The therapist has worked up to this stage with considerable elegance. No one in the family appeared threatened by this shift in focus. Once more, the family's lack of resistance reassures the therapist that she and the family are beginning to share a common conceptualization of Maria's depression in the context of the family situation.

Session 4: The Couple *(Maria's BDI = 32)*

During this first couple session, the therapist's primary goal is to discern how Michael and Maria function as a couple and how their communication style and pattern of interactions are related to Maria's depression. If the children were successful in their task of remaining outside the boundary of their parent's relationship, a more informative picture should emerge. Indeed, Maria and Michael reported that the children had generally done a good job of following the therapist's directive. Both admitted that it had been noticeably difficult for Elise to refrain from her typical efforts of comforting her mother. Maria reported that it was also difficult for her not to receive this attention and support. Elise's approach to this stressful situation was to seek reassurance from her mother that in fact she was not supposed to try and comfort her. Maria's confirmation that this was so then allowed Elise to hold back. The therapist conjectured that without her mother's assurance, Elise would not have been successful at holding back. In one sense, David was better able to fulfill his responsibilities in the directive, in that he did not exhibit any major noncompliant episodes during the entire week. He did, however, have one soiling incident. The therapist wondered if this was his own internal reaction to a stressful week in which previous options (e.g., acting out) had been closed to him.

The therapist proceeded to obtain a detailed account of the week's events from Michael and Maria. Both readily agreed that this was one of the toughest weeks they had experienced in a long time. Ironically, this was good news for the therapist. It was indicative of progress in therapy, in that with opportunities for detouring or sidetracking limited, Michael and Maria were getting closer to the heart of their problem. Michael's perceptions of his interactions with Maria followed the theme alluded to in the last session — nothing he did this week pleased Maria. When he cleaned out the garage (which she had been asking him to do for weeks), Maria was annoyed because it was such a beautiful day that she would have preferred for the family to go for a ride in the country. In addition, Michael's attempts, following an argument between Maria and her mother, to offer Maria suggestions as to how to deal with her mother were met with accusations of interfering in that relationship. Finally, Michael felt that his attempts to give Maria some space one evening were interpreted by her as rejection and a reluctance to be close with her. Despite Michael's protestations that he had only concern for his wife and would do whatever was necessary to help her out of her depression, his feelings of frustration and hostility were apparent. Therefore, Maria's feelings of negativity from Michael clearly had some basis in reality.

Maria's account of the interactions between her and Michael was similarly negative, but with a different slant. Maria began by explaining that, right from the beginning, her week had started off badly. During a conversation with her mother in which she was describing the goals she had set for herself in therapy, Maria felt criticized and degraded, primarily because her mother disapproved of her attempts to add more pleasurable activities to her life (a goal described in the previous chapter). Maria was accused by her mother of being selfish and inconsiderate and of failing to place her husband and children's needs above her own. Maria felt guilty and torn, half accepting her mother's value system and half rejecting it as archaic and unreasonable. At times, Maria felt that she could deal effectively with her mother's expectations and value system, but at other times she just could not shake off the weight of her mother's disapproval. Because of Maria's feelings of rejection from her mother, she turned to Michael for reassurance and support, but felt that he reacted with impatience and withdrawal. Maria agreed that Michael did offer advice, but that is not what she wanted. Moreover, she felt that Michael had avoided her all week. For example, she stated that he cleaned the garage only so he would not have to spend time with her. Similarly, one evening when Maria was feeling in particular need of nurturance and intimacy, Michael retreated to his study. An even more striking event, which underscores the negativity in their relationship, occurred the evening Michael did respond to her need for closeness. He agreed to watch a movie with her, and sat the whole time with his arm around her and at times caressing her. Although Maria did not say anything to Michael at the time, she felt that this was a sympathy gesture, rather than a genuine expression of his feelings for her.

The material provided by Michael and Maria highlights the negative path this couple has carved out for themselves. Neither partner knows how to extricate him- or herself from this interactional pattern that, consistent with the description outlined in Chapter 2, is implicated in the maintenance of Maria's depression. If we consider the sequence of events involved in the development and maintenance of Maria's depression, the following steps are encompassed. (However, this is only one set of interactions, and there may be others that begin with a different stressful event.) Maria has an overly-involved relationship with her mother, as evidenced by her sensitivity to her mother's reactions and expectations of her. Following a conversation with her mother, Maria experiences disapproval and rejection. To compensate for this unsatisfying relationship and to ameliorate these feelings, Maria turns to Michael for reassurance that she is indeed a valuable and worthy person. Instead of this response, however, Maria perceives unemotional advice and withdrawal. Her feelings of rejection and inadequacy are now confirmed by another source. Despite her failure to receive the support she desires, Maria continues to seek it in similar ways, likely because she was able to obtain support in these ways at an earlier period in this repeating pattern.

Michael's attempted solutions to Maria's depression follow a similar pattern and can also be separated into discrete steps. First, Michael tries to give Maria advice and alternatives to the way she is feeling. As she continues to reject these attempts, he grows increasingly frustrated and intolerant of her depressive symptoms. The next step for him is to try and do what he feels Maria wants of him. As described, however, these behaviors are interpreted by Maria as Michael only going through the motions. The third dimension to Michael's attempted solution is to keep out of Maria's range to avoid triggering an argument. Michael's attempts to deal with Maria's depression are best viewed as different facets to an overall solution, rather than as steps that occur in any particular sequence. It is important to mention again that this pattern persists, despite failure or even worsening of the problem, because it is viewed by Michael as the only logical or reasonable reaction to the situation.

The therapist's responsibility is to reframe the problem and the solution in a way that provides an opportunity to produce, first, a different conceptualization of the problem, and then a different set of responses.

Therapist: I can understand your concern about your wife, Michael. It is obvious to me already how much you care about her. Whenever Maria gets depressed, you worry very much about her, and you try all the different ways you can think of to help her get better. I can sense your growing frustration with all your failed attempts to make things better for her. As you have described different situations to me, I see how you often walk on egg shells around your wife — almost as if you are afraid that she is fine china and might shatter. In many ways, and although Maria might not recognize it, you have been trying too hard. Like anyone who tries too hard to improve a situation, you end up seeming less genuine, less sincere, and not yourself. Maria, you sense that difference in Michael. He does not seem sincere in his efforts to help you, and understandably, this makes you feel even worse. Now on top of your already feeling depressed, it seems as if Michael is becoming disappointed in you. It also feels like he doesn't understand you and probably even at times as if he doesn't care. Despite these unpleasant thoughts, you still try and protect him. You keep many of your feelings to yourself because you don't want to burden Michael. What really strikes me as ironic about your situation is that the main reason I think you have become so entrenched in this rut is that you have both been trying too hard to protect the other person, and once the cycle is activated, both of you somehow lose sight of each other's strengths.

Maria: (with a big sigh of relief) Somehow that makes this whole situation seem more reasonable. I feel like a big weight has been lifted off my shoulders, although I'm not exactly sure why.

Michael: I'm glad you were able to see how hard I have been trying, and I think Maria is beginning to recognize it as well. I don't know how things got this bad. I never realized before just how frustrated and upset I've been feeling.

The therapist has redefined Maria's depression and Michael's reaction to it such that neither person has to feel guilty. Both spouses have been acknowledged for their efforts and their concern. Moreover, Michael and Maria have been given an interpretation that captures their feelings about the problem, that makes sense to them, and yet that significantly alters their previous definition of the problem, thereby paving the way for a different set of responses. The final task in this conjoint session is for the therapist to describe an alternative set of behaviors designed to ply this couple out of their dysfunctional pattern of relating to each other.

> *Therapist:* Although this may sound a little odd to you, I think the only way out of this rut is for both of you to stop being so protective of each other and to recognize just how strong the other person is. For you, Maria, that means to stop trying so hard to feel cheerful all of the time. Share more of your feelings with Michael, whether they are hopeful and cheerful or gloomy and pessimistic. Michael, you'll need to stop feeling so responsible for how Maria feels. If she has had a tough day and is feeling discouraged, just let her tell you about it. It's not your job to try and make her feel better. In a way, you both need to prove to the other just how strong you are. I suggest that over the next week or so, even if you feel close, test each other out by bringing up a difficult topic, just to prove to yourselves that neither of you is going to fall apart and that you can in fact deal with the issue. Do you think that you can manage that task?
>
> *Maria:* I think so.
>
> *Michael:* It sounds pretty interesting, we'll give it a try.
>
> *Therapist:* Now, before we stop for today, Maria, I would like you to come in for the next session by yourself. It sounds like there might be some important issues between you and your mother that sometimes make you feel pretty rotten. Maybe we could spend some time looking at that relationship. Is that OK with both of you? Good. Then the session after that, I will want the whole family to come back again. At that time we can review the progress we are making so far. Also, maybe during the week you can look over our contract and see if you are making the changes we specified there.

This conjoint session was quite effective in removing the problem (Maria's depression) from being solely her problem to one that became unmanageable as a result of both of their attempts to deal with it. Both Michael and Maria left the session feeling less defensive and hostile than they had for some time.

Session 5: The Individual *(Maria's BDI = 35)*

As outlined in Chapter 3, the major focus of this first individual session with Maria is to help her both recognize the effects of her depression on her family and understand how she may be attending more strongly to the negative aspects of her environment and situation. Moreover, the therapist must teach Maria effective techniques and strategies for attenuating this negative "tunnel vision." All of this must be accomplished, however, within a systems conceptualization of depression. Therefore, Maria must not be made to feel a burden or problem for her family, who are merely victims of her depression. These relatively traditional individual therapeutic techniques should therefore conform to the general principles that are central to our interpersonal systems orientation.

Because this treatment approach to depression encompasses interventions at several levels (e.g., individual, couple, and family), the therapist must become skillful at balancing his or her relationship with all members involved in the treatment process. The therapist must take steps to ensure that she or he does not unknowingly support hidden loyalties or coalitions or become viewed as an ally to one or two of the family members. Yet, at the same time she must develop an open and trusting relationship with all family members. The technique of joining is a highly useful one in this approach, as it can be utilized at all levels of involvement. Indeed, the therapist's first goal in the individual session with Maria is to promote the therapeutic relationship through a joining maneuver.

Therapist: Come in, Maria. You look nice and "summery" today; those colors look really striking on you.

Maria: Oh, thank you. I read a book on colors, and decided I was a "spring."

Therapist: Well, I'm impressed at your talents, Maria. Have any of your friends asked you to figure out their colors?

Maria: As a matter of fact, several have. I was scared to do it at first, in case I made a mistake, but they pressured me into it. It seemed to turn out OK. I do a lot of sewing, and I buy most of my material from one store in town, so they know me pretty well there. So when I asked for a whole bunch of swatches of different colors of materials, they said that would be fine. I made up little booklets for my friends, just like the professionals do.

Therapist: It sounds to me like you did just as good a job as the experts do. Every time you have been here you always look very attractively dressed.

Maria: Yes, I love clothes.

Through her appreciation of Maria's style of dress, the therapist is establishing a common area of interest, a very powerful method of joining with an individual. Maria was obviously pleased with the therapist's appreciation of her sewing and color coordination talents. Once the therapist felt that she and Maria were communicating well, she proceeded to review with Maria how her week had been.

Therapist: I asked you and Michael last week to try to not be so protective of each other and to try to recognize how strong the other is. Although I would like to review this in detail when Michael is here, maybe you can just give me a brief description of how you felt things were between you and Michael this week.

Maria: Well, the first couple of days were actually pretty good. Michael didn't work late, so we were able to eat dinner together and spend the evening together, too. Even the kids were pretty good. Then everything just started to go downhill. Michael seemed upset with me, for no reason that I could figure out. He hardly talked to me the rest of the week. He started working late again, which is what he does when he doesn't want to face me. David and Elise were at it again, too. I'm telling you, by last night I was ready to pack my bags and leave home. I just asked myself what was the point of it all; no one appreciates me anyway.

Therapist: So, it seems that there was an improvement for a few days, and then things just seemed to start to slip. When things were going well, you and Michael were closer and got along much better.

Maria: That's right. For a while, I started to get my hopes up, and then I felt crushed again.

Therapist: Why do you think things were better at the beginning of the week? What were you and Michael doing differently?

Maria: Well, we thought that what you said last week made a lot of sense, and it just seemed to break the ice between us. We talked about things that we haven't talked about for a long time. It was really nice.

Therapist: I guess I'm a bit surprised that you two started to make some changes so quickly. It usually takes longer than that to start to see improvement. So I guess in some ways I am actually more surprised to hear that the week started off well than I am to hear that it ended badly. I wonder what happened to make the situation start to backslide?

Maria: I honestly don't know. I had a feeling that it would, though. I knew it was too good to be true.

Therapist: You know, Maria, a lot of people who get depressed seem to have very similar experiences. For some reason, they become extremely sensitive to every bit of unpleasantness around them. It's almost like they put on glasses that filter out all the pleasant and rewarding situations and leave only the negative and discouraging ones. Even though positive situations are still occurring, they seem to be missed. If the depression continues, that person becomes even "better" at filtering out more and more positive aspects of their environment and at concentrating harder on the negative aspects. After a while, it feels like everything is just plain wrong. We're not exactly sure why this happens, but it does happen for most depressed people. Does that make sense to you?

Maria: Yes, I guess so, except that I'm almost positive, at least in my case, that my family *is* doing more things that are annoying.

Therapist: That's a good point, Maria, and I believe that you are probably right. What I've seen with many families is likely happening with yours as well. When your family sees that you are beginning to get depressed, they try to help. They try to do whatever they think will cheer you up. Unfortunately, however, most people are not very good at meeting the depressed person's needs. This is true of your family; their solutions didn't make things better for you. What seems to happen next is that for each person, part of them continues to try to be helpful, but another part of them is frustrated and angry because they feel like a failure in not being able to cheer up the depressed person. Being depressed, you tend to notice more those behaviors that reflect the frustration, and *not* those that are supportive and caring. The same is true for yourself. You notice all your thoughts, feelings, and circumstances that are negative ones or failures, but not positive ones or successes. If you started to listen to the kinds of things you were saying to yourself, you would be amazed. You might even discover that you sounded like a critical mother. In fact, one thing I will ask you to do for homework this week is to start becoming more aware of your thoughts and perceptions. This is going to seem like a lot of work, but I think you will find it helpful. I would like you to record some information in a diary each time during the next week when you find yourself getting upset in a situation. For example, if Michael comes home late for dinner and you get annoyed, write down the circumstances of the incident, what you are feeling, and as much as possible what you are thinking, especially with regard to how you are interpreting the event, such as "he's late because he's avoiding me." I'll write this out for you before you leave today.

Maria: I'll admit that I do tend to feel more negatively when I'm depressed, but I certainly agree with you that I know at times my family is acting pretty rejecting towards me.

Therapist: That's true, Maria. During the times you have been to see me, I have seen your family appear both rejecting, such as when Michael stops talking, *and* supportive, such as when Elise gives you a hug whenever you become upset. The reality is that they do both, but you only notice the negative and then your feelings become lopsided — there is nothing to offset or balance those negative feelings. That is one thing we need to help you to do: to get a more balanced perspective of your environment and relationships.

Maria: I guess if I really think about it, everything isn't negative, but you're right — I sure do have a hard time seeing the good things. I just feel weighed down by so many situations that feel so overwhelming.

Therapist: The way I sometimes think about it, Maria, is something like one of those slinky toys on the top of a staircase. One end falls down and the weight of the drop pulls the other end down, which in turn pulls the first end down again, and so on. Someone in your family does something that upsets or annoys you, so you react, but your reaction makes them feel rejected, and their reaction subsequently hurts you, and so forth. Do you get the idea?

Maria: Yes, I guess I never thought of it that way before. I think I just saw it as one-sided. Sometimes it's not even Michael or one of the kids who upset me, but maybe I take it out on them.

Therapist: Can you think of an example of that, Maria?

Maria: Well, in particular, I'm thinking of my mother. Sometimes she makes me want to scream, but I never seem to be able to stand up to her. She is so pig-headed. Everything always has to be her own way. Maybe I take my feelings out on someone in my family.

The therapist and Maria continued to talk about Maria's relationship with her mother and some of the points of frustration and conflict in their relationship. The therapist made a point of emphasizing all the points just conveyed to Maria in the context of the relationship with her mother. In summary, the therapist discussed Maria's tendency to notice only the negative events and situations, while ignoring the positive ones. This was conveyed to Maria within a systems framework, with its concomitant emphasis on circular or reciprocal interactions. In this regard, Maria was also given some insight into how her depression is perceived by her family and the impact it has on them, and how their reactions, in turn, are perceived by and affect Maria. Their attempts to help Maria, although unsuccessful, were then described. The therapist went on to point out how she had witnessed in their therapy sessions both positive and negative behaviors from Maria's family. Finally, the therapist gave Maria a homework task designed to help her monitor her thoughts in order to become more aware of her negative cognitive set.

Maria was given written instructions for her homework task and was reminded that the next session was for the whole family.

Session 6: The Family *(Maria's BDI = 21)*

The first task of the therapist in this family session is to review the homework assigned during the previous family session. Specifically, the therapist had requested that Elise and David try their best to refrain from becoming involved either when their parents quarreled or when their mother became upset. The major goals of this directive were twofold. First, it was intended to prevent the marital conflict from being defused, sidetracked, and perhaps detoured through the children. Once these distractions are eliminated, it is then possible to get to the heart of the matter. Second, in the context of our discussion of the role of family boundaries, this directive was expected to make more explicit the boundary between Maria and Elise and weaken the wall between Michael and Maria. Thus, instead of Maria turning to her daughter for comfort and support, the objective is to promote her having these needs met through her marital relationship.

A second objective of this family session, as indicated in the previous couple session, is for the therapist to assess the progress of the family members, and to evaluate the need for further sessions with the entire family. If the children were successful with their homework assignment and were able to remain removed from their parent's conflict and their mother's depression, it is likely that future therapy sessions will involve only the marital couple and Maria alone. If, however, the children were unable to perform that task (which would be symptomatic of severe overinvolvement on their part), further family sessions would be advisable.

In conducting this assessment, the therapist will utilize both formal and informal evaluation procedures. Specifically, the therapist will request that each family member comment on how they are feeling about the family situation in general as well as on Maria's depression. In addition, comments concerning Michael's involvement with the family will be solicited, as will information regarding David's encopresis. Some of the formal assessment devices completed earlier will be readministered. These measures will include the BDI for Maria, the CDI for David, and the Dyadic Adjustment Scale for Maria and Michael.

The Richardson family arrived for their family session in relatively good spirits. The children proudly reported that they had been "almost perfect" in completing their homework assignment. David found his part to be somewhat easier than did Elise. Moreover, he provided numerous incidents wherein he could have created problems, but instead was able to remain uninvolved. His job was made easier by the warm weather, which afforded numerous opportunities for him to be outside playing with his friends. Of significance too was the fact that during this time David was accident-free. This latter event strongly supports the validity of the therapeutic goal of extricating the children from the marital conflict and Maria's depression. Elise, however, admitted that it was often difficult for her not to comfort her mother when she saw her upset or sad. Elise was particularly concerned that if she did not comfort her mother, Maria would become even more distressed. Upon further questioning from the therapist as to how she was able to complete her assignment despite its difficulty, Elise acknowledged that both David and her mother were helpful in reminding her (i.e., giving her permission) not to intervene. Somewhat surprisingly, Elise volunteered that there were several occasions during the past couple of weeks on which her mother seemed quite cheerful, and this helped her to hold back during those other times when Maria clearly was not happy. It was obvious from Elise's reaction, however, that unless Maria's depression was significantly ameliorated or she received more support from Michael, Elise would not be able to continue her uninvolved stance.

Both Michael and Maria agreed that their children had been able to follow the therapist's instructions well. Moreover, they expressed surprise at the behavior of their children the past few weeks. David, in particular, had been cheerful most of the time and had been cooperative and helpful around the house. A phone call from his teacher revealed her pleasure at his improvements in school as well. The teacher reported that David was noticeably happier, getting along better with the other children, and more productive in his school work. In view of David's positive changes, the therapist decided to review the current level of family functioning with him.

Therapist: David, your parents sound very pleased at how well you've been doing the last while. I'm very impressed. How come you've been able to make all these improvements?

David: I don't know. I just felt like it, I guess. I feel happier, and no one has been bugging me at home.

Therapist: Do things at home seem different to you?

David: Well, if you ask me, I think everybody in our house has been feeling better. Mommy doesn't seem to be so crabby . . . she even played some computer games with me. My dad and I went fishing together, and we went for bike rides. We had a lot of fun together.

Therapist: (to Michael) It sounds like you have been doing better at finding more time to spend with David. Have you been able to do this with the rest of the family as well?

Michael: I think I have. Maria and I have gone out to dinner twice, and we even made it to a movie, which we haven't done in years. We almost arranged a weekend away, but at the last minute our baby-sitter cancelled. And since the weather has been so nice, the whole family has been able to go for rides in the country. Everyone seems to enjoy that.

Maria: Michael really has been around more, especially the last week. I can't tell you how pleasant it has been. I can hardly believe it, but we have actually been having some fun together.

Therapist: You certainly seem happier, Maria. Do you think you have been feeling less depressed?

Maria: Kind of up and down, but overall I would say I have been less depressed. (Her BDI score of 21 reflects this relatively decreased level of depression.) I just wonder if things are going to stay this way.

Therapist: How about the rest of you, do you think Maria is happier?

David: Yes, definitely.

Michael: We have had a couple of really rough times, but especially the past week, she has been really cheerful.
Elise: Sometimes, but I'm still worried about her.

The foregoing information suggests not only that Maria has begun to feel less depressed, but also that her whole family has begun to experience less stress. David, in particular, feels that a burden has been lifted from his shoulders. In this session all problem areas and treatment objectives have been reviewed, and the family discussion reveals some positive changes. Michael, for example, is finding more time to spend with his family, and his somewhat increased DAS score of 100 reflects this improvement. Because Maria's DAS of 87, although also somewhat increased, is still relatively low, the therapist decides to continue to see Michael and Maria together. David has had considerably fewer encopretic incidents than previously, and appears happier and less withdrawn. (This is also indicated in his lower CDI score of 7.) The therapist decides that further therapy sessions with the entire family are no longer necessary.

As outlined in Chapter 3, one technique that can be used once a family or individual demonstrates changes is to caution them to go slowly and to not change too quickly (cf. Coyne & Segal, 1982). This warning can actually help the family to feel more confident in their efforts to continue to grow and can help to maintain the changes. In addition, it can help prevent discouragement in the event of "backsliding." The therapist determined that this technique of restraining was appropriate at this point in therapy.

Therapist: I must tell you all that I am very impressed at how quickly you have made improvements. From what you have said today, I can see that everyone is feeling happier. You have talked more with each other today, and there has been more laughter. David seems energetic and in good spirits, Maria and Michael are sitting together on the couch, and Elise doesn't seem as worried as she did in previous sessions. That all sounds *very* positive, and I think my only concern is one that is perhaps shared by both Maria and Elise, that is, "Can this really last?" In some ways, change is always a little scary, even if it is a positive change. It might be best if you did not try to change too quickly. If you find the situation at home getting too good too fast, try to slow it down a bit. I know you may find that a little strange, but it is important not to change *too* quickly.
Maria: I don't think we will improve faster than we can handle it. I'm more concerned that things will continue to go up and down; that's what I have trouble coping with.
Therapist: In a way, Maria, that is what I am afraid will happen if you try to improve the situation too quickly. Let's just take it one step at a time, OK?
Michael: Well, we'll try, but if we are all getting along and feeling good, I don't think we're going to stop and say, "alright now that's enough for today."
Therapist: I understand what you're saying, Michael. I just want to encourage you to move ahead slowly.

The family reluctantly agrees to this strategy, but also indicates to the therapist that they are determined to make changes despite her warning to move slowly. The therapist ends the session by indicating that the next session will be an individual session for Maria, followed by two sessions for both Michael and Maria. She asks the children if they mind if she only sees their parents for the next 3 weeks. They tell her that they do not mind.

The therapist ends this family session by spending a few minutes alone with Maria. To prime Maria for a major objective of the next session (to help Maria become more aware of positive aspects of her environment), she was given the Pleasant Events Schedule (described in Chapter 3) to identify more specifically the activities she would typically find pleasurable. She was asked to complete it the day before she was scheduled to attend her next individual session. The rationale for the delay in completing this inventory was based on the therapist's belief that before helping Maria focus on the more positive aspects of her life, Maria would first have to recognize her tendency to selectively attend to negative situations, and she was already keeping a diary of these events. Once cognizant of this negative bias, Maria would be more open to broadening her perspective to include pleasant events as well.

Session 7: The Individual *(Maria's BDI = 17)*

This session with Maria continued with the same themes explored in her previous individual session. She had diligently completed her homework assignment and had copious notes describing how she had felt during the past 2 weeks. She felt that her diary included virtually all of the incidents in which she had been upset or depressed during that period. She was able to describe how she felt about each incident as well as her interpretation of each event. In reviewing these notes, Maria was surprised by how few incidents involved her children; she had thought previously that David was a primary source of her frustrations and subsequent feelings of depression. Maria had also noted (on her own) that she had interpreted *all* of the negative situations or interactions as rejections or criticisms of her. Seeing it written down and repeated so frequently struck her as unrealistic. Maria told the therapist that when she viewed each incident in isolation, the interpretations seemed reasonable, but when she collected them in her diary and reread her entries, the incidents had an entirely different impact. The therapist noted that clearly fewer incidents were recorded in the second week than the first and questioned Maria regarding this discrepancy. Maria explained that she had felt much happier during the second week, in part because she was doing more of the activities that she found pleasurable (she had also recorded each of these events) and in part because she felt that the recording task itself was somehow making her view situations in a slightly different way. Although Maria could not articulate this perception well, she was obviously affected by the recording process, which essentially forces the individual to stand back and view situations more objectively.

Maria and the therapist also explored changes in Maria's reactions to situations and people. Because Maria had been so thorough in her homework, she had become noticeably more aware of how negative she was in many situations. Indeed, even before she and the therapist discussed in detail the contents of her diary, Maria had become cognizant of how readily she had assumed the worst in most cases. Maria was clearly ready to be assigned the second stage of her individual homework procedure (outlined in Chapter 3). Specifically, Maria was asked to continue this daily recording, but in addition was required to record the occurrence of positive events and the positive behaviors of others. Thus, for the next 2 weeks, Maria was to record both negative and positive situations in the same way she had previously been recording only negative events. Furthermore, to facilitate Maria's attention to positive occurrences, her responses to the Pleasant Events Schedule were reviewed. As with most depressed people, Maria had endorsed a number of activities, indicating that she found these to be pleasurable when she was not feeling depressed.

The second part of Maria's homework involved encouraging her to engage in more of the enjoyable activities she had identified. Thus, in addition to recording negative and positive events, Maria was asked to develop a daily schedule for herself in the form of an itinerary, in which she included a number of these events. Maria and the therapist agreed on which activities Maria would attempt and together drew up a reasonable schedule for the next week. A major consideration in constructing this schedule was to arrive at activities that were only slightly more than those Maria was currently involved in and not significantly more so that Maria might feel overwhelmed and experience failure if she was not able to complete them. The ultimate goal of this strategy is to gradually increase the number of activities until they reach a satisfactory level for Maria. The guidelines outlined in Chapter 3 for setting up this schedule were also followed.

The final area pursued in this session was Maria's interactions with her mother during the past 2 weeks. Maria was strongly affected by expectations and demands from her mother. The therapist offered Maria an observation concerning her vulnerability to these pressures from her mother. The following dialogue conveys the therapist's interpretations regarding this relationship.

> *Therapist:* I've been thinking a good deal, Maria, about your relationship with your mother, and something puzzles me. I've been wondering why sometimes you seem to be so affected by her, and at other times you seem so strong and able to withstand pressure from her.
>
> *Maria:* I know that happens, but when I'm depressed everything just upsets me more, not just my mother.
>
> *Therapist:* I understand that, but somehow it seems to be more than that. It seems that when your relationship with Michael is problematic, you turn more to your mother for companionship and support. I wonder if at these times you become more susceptible to her criticisms and demands. However, when you and Michael are getting along well, you don't need as much from your mother and consequently aren't as affected by her.
>
> *Maria:* That sounds reasonable, but I'm just not sure if that is what happens.
>
> *Therapist:* Well think about it, and maybe we can talk more about that next week when both you and Michael will be here.

The therapist ends the session by acknowledging that she has asked Maria to do a lot in her homework assignment and asks Maria if she feels it is too much. Maria assures the therapist that she can manage it. Indeed, Maria has given the therapist the impression that having concrete assignments to complete is helpful to her.

Sessions 8 and 9: The Couple
(Maria's BDI = 15, 10)

Because the therapist's earlier assessment highlighted the role of the marital relationship in Maria's depression, the outcome of the couple sessions is considered crucial to the success of therapy. As we already noted, the number of sessions and the goals of therapy are not set in stone. If events during these two sessions indicate the need for changes in the contract, the therapist will readily negotiate these with the couple. In general, the more resistant a couple is to change, the more sessions will be required. Moreover, when a couple does not specifically request marital counseling, the therapist must be more creative in the interventions. We noted earlier with the Richardsons a basic defensiveness to admitting marital problems, but also an openness to trying different approaches to their problems.

We mentioned earlier that the technique of joining can be employed at different stages of therapy. Because this is the second couple session, and because there have been several sessions in the interim, the therapist must ensure that Michael is not feeling isolated or alienated. Therefore, the therapist begins the session with Michael.

Therapist: You seem a little more relaxed lately, Michael. Has your work situation calmed down a little?

Michael: We went through a very tense time for a while because of a major contract we landed, but now things are starting to fall into place. That's how things seem to happen at work — we seem to go through cycles of peaks and valleys.

Therapist: It sounds like you have learned how to adapt to those cycles. It seems that would be pretty stressful, especially with all those fluctuations. Do you usually know ahead of time what's coming up?

Michael: Well, I am getting better at handling the work load, and it is easier when we can predict what is coming up. But that only happens about half the time.

Therapist: When Michael is under these pressures at work, Maria, do they seem to affect the home situation as well?

Maria: I would say so, especially because we are such a close family. When Michael is stressed, it affects the whole family, just like when I am depressed, everyone feels the impact.

The therapist has joined with Michael by sharing his interest in his work. While doing this, she used body gestures and language that were similar to Michael's. This is another highly effective way of joining with an individual or couple. Moreover, by gradually bringing the conversation around to include

Maria, she has brought the focus onto the couple in a nonthreatening way. Maria's unsolicited comment about the similarities between Michael's mood and her depression both having an impact on the family highlighted a parallel between Maria and Michael and, in addition, emphasized the theme of closeness. This latter comment is viewed by the therapist as a positive change, as it suggests that Maria is feeling more like she and Michael are a couple.

The next step in this session is to review the homework assignment Michael and Maria were requested to complete at the previous couple session. Specifically, they were asked to be less protective of each other and to try and recognize the strengths in each other. Michael explained that he had some difficulty with this task, because he felt that part of his role as husband and father was to protect his family. He did, however, admit that Maria was a highly competent mother and that he trusted her judgment in virtually all family matters. He did worry about her when she became depressed, and he felt that at these times he was more likely to handle her with kid gloves. Despite these concerns, Michael did mention several incidents in which he was direct with Maria and was surprised by her reaction. For example, one evening he came home after a particularly rough day at work. Typically, Michael would have gritted his teeth and tried to appear as calm and cool as possible not to upset Maria. On this evening, however, he immediately revealed to Maria how difficult his day had been, detailing some events of the day and describing how he was feeling burned out and needed a drink and a chance to unwind. Rather than giving him the criticism he was anticipating, Maria responded with support and nurturing. Both spouses felt extremely positive about this interaction. Similarly, Maria had been more open with Michael about her bad days, although not as frequently as she would have liked, and at those times gave only short accounts. Michael agreed with this assessment. After several other examples were discussed, both Maria and Michael were left with the feeling that the other person had more strengths than they originally thought.

This dialogue led naturally into a discussion of how this couple's relationship had generally been over the past few weeks. Michael was quick to respond that he felt that he and Maria had become closer, that he looked forward to coming home at night, and that Maria was much more enjoyable to be around. He added that the children were more pleasant and cooperative and seemed to be fighting less. Maria also painted a positive picture, but gave greater credit for the change to Michael's increased availability. She was happier because Michael was home more often and was spending more time with her. Maria believed that the children were better behaved and easier to get along with because their father was becoming more involved with them. Despite this rather glowing picture, there was still a noticeable undercurrent of tension. The therapist decided to pursue the issue of Maria's depression by having both Michael and Maria comment on the current status of her depression and any changes each felt had occurred.

Therapist: Because one of the main goals of our therapy is to help reduce Maria's depression, I think that now would be a good time to review how both of you are currently feeling about that problem and to discuss any changes that might have developed since our first meeting. Maybe you could go first Michael.

Michael: As I said earlier, I think Maria has been much happier lately. She laughs more, she's not as moody and grumpy, and she doesn't complain all the time. I guess in general she's not so sensitive and emotional. We get along so much better when she's like this. When Maria is not depressed, she's a lot of fun. It sure would be nice if she could always be like this.

Maria: If you were always around as much as you are now and paid this much attention to the kids and me, I might not get depressed as often. I don't think you realize how much our family is affected by your mood. You think you're always calm and easy going, but sometimes when work is tough, you come home and hardly speak to any of us. You never tell me what's going on — you just shut me out. Even when I ask you if something is bothering you, you always say, "no, everything is fine."

Michael: I don't think you're really being fair. I know you sometimes have tough days at home too, and I don't want to come home and burden you with my troubles. And I don't shut you out. I just sometimes need some peace and quiet. Besides, I think that when you get into one of your moods, you're not much fun to be around.

Because Michael and Maria are expressing their feelings in a more direct and honest way than they typically do, the therapist takes advantage of this naturally occurring enactment to reinforce their openness in the interaction.

Therapist: Excuse me for interrupting, but I must point out how impressed I am by this conversation you're having. This is a perfect example of being more open with each other and not being overly protective of each other. You are both doing a splendid job of telling the other person what you are feeling, and neither of you seems to be worrying that the other person is not strong enough to hear it. You are both obviously more aware of each other's strengths; otherwise, I don't think you would risk being so honest. In fact, I am particularly struck by Michael's willingness to talk about his feelings, especially because we talked earlier about how hard that is for you to do, Michael.

Michael: (somewhat taken aback by the therapist's comment) Well, now that you mention it, I guess you're right . . . we are being more open with each other. Actually, that didn't feel too bad either. I think I'm usually afraid that if we are too honest with each other, we might say something that really hurts the other person, and that's the last thing I want to happen.

Maria: When you talk to me like that, I feel that we are equals, that we are sharing our feelings with each other. Believe it or not, it just makes me feel closer to you. It makes me think you really do care. Sometimes I just get so frustrated that I don't seem to be able to reach you, like we're miles apart.

Therapist: We talked earlier about one thing this family might need in order to feel close, to feel that you are all on the same team, and that is that perhaps the men in this family need to contribute more to expressing feelings. Remember we said that they didn't need to describe mushy or sentimental feelings; they just had to be a little more expressive about what they were feeling. I think this interchange captures exactly what we were talking about. In fact, Michael, if

you were able to set this kind of example for David, it might ease some of the
pressures he sometimes feels when he is upset and doesn't know what to do
about it. I can't emphasize enough how important I think this is for the continued well-being of your family.
Michael: I think I understand pretty clearly what you are saying, but do you really
think that David's and my expression of our feelings more is going to make such
a big difference to the happiness of our family?
Maria: I think it would make a tremendous difference.
Therapist: I think that you and Maria are both sensitive people, sensitive in the
sense that neither of you is immune to people's feelings or circumstances. Consequently, you both know when something is upsetting the other or any member of your family for that matter. If you don't deal with whatever those feelings
are, or if you more or less deny that something is wrong, then relationships in
the family will feel somehow "out of synch." If this pattern persists, tensions in
the family will mount, because inevitably one or more family members will feel
that things are not right, but yet not be able to do anything about it. I know that
asking you to be more expressive with your feelings is asking a lot, Michael, but
it would be a sacrifice that your whole family would benefit from tremendously.
I also think that you and Maria need to talk about this at greater length before
you decide if and how you can do that. (It was important that the therapist not
pressure Michael into agreeing to this request, but rather that he and Maria
come to an agreement on their own.)

These two couple sessions ended with a more detailed discussion of the
changes that both Maria and Michael felt had occurred since the beginning of
therapy. In addition, the therapist perused Maria's diary records. It was clear to
both the therapist and Maria that she was becoming more successful at recognizing and attending to the positive aspects of her relationships and environment. In addition, her daily schedules strongly supported her goal of
participating in more pleasurable activities. One session still remained in the
contract, and both the therapist and this couple felt that they were ready to terminate therapy. Consequently the final session was scheduled as a family session
to tie up loose ends and to highlight any residual issues on which this family
might continue to work on their own.

TERMINATION

Session 10: The Family *(Maria's BDI = 7)*

The modal result of the "final" session is termination, although sometimes
new goals are agreed upon and treatment is continued. In this session the therapist and family must review the original presenting problems and treatment
goals; if necessary, additional treatment objectives can be established. This is
typically a fairly relaxed session, with more "social" interactions than previous
sessions. All members involved in the therapy process should attend this session. Moreover, each person is asked to give his or her opinion on the progress
made towards each of the treatment goals, and the therapist observes the family
interactions to ensure that they are consistent with the family's verbal accounts

of the progress they have made. To substantiate these subjective impressions of change, all psychological inventories are readministered. Finally, general issues of separation related to termination are addressed. One effective way of dealing with anxieties about termination is to schedule a follow-up session in 3 to 6 months as well as to extend an invitation to the family to call if other issues arise. Simply having these two options available to the family often allays their concerns about terminating therapy.

Termination, as opposed to continuing treatment, is indicated under a number of circumstances. Termination is warranted, for example, if the individual or family has made the changes and gains agreed upon in the initial sessions. This point also highlights the need for goals and changes to be well-defined and measurable. Even if the original objectives have not been met, termination may be still be indicated if the family has changed sufficiently that they now possess the resources to deal effectively with the family member's depression. Finally, termination may be indicated if therapy seems ineffective in helping alleviate the depression. In this case the therapist must attempt to determine the reason for this lack of progress. Perhaps the original goals were too high, the couple or family was not ready to make further gains, or the therapist was unable to break through the family's resistance. Any of these possibilities necessitates a decision regarding the viability of the original goals and the couple or family's continued involvement in therapy.

The final session with the Richardson family revealed significant improvement. According to both self-report measures and the therapist's observations, Maria was no longer depressed. Her BDI score of 7 corroborated the SADS interview in indicating a significant decrease in depressive symptoms from the beginning of treatment. David's current CDI score of 4, too, fell within the normal, nondepressed range, a decrease from his initial elevated score of 17. In addition, the encopresis was also under much better control. Maria and Michael's Dyadic Adjustment Scale scores of 110 and 114, respectively, indicated that both showed improved marital satisfaction from their initial pretreatment levels. The family's responses on the Family Environment Scale, however, indicated several areas of change from their original scores (Figure 6.1). Specifically, both Michael and Maria showed considerable improvement in the "Relationship" dimensions subscales of cohesion, expressiveness, and conflict. In addition, they also obtained higher scores on the Active-Recreational Orientation subscale of the "Personal Growth" dimension, largely because of their increased participation in family recreational activities. The relative lack of change in the remaining subscales may reflect residual problems in the family or an insufficient time period for changes to permeate individuals' perceptions and behaviors within the family.

The therapist reviewed the family's progress towards the goals agreed upon in the initial assessment session. Maria's responses to the Pleasant Events Schedule indicated that she was engaging in an increased number of hobbies. Maria also

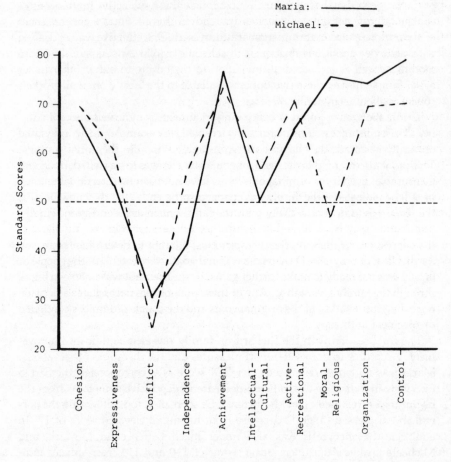

FIGURE 6.1. Termination Family Environment Scale Profile.

reported that the family was trying to spend at least 3 hours more per week together and that she was satisfied with their effort. She had become much closer with one of her friends, and they were indeed spending a half day together each week. David's frequency of encopresis had been reduced from several times a week to approximately once a month. Although this behavior still disturbed Maria, she felt that this frequency was tolerable. Finally, Michael reported that he was able to meet most of his goals and was working on meeting the others. For example, he was able to plan one family activity each week and to spend one evening each week alone with Maria. Although he was by no means expert by this point in sharing feelings with Maria about his work, Michael reported that he was slowly getting better at doing this and Maria corroborated this perception. Finally, the children and Maria all reported feeling happier with Michael's increased involvement in the family. David and Elise also noted that their parents were getting along better, and Elise volunteered that she did not have to worry about her mother as much. This family generally was functioning in a much more positive way than during their initial session. There was more laughter, spontaneity, and closeness. The children were more responsive to requests from their parents and interacted with each other with more warmth and friendliness. The initial strong undercurrent of tension was gone.

The therapist ended the session by summarizing the progress the family had made, and congratulating them on how well they had all done. She again cautioned the family that they had made some impressive gains very quickly and that they might experience a few setbacks in the months ahead. The therapist did, however, remind the family of their strengths and encouraged them to remember these strengths when they encountered rough times. She reminded Michael and Maria of how much better their relationship was when they were being honest and direct with each other. The therapist also encouraged David and Elise to be the children in the family and to let their parents take care of the family and do whatever worrying was necessary.

The final task faced by the therapist was to broach the subject of a follow-up session. As we stated in Chapter 4, we believe that a follow-up session is an integral part of this treatment. Only by remaining in contact with the patient after termination can the therapist evaluate the longer-term efficacy of intervention. As "motherhood and apple pie" as this procedure seems, however, the therapist must recognize that the couple or family can all too easily interpret this request for them to return in 6 months as the therapist's belief or expectation that they will require further treatment at that time. Consequently, the therapist should word this request very carefully. We have found that if the therapist presents this request to the couple or family as a standard policy followed with all patients, a procedure that allows the therapist to see how her or his patients are getting along, they are much less likely to perceive it as a treatment-oriented request.

Following this procedure, the therapist asked the Richardson family to return for a 6-month follow-up session, and they agreed to do so.

FOLLOW-UP

Six-Month Follow-up Session: The Family
(Maria's BDI = 6)

The primary objective of this follow-up session is to assess the stability of the gains made at the end of therapy. Again, all relevant psychological inventories are readministered, the original treatment goals and gains are reviewed, and the family's current level of functioning is discussed. If necessary, a limited number of treatment sessions with a specific set of goals can be negotiated.

Overall, the therapist was pleased with the Richardsons' continued improvements. Despite a few setbacks, they had managed to function well. During the

6-month interval, Maria had experienced a few "down" periods, but nothing that she labeled depressed. Her family concurred with this assessment. Moreover, Maria's current BDI score of 6 was essentially the same as her score of 7 at the end of treatment, and she also no longer met DSM-III criteria for a Major Depressive Episode. Michael and Maria were still struggling with their relationship, but both were basically happy with their progress. They were spending more time together as a couple, and these occasions were more enjoyable than they had been for some time. These verbal reports were substantiated by Maria and Michael's responses on the DAS (Maria, 111; Michael, 119). The Richardson family's FES profiles were similar to their termination profile, with improvement in the areas of help and support among family members and involvement in activities outside the home. With regard to the original goal of increased involvement by Michael in the family, continued improvements were also noted. Although Michael's work demands still resulted in fluctuations in his level of involvement, the other family members were better able to deal with this. David still had incidents of soiling, but these were less frequent. In sum, the Richardson family was content with its situation and felt that further appointments were unnecessary. They did, however, agree to contact the therapist if the need arose.

The dynamics of this family provide an excellent opportunity to illustrate many of the therapeutic strategies used in the interpersonal systems approach to treatment described in this guidebook. In addition, this case illustrates both the range and the variety of levels at which interventions can be focused (i.e., individual, couple, and family) to provide a comprehensive and flexible treatment plan. Despite the apparent independence of these levels and intervention procedures, they can nevertheless all be conceptualized and implemented within an interpersonal systems framework. Even when relatively traditional "individual therapy" strategies were employed, they were utilized in a manner consistent with this perspective. Therefore, this treatment approach can be implemented even in those cases in which it is impossible to involve the family "physically" in the therapy process. One of the case examples presented in the following chapter, in which a young college student is treated for depression, illustrates this point in greater detail.

Chapter 7
Case Examples

Through three detailed case examples, we will highlight many of the points made and issues dealt with in the previous chapters. Using these examples, we will guide the reader through the process of therapy from an interpersonal systems perspective, and will illustrate how this approach may be utilized with a diverse range of clients. Beginning with the initial referral, we will indicate how information obtained through appropriate assessment procedures can be used to lead to interpersonally-based case formulations and, consequently, to specific interpersonal systems intervention strategies.

CASE 1: A DEPRESSED CHILD

Ten-year-old Graham Jones was referred for treatment by his family physician. At the time of the referral, Graham had been depressed for about 4 months, experiencing loss of appetite, difficulty sleeping, restlessness, inability to concentrate at school, lack of interest in playing with other children, and moodiness (e.g., crying for no apparent reason and sudden outbursts of temper). In addition to concerns about his depression, Graham's parents were also worried about the amount of school he was missing.

We noted in Chapter 4 that when a child is referred as the identified patient, the therapist should also involve the parents in treatment. Consequently, Mr. and Mrs. Jones were asked to accompany Graham to the initial interview. Mrs. Jones immediately volunteered that neither she nor any member of her family had ever seen a therapist before and that they were all feeling uncomfortable about coming to the session. Mr. Jones avoided eye contact with the therapist and sat with his head down, fidgeting with his hat. Graham chose a chair near his mother, and he too sat slouched in his chair, staring at the floor. On the basis of this seating arrangement and the Jones' behavior, the therapist hypothesized that Mrs. Jones was emotionally closer to Graham than was Mr. Jones, who was also likely somewhat detached from his wife. The therapist plans to assess this hypothesis by having Mr. and Mrs. Jones later complete the Dyadic Adjustment

Scale (DAS). Immediately recognizing this family's difficulty in participating in the therapy process, the therapist engaged in a rather lengthy social stage, during which he actively joined with the family. Once the family's overall anxiety level had decreased and they were feeling reasonably relaxed with the therapist, they provided the following information.

Graham was an only child who, before the family's move to the city 6 months ago, had lived in a small rural community next door to his maternal grandmother. In addition to the grandmother, several other members of his mother's family lived nearby. Mr. and Mrs. Jones (Mrs. Jones in particular) described themselves as strongly family-oriented. Indeed, most of their previous social life had centered around activities with relatives. Graham was described by his mother as a boy who was "happy-go-lucky" before the move and who, although quiet, was far from shy. Graham reportedly had several close friends with whom he played regularly.

During the initial interview, the therapist requested that the family enact an incident that had occurred the previous morning, wherein Graham had stayed home from school. Although the Jones family had to be strongly encouraged to participate in this exercise, they were ultimately able to do so. This enactment was critical in revealing a pattern of interactions that seemed to be strongly involved in the maintenance of Graham's depression. In brief, Mrs. Jones' first comment to Graham that morning was that he looked pale, and she questioned whether or not he was feeling well. Mr. Jones accused his wife of pampering Graham, and stated that he did not look at all pale. Mrs. Jones then felt she had to support her perception and checked Graham's forehead, triumphantly announcing that he felt feverish. Mr. Jones became disgusted and retorted that her coddling Graham was enough to make anyone feverish. As this dialogue escalated, Graham grew increasingly upset and finally broke into tears. Mrs. Jones glared at her husband and retorted, "Now look what you've done." Mr. Jones stomped out of Graham's room in disgust, and Mrs. Jones turned her affection and attention to her son. This scenario offered support for the therapist's preliminary hypothesis of an overly involved mother-son subsystem and a weak marital subsystem.

The therapist probed for further information about how this family was functioning now, as compared to how they had interacted before the move. The ensuing discussion indicated that Mrs. Jones had previously had many of her needs for intimacy and support met through her family of origin. Mr. Jones was seemingly content to be a part of this system, but felt more comfortable "watching from the sidelines" rather than being involved more directly. With her primary source of support eliminated by the move, Mrs. Jones turned her attention to her son and had become increasingly involved in his life. Graham had provided an easy opening for this reaction through his mild problems adjusting to the move and difficulties with entering a new school.

Mrs. Jones initially dealt with Graham's anxieties about going to a new school by being supportive and reassuring. Although this was at first helpful for Graham, it unfortunately also provided him with increased opportunities to avoid school. Moreover, Mrs. Jones' overattentiveness quickly became reinforcing for Graham. Consequently, not only was Graham allowed to avoid an uncomfortable situation (school), but he also received considerable attention for doing so. Further inquiry suggested that Mrs. Jones' willingness to allow Graham to stay home from school reflected, in part, her own need for companionship. Because she neither worked outside the home nor belonged to group or community organizations, she lacked an obvious avenue for developing her own friendships. Indeed, having lived all her life in the same village, Mrs. Jones had never before been in the position of having to initiate and cultivate relationships. Therefore, she was not particularly skillful in this area.

In the more formal assessment phase, the therapist met with Graham alone and with Mr. and Mrs. Jones together, without Graham. In addition, the therapist had Mr. and Mrs. Jones complete the Beck Depression Inventory (BDI) and the DAS, while Graham completed the Child Depression Inventory (CDI). The results of both this formal assessment and the interview led the therapist to the following conceptualization of the Jones family: Before their recent move, Mr. and Mrs. Jones had a stable but somewhat detached marital relationship. However, they were both happy with the amount and type of involvement with each other. Mrs. Jones was busy with various community activities and with her extended family, and Mr. Jones enjoyed his work and generally had no complaints about his life. The Joneses spent most of their social time in group activities, rarely spending time alone as a couple. Graham was doing well in school. He enjoyed the time spent with his friends and also liked to accompany his parents on their outings with their extended family. The Joneses had never been exposed to any serious stresses, and so had never been required to develop strategies for dealing with major problems.

Following the move, however, they found themselves isolated and without the resources necessary to pull themselves together as a strong family unit. Mrs. Jones secretly blamed her husband for their current situation, although she had never directly confronted him with her feelings. Similarly, Mr. Jones covertly expected his wife to provide the same harmonious and stable family and social life they had previously experienced. Some of his frustration and anger with his wife over how she was treating their son appeared to be a displacement of his general disappointment in her. (Indeed, the therapist's observation sheet indicated that during the marital session, Mr. and Mrs. Jones engaged in a high proportion of negative communications, most of which was initiated by Mr. Jones.) Sensing this hostility, Mrs. Jones was turning increasingly to her son for closeness and companionship. As a result, Mr. Jones felt even more alienated and expressed his resentment through criticisms of his wife's pampering of Graham. Mrs. Jones responded to this criticism by becoming even more involved with her son. Graham was caught in the middle and lacked the skill to escape. By the time the family sought therapy, they were all feeling discouraged and depressed. Both Mr. and Mrs. Jones' DAS scores were below 90, corroborating the therapist's more subjective impression of a fair degree of marital dissatisfaction. Graham met diagnostic criteria for depression, and consistent with this, his CDI score was significantly elevated (24). Interestingly, both Mr. and Mrs. Jones obtained BDI scores in the mild-to-moderately depressed range (Mr. Jones, 13; Mrs. Jones, 18).

Because this family was neither psychologically sophisticated nor particularly verbal, the therapist had to approach them in a matter-of-fact, concrete manner. He began by educating the family in simple, straightforward terms about the process of therapy. After a detailed negotiation, the therapist and family agreed to the following sub-goals, intended to meet the ultimate goal of reducing Graham's level of depression: (a) to increase the number of days Graham attended school; (b) to help Graham develop at least two friendships with children in his new school; (c) to help Graham decrease the periods of withdrawal and temper outbursts at home; (d) to help Mrs. Jones find at least one activity or organization she could join; and (e) to help this family feel less isolated and lonely by helping them find a social activity they could join together. The intended result of the successful completion of these goals was that each family member would obtain a lower score on the depression inventories at the end of treatment, as compared with their pretreatment scores. The therapist also predicted that Mr. and Mrs. Jones' DAS scores would improve as a result of the intervention.

Because both Graham's depression and the Jones' marital tensions were relatively recent occurrences, the therapist determined that the goals of therapy could likely be adequately met within six sessions. Furthermore, because it was a child who was exhibiting the major symptoms of depression, the whole family was requested to be involved in the treatment process. Therefore, the family contracted for three family and three couple sessions, each to be 1 hour in length. The therapist informed the family that both the treatment goals and number of sessions could be renegotiated if necessary.

One of the first intervention strategies employed by the therapist was to reframe the presenting problem. Reframing was employed to motivate Mr. and Mrs. Jones to pull together more and take the burden of worrying from their son. It was also intended to begin the important therapeutic process of altering the family boundaries by strengthening the marital dyad and weakening the mother-son subsystem. Graham's depression, which was viewed by Mr. Jones as resulting from his wife's overprotection and pampering of their son, and by Mrs. Jones as primarily a medical illness, was reframed by the therapist as follows:

> This whole family has undergone a major upheaval. Moving to a big city after having spent your entire lives in the same small village is pretty traumatic. Adding to this trauma is the fact that you have left behind so many people who are very close to you. Here you all feel alone and have not yet found activities and friends to replace your old ones. Graham is having trouble adjusting both to these changes

and to his new school. I think his problems are intensified because he is torn between wanting to start a new life and wanting to stick to his family. Without realizing it, I think, Graham is afraid that if he goes to school every day and begins to make friends with the children at school, he will be abandoning his parents. Not only is he worried about his own acceptance here, but he is also worried that his parents, and particularly his mother, will not fit in. He is not used to seeing his parents having trouble coping. All of this worrying about his family is understandably making him feel depressed.

The therapist also challenged the family structure, by which Mrs. Jones was unknowingly reinforcing her son's school-avoidance behavior. This task was accomplished by reassuring Mrs. Jones that she had been supportive and understanding of her son's difficulties long enough, and that it was now time to encourage him to be a little braver and more determined. To increase Mr. Jones' involvement with the family, he was requested to help his wife with this task and was told that it might take both their efforts working together to help Graham overcome his feelings of helplessness and discouragement. As a result of the reframing and restructuring strategies (which also offered Mrs. Jones an alternative way of being helpful to her son), Mr. and Mrs. Jones were able to make some changes around their handling of Graham's avoidance of school. They decided that each morning, Mrs. Jones would prepare her son a healthy breakfast and Mr. Jones would drive him to school. If Graham got upset or felt ill at school and wanted to come home, he had to call his father at work and discuss the matter with him first. The intention of this procedure was twofold: to weaken the overly involved mother-son relationship, which was contributing to the maintenance of Graham's depression, and to promote greater involvement by Mr. Jones. For these efforts to be effective and long-lasting, the therapist had to quickly help Mrs. Jones find other interests she could pursue.

Each family member was asked for ideas on what Mrs. Jones could do to develop some new interests and activities in the community. Emphasizing the family's strengths, this discussion involved commenting on Mrs. Jones' talents, what the family members thought she would need to feel happy in her new home, and how she might implement some of their ideas. The result of this discussion was a list of four activities that Mrs. Jones could pursue. Before she attempted them, however, she would first need to develop a specific plan of action. This area of discussion was pursued in one of the couple sessions, in which the therapist worked some very specific strategies to help Mrs. Jones effectively join in and meet people. The therapist carried out this task in a couple session, because he felt that both Mr. and Mrs. Jones could derive benefit. The list of strategies was ordered from the easiest to the most difficult task, and Mrs. Jones agreed to a time frame to achieve the first objective. In addition to helping Mrs. Jones develop interests in the community, the issue of what this couple and family could do to develop a social life was pursued. This couple finally decided that the first step would be to join the Newcomers Club. To maximize the generalizability and maintenance of treatment gains, the therapist periodically continued to appeal to the family's strengths to generate their own ideas and solutions.

By the sixth session, the family and the therapist both agreed that the family members had successfully accomplished all of their goals. With help from his parents, Graham was able to overcome his fears of starting a new school. A call from Mrs. Jones to Graham's teacher had alerted her to his problems and the teacher followed up on this information by having one of Graham's classmates volunteer to be his "buddy" and show him how the school operated. Graham's few attempts to backslide were successfully countered by talks with his father. By the sixth session, Graham had not missed any school in almost 3 weeks. Moreover, he had joined the soccer club, had made some friends, and now eagerly looked forward to going to school. Graham also had not had a temper tantrum at home in the last 3 weeks. His two most recent CDI scores of 6 and 4 were both in the nondepressed range, and he no longer met diagnostic criteria for depression. Both Mr. and Mrs. Jones happily reported that the "moody" Graham was gone and felt that they had their old son back. Mrs. Jones had completed the second item on her list and was beginning to feel hopeful about finding a niche for herself in this new community. She had begun a friendship with her next-door neighbor, which had made a big difference. Finally, through the Newcomers Club the Joneses had taken the first step to developing a social life for themselves. Corroborating the success of this intervention, both Mr. and Mrs. Jones' scores on the BDI were now in the nondepressed range (Mr. Jones, 3; Mrs. Jones, 7), and their DAS scores were now both slightly above 100, a moderate improvement from their pretreatment levels.

The therapist informed the family that he would like to see them again in approximately 4 months to ensure their continuing gains. The family agreed to this recommendation. However, a few days before this scheduled appointment, Mrs. Jones telephoned the therapist to tell him that everything was going so well that they felt it was not necessary to return. Mrs. Jones was cheerful on the phone and was happy to tell the therapist about what had been happening with the family. Graham was doing very well in school and had virtually a perfect attendance record. Moreover, a recent report card was very positive. He was involved in several sports activities in school and had made many new friends. Mrs. Jones had no residual concerns about his adjustment. As for herself and her husband, Mrs. Jones reported that they regularly attend Newcomers Club functions and had made several friends. Finally, Mrs. Jones revealed with pride that she had secured a part-time filing job with a group of physicians, and was receiving positive reports from her employers. The therapist was satisfied that this family was functioning well and agreed that they need not keep their appointment. He did remind Mrs. Jones, however, that they could contact the therapist if the need arose in the future.

CASE 2: A DEPRESSED UNIVERSITY STUDENT

Paul McKenzie was a first-year university student who sought counseling because of general difficulties adjusting to his first year away from home. He felt lonely, tired, unable to do his school work, unmotivated, and generally depressed. School was in its fifth month, and Paul had not yet developed any social life. He spent his days entirely in class, at the library, or alone in his apartment. He occasionally went to a movie alone, but typically returned from these outings feeling even lonelier and more discouraged. Although school had always presented difficulties for Paul, he obtained passing grades through hard work and dedication. Currently, however, he was in serious jeopardy of losing some credits, if not failing the whole year. Paul felt that the reason for this situation was primarily that he missed too many classes; he further reported that he was unable to concentrate even when he did attend class.

Paul presented as a shy and anxious young man who lacked self-confidence. He avoided eye contact with the therapist, repeatedly cleared his throat, and shifted nervously in his chair. As with many depressed patients, the therapist had difficulty engaging Paul, and even social conversation was not productive. Moreover, Paul had difficulty articulating his feelings and describing the particular difficulties he was experiencing. He tended to speak in vague generalities instead of describing specific details. A SADS interview resulted in Paul receiving a diagnosis of Major Depressive Episode, and on the basis of this interview and of Paul's responses to the Beck Depression Inventory (total score 32), the therapist ruled out the possibility of suicide. When questioned about his reasons for seeking therapy at this time, Paul replied that his parents (particularly his mother) had strongly recommended it. The therapist hypothesized that Paul still had strong attachments to his family, a belief supported by Paul's admission that he had never been away from home before.

Paul's family lived too far away to participate in therapy, but because of the therapist's conviction concerning the important role of Paul's family in contributing to his depression, the therapist decided to try to "involve" them in the therapeutic process by finding out about them and by having Paul comment on various aspects of the therapy process as he believed members of his family would. Paul revealed the following information about his family: He was the younger of two siblings. His older brother, Kevin, appeared to be the star in this highly success-oriented family. Kevin was described by Paul as outgoing, bright, athletic, and well-liked by most people. He was currently a junior executive for a large bank, and Paul felt that Kevin was destined to move ahead quickly. Paul reported that whereas Kevin and his father were very close, he was closer to his mother. Although Paul described his father in positive terms, there was an undercurrent of anger and hostility. Despite Paul's reports that he and his father were not close, that his father got easily frustrated with him, and that his father expected perfection from his family, Paul denied any feelings of anger or resentment towards his father. He painted a picture of his mother as a rather unhappy woman who had a long history of medical and psychological problems. She typically came to Paul's defense when he was being berated by his father. Although Paul was somewhat vague about the relationship between his mother and brother, the therapist was left with the impression that there was a history of tension and conflict between the two.

In a case such as this, the decision of who to see in therapy is predetermined. Nevertheless, it is important to retain an interpersonal systems focus by continually drawing in family members. A simple but effective method for achieving this goal is to request that the individual in treatment describe how a family member would respond to a particular question or issue. The therapist can also request that family members be given questionnaires to complete and mail in. Thus, in this particular case Paul was given the Family Environment Scale (FES) to complete and, in addition, to send to his parents, to be returned to the therapist. Given Paul's difficulty in expressing himself, as well as the unavailability of his family to participate in the therapy process, the therapist decided that Paul would require at least 10 sessions to make significant progress. Despite some initial difficulty, the therapist and Paul agreed on three treatment goals: (a) to decrease Paul's feelings of depression, as evidenced by lower BDI scores and increased participation in pleasurable activities (playing hockey, skiing, and listening to music); (b) to increase Paul's feelings of self-confidence and independence, which would be reflected in his developing two or more friendships and participating in at least one social activity each week; and (c) to decrease Paul's school problems, as evidenced both by increased attendance in class (i.e., missing three or fewer classes a week) and by self-reports that his concentration was greater.

Given Paul's previously mentioned difficulties in opening up with the therapist, ongoing attempts were engineered by the therapist to join with Paul through a mutual interest in sports and discussions of the difficulties inherent in being the youngest child in the family. These attempts were only moderately successful, however, and for the most part, Paul remained guarded and defensive. Some understanding of this behavior was gleaned from an enactment in which Paul was asked to portray his father's reactions to his bringing home a poor report card. His father's behavior, as displayed by Paul, was reserved, unemotional, and detached. Ultimately, his father delivered a lecture on the consequences of doing poorly at school. Although he had more difficulty in role-playing his mother's reactions to the same situation, Paul portrayed her as much more emotional and reactive, but also as more understanding and supportive. Therefore, it seemed that Paul took his cues from his father with regard to revealing his feelings.

From the FES profiles returned by Paul's parents, Paul's FES responses, and additional information obtained through the interview process, the therapist was able to piece together the following case formulation. The McKenzie family was highly achievement-oriented. Because Kevin and Mr. McKenzie were more successful, they held the positions of respect and esteem in the family. Paul and his mother, conversely, were viewed as less capable and more needy. As a result of Mr. McKenzie's longstanding devotion to his work, he was often unavailable to his family. As Kevin embarked on his education, he too became overly involved in his studies and in extracurricular activities. As a result of these two events, Mrs. McKenzie felt that her only support in the family came from Paul. She typically relied on him to take care of her when she was sick and to keep her company when she was lonely. As a result of Paul's attachment to his mother, he had failed to develop the autonomy and independence typical of an individual his age. Given the importance Mr. McKenzie placed on independence and success, it is likely that he was disappointed in his younger son. Compounding this situation was the fact that Paul's move to the university had deprived him of the one "task" at which he felt competent (i.e., taking care of his mother), and this competence had not been replaced by another (i.e., academic success). Indeed, Paul currently viewed his problems adjusting to university as incontrovertible evidence of his incompetence. The more critical he was of himself, the more depressed he became, and as his depression increasingly interfered with his studies, he felt even more inadequate.

A major task facing the therapist was to reframe Paul's depression in a less self-defeating manner using the information obtained from the formal assessment. The therapist began the reframing by telling Paul how impressed he was at the sacrifices Paul had made over the years to take care of his mother.

> Not many sons would have been as devoted as you have been to making sure that their mother was not lonely. You have always been there for your mother when she needed someone. To do this, though, you've had to give up many things, such as friends and parties, that would have made you feel happier. But now you are away from home, and I think that perhaps without even realizing it, you are afraid that no one will be there for your mother. In fact, in some ways it seems like you are worried that if you do really well at university, making some good friends and doing well in your studies, your mother may feel that you have joined your father and brother's side and have deserted her side. It may even be that you are afraid your father cannot take care of your mother or be good company for her. I wonder how he would feel about that?

As the therapist anticipated, Paul's reaction to this reframing intervention was to defend his father's ability to be a good husband to his wife. Indeed, the success of this strategy was to put Paul in such a position that the only way he could continue with his current depressive behavior was to admit that his father was incapable of managing his home situation. Because Paul's father was viewed as so successful, the therapist reasoned that it was highly unlikely that Paul would be able to agree with this. In addition, an indirect target of this reframing was a longstanding family belief that although half the family members were competent and successful, half were not. To ensure that this reframing had a lasting effect on Paul, the therapist repeated it in different ways several times.

The therapist also believed, however, that before Paul could make significant progress towards reaching his goals, he would need to reassure himself that there would be no serious consequences of his doing well. Therefore, the therapist used a restraining strategy, cautioning Paul not to make any hasty improvements until he proved to himself that his mother would not suffer if he became a "success." Therefore, the therapist assigned Paul the task of going home for the weekend and assessing whether or not his father was able to make his mother happy. He was instructed not to fall back into his old role of being attentive and understanding with his mother, or else he would not discover whether or not his father was truly capable. Paul was also instructed to tell both his parents about a high grade he had received on a paper and then to watch carefully the reaction that this news elicited from both parents. In so doing, he was checking for himself whether it was really all right for him to do well. Because Mrs. McKenzie had indicated on the FES questionnaire that she too valued success and accomplishments, the therapist was confident that she would be proud of her son's high grade. To ensure that Mrs. McKenzie would not feel neglected, Paul was directed to let his mother know how much he missed her good home-cooked meals and how much harder it was to not have her around to do things for him.

Paul was given the same assignment for two consecutive weeks and returned from the second weekend noticeably more confident that it was permissible for him to do well after all. One factor that seemed to make a significant difference for Paul was a change that was beginning to develop in his relationship with his father. The two had talked more and had been closer over these two weekends than they had been for years. Perhaps without Paul for support, Mrs. McKenzie was making an effort to become more involved with her husband, and he in turn was no longer feeling excluded by his wife. Paul's growing acceptance by his father was helping Paul to feel more self-confident. Moreover, as Paul was able to determine for himself that his father was capable of being supportive and understanding of his wife, he was able to slowly move out of his overinvolved relationship with his mother. Therefore, the marital dyad was growing stronger and the mother-son subsystem was weakening. To ensure continued growth in this direction, the therapist cautioned Paul to develop his own life only in direct proportion to the confidence he felt in his mother's ability to manage without him. In part, Paul's reluctance to see himself as overinvolved with his mother motivated him to try harder to establish an independent life.

Interspersed with these "family-related" tasks were individual therapy strategies and techniques described in Chapter 3. The therapist educated Paul about the interpersonal aspects of his depression and about the cognitive style of depressed individuals. Paul was instructed to monitor and record his perceptions and cognitions surrounding, first, negative "critical incidents" and then both positive and negative events. In the fourth session, the therapist began to encourage Paul to increase his involvement in enjoyable activities (as agreed upon for the first treatment goal). To help Paul identify these activities, he was requested to complete the Pleasant Events Schedule. The therapist then worked with Paul to generate a daily schedule for him, in which he gradually became increasingly involved in hockey and skiing.

As with many depressed individuals, Paul seemed uncomfortable around other people and appeared to lack the skills necessary to elicit positive responses from them. Because the second treatment goal involved the development of new relationships and involvement in social activities, the therapist decided to work toward this goal through the use of role-playing and behavioral skill-training. The therapist engaged Paul in frequent role-plays centering around how he could meet and introduce himself to other students. With support, encouragement, and relevant homework assignments from the therapist, Paul was able to initiate several appropriate conversations, one of which was particularly fruitful. On one trip home he started up a conversation with a young woman who was waiting for the same train. She was a student at the same university, and the train ride marked the beginning of a romantic relationship. This was Paul's first real involvement with a woman, and despite some rough times ahead, the relationship greatly increased his self-esteem.

As Paul's relationship with his father improved and his romantic relationship developed, so did his school progress. He was not missing classes and reported that he was able to concentrate much better. Because these changes were not sufficiently stable by the end of the 10 sessions originally contracted for and Paul's BDI of 13 was sufficiently high, Paul and the therapist mutually agreed to contract for 5 more sessions. At the end of the fourteenth session, Paul reviewed the changes he had made and reported that he had accomplished all of his original treatment goals. (Note again that defining the treatment goals as behaviorally as possible simplifies the issue of evaluation of progress.) Paul's BDI scores for the last two sessions were both below 6. As is often a good idea when this treatment approach is used with an individual alone, however, Paul was asked to provide information on changes his family believed he had made. Instead of asking Paul to conjecture, he was asked to directly solicit this information from each family member. He returned for the final session (BDI of 3) with reports that everyone saw him as more mature, less "uptight," more open and involved with his family, and more energetic and enthusiastic about his life. His father in particular voiced his pride in his son's accomplishments. Although Paul's grades had improved, he was unlikely to ever be an "A" student. Nonetheless, his family appeared to be more accepting of this level of accomplishment than they had been in the past. Finally, Paul no longer met DSM-III criteria for Major Depressive Episode.

Although the therapist thought that Paul still had significant gains to make in becoming more mature and responsible, he did not feel that these goals required the intervention of a therapist. At a follow-up appointment at 6 months, Paul appeared to have maintained his previous therapy gains. His BDI score of 3 was clearly in the nondepressed range. Paul was still involved in the same romantic relationship, but at the same time had increased the time spent with male friends. As Paul's social life had improved, his grades had suffered somewhat, but he nevertheless had managed to obtain all of his credits. Paul reported that his relationship with his family was getting better and that his parents were more active and involved with each other than he had ever known them to be. Indeed, they had taken several trips together. Although his mother continued to have her ups and downs, Paul was less reactive to them. He felt that he did not need any further help at this time, but agreed to call the therapist if problems arose.

CASE 3: A DEPRESSED MARRIED WOMAN

Jennifer Munroe was referred for treatment, at her request, by her family physician. Jennifer had had a few counseling sessions with a previous therapist, but had terminated treatment because it was unproductive. She had been feeling depressed since the birth of her son almost 2 years earlier, which she felt had had a disruptive effect on both her and her husband, David. She had given up a high-level management position to stay home with their child and felt that David did not appreciate how tiring raising a child was. Moreover, Jennifer felt that David was having difficulty accepting the responsibilities of parenthood. Before the birth of their son, she and David had led an active life. Because of their solid financial position and childless state at that time, they had had considerable flexibility to travel, entertain, and pursue many hobbies (e.g., flying, windsurfing, sailing, and collecting antiques). The birth of their son had restricted their freedom and reduced their income. Jennifer was feeling depressed and unable to cope with the stresses in her life. On the basis of the information provided over the telephone, the therapist strongly felt that Jennifer and David would both be needed in the therapy process to help the therapist obtain a comprehensive understanding of Jennifer's depression, establish appropriate treatment goals, and most importantly increase the effectiveness of therapy. Because their son was only 2 years old, the therapist decided that it would not be appropriate to include him in the therapy process.

The Munroes arrived at the assessment interview with Jennifer looking very depressed and David appearing aloof and uncomfortable. A more extensive review of their current situation revealed that David and, to a lesser extent, Jennifer, were both feeling angry, frustrated, and discouraged about Jennifer's depression, and hopeless about the possibility of being able to resolve her condition. David felt particularly resentful that his wife was no longer fun to be with. He was able to describe at length the pleasurable and exciting times they used to have together and reported that he wanted his "old Jennifer" and their previous lifestyle back.

During the formal assessment stage of the initial interview, both spouses were asked to complete the BDI and the DAS. In addition, the therapist engaged Jennifer in an individual diagnostic interview. David thought that the task of filling out questionnaires was unnecessary, stating that it was clear to him that if his wife would just shape up and get back to her energetic and fun self, they would have no problems. Jennifer accused David of being a dreamer and told him that they could not ignore two important changes in their lives—a new baby and a reduced income. Although this couple denied marital problems per se, both obtained scores on the DAS that reflected a significant level of dissatisfaction with their marriage (Jennifer, 84; David, 90). The structured interview with Jennifer indicated that she met diagnostic criteria for Major Depressive Episode; in fact, Jennifer also met the criteria for endogenous depression presented in Table 4.1. She reported that her depression seemed worse in the morning, and this, combined with feelings of guilt about her depression, early morning awakening, distinct psychomotor retardation, poor appetite, and a recent weight loss of 12 pounds, prompted the therapist to refer Jennifer to the clinic psychiatrist for antidepressant evaluation. Corroborating these interview results, Jennifer obtained a BDI score of 42. Interestingly, as is often the case with couples in which one spouse is clinically depressed, David's BDI score of 16 also indicated moderate depressive symptomatology.

Both Jennifer and David were strongly committed to the idea of having and being part of a family and, consequently, were reluctant to acknowledge any problems that might threaten their relationship. David in particular was concerned with his image as a family man and was worried about the possible reactions of his parents and friends if they found out that there were problems in his family. This information helped to explain somewhat the urgency with which David felt that his wife should get back to her "normal" self. Jennifer, however, while agreeing that her depression represented a significant part of their problems, also felt that David's lack of responsibility contributed to their present state. In comparing this couple's verbal account of the problem with their responses to the structured inventories and the undercurrent of tension in the room, the therapist began to feel that this case was more complex and demanding than it had originally appeared.

The therapist's next step in the therapy process was to employ the strategy of joining, which, as we noted in Chapter 3, is an important first step in the treatment process. The therapist felt that this task was especially important because she had already been warned that Jennifer had discarded a previous therapist for his lack of understanding and perceived inability to help. The therapist was able to join with this couple by listening intensely and by reflecting back their feelings of frustration and despair. She altered her joining efforts between husband and wife, and David and Jennifer ultimately stated that the therapist clearly understood them. This couple was very verbal and they appreciated the therapist's active involvement in the therapy process.

The therapist required little planning to stimulate an enactment, which was intended to help her better understand the role of Jennifer's depression in the marital relationship and how the specific interactional patterns of this couple might be maintaining her depression. The Munroes were able to generate a situation for enactment that developed out of a discussion regarding the various circumstances that contributed to Jennifer's depression. Specifically, Jennifer felt that David completely "tuned her out" whenever she touched on a sensitive topic. The therapist asked them to identify one of these areas and to replay for her how their conversation about that area typically unfolded. Jennifer raised her suspicion that David might be having an affair. David countered that this was ludicrous and blatantly denied having an affair. Jennifer began to recount a variety of suspicions and then demanded that David account for his time. Her concerns involved such issues as why David hung up the phone so frequently when she arrived home, why he had so many early morning meetings with business clients, and why he denied being downtown on a particular day when she had seen his car parked there. Her suspicions seemed endless. For each circumstance described by his wife, David was able to offer an explanation. Although he believed that these explanations were satisfactory, Jennifer felt that they were all fabricated. As the therapist observed this interaction, she saw just how deeply the roots of mistrust, resentment, and anger ran. Neither spouse demonstrated any attempt to understand how the other was feeling, or to console each other. Minimal eye contact was exhibited by the couple, and both made frequent attempts to entice the therapist to side with him or her. David and Jennifer were clearly locked into a trap of perpetrator and victim. Interestingly, both felt they were the victim and the other spouse the villain.

As the therapist continued to study and observe David and Jennifer's enactment, she recognized how easy it would be to be drawn into the web woven by this couple. She observed that when the conversation became heated, neither couple displayed good listening skills and that most statements were either accusatory, defensive, or attempts to induce guilt. At one point, David accused Jennifer of deliberately becoming depressed to deprive him of all the exciting and pleasurable activities they used to pursue. Jennifer, in turn, told David that if he were more helpful around the house, they would have more time in which to pursue these activities. She also accused David of being unable to understand that giving birth to and raising a child was exhausting work. As the therapist observed this sequence of interactions, she noted numerous instances of negative reciprocity. The Munroes had dug themselves in so deeply that at this point any concession or compromise would be viewed as a weakness or an admission of guilt.

We can see in this example that, as is often the case, depression in one spouse is an indication of difficulties in the marital relationship. Because this pattern of marital interaction may not have been gleaned from an interview with Jennifer alone, it was important that the therapist requested that both spouses attend the initial session. Given this strong marital conflict, it is unlikely that simply treating Jennifer's depression alone would have been completely successful.

The therapist was now faced with the challenging task of trying to reframe Jennifer's depression to facilitate healthier and more productive marital interactions. After careful consideration, she produced the following statement:

> Jennifer is clearly depressed. And despite David's reluctance to accept it, I think he is somewhat depressed as well. From what you have told me, the two of you used to lead an exciting and stimulating life, one that many people would envy. You did a lot together and never really had to worry about such issues as finances or children. But then your life changed. You had a son and had to give up a portion of your income through Jennifer's decision to stay home and raise your child. Hearing the situations and feelings you have both described to me, I can understand why you are both feeling depressed and, indeed, why you have been for some time now. In fact, given some of the major changes you have undergone, I am surprised that you are not both feeling even more depressed. From what you have both said, it sounds like your relationship has been gradually deteriorating since the birth of your son. Yet neither of you has crumbled. At some level and in some way you both feel a strong devotion to each other, but a lot of surface aggravations are temporarily covering that up. Jennifer, you are disappointed in yourself that you can no longer live up to David's expectations. You feel that in some way you have let him down. Thinking like this makes you feel depressed and this depression is reinforced by the reality that when you have a child, you do not have the freedom you previously did. It even seems that the more David tries to encourage you to become more active, the more fearful you become that once again you will be unable to follow through with your plans. Thus, you try to make excuses beforehand, attempting to prevent David's subsequent disappointment. At one point I even wondered, David, if some of your complaints and dissatisfactions with Jennifer were your unconscious attempts to distract her from the boredom and lethargy she was feeling being stuck at home. Perhaps as we work together this will become clearer to us all.

In offering this perspective, the therapist is attempting to build on the couple's strengths. The Munroes expressed both surprise and satisfaction at this new perspective and seemed willing to continue. Therefore, the therapist's next task was to work with this couple in formulating appropriate treatment goals. However, this task too proved frustrating. For example, David wanted Jennifer to try harder to be less depressed, more outgoing, and at least attempt more activities. Jennifer countered that she would be willing to try this if she felt less pressure and more support from David. She added that before she would be willing to make a strong effort, she would have to feel more assured that David was not involved in an affair. Because of this couple's style of attack/defend, it took an entire session of much arguing, disagreeing, tears, accusations, and hurt feelings before they could agree on a set of treatment objectives. The two general goals were relatively easy to define: (a) to decrease the level of Jennifer's depression and (b) to improve the overall quality of their marital relationship. The therapist hypothesized that meeting these two goals would also reduce David's moderate level of depressive symptomatology.

To decrease the level of Jennifer's depression, the therapist felt that Jennifer had to be encouraged to engage in more pleasant activities. Therefore, it was agreed that Jennifer would take one afternoon off each week and leave their son with a sitter. During this time she would pursue some of her former interests (e.g., playing tennis, visiting friends, and visiting art galleries or museums). In addition, because most of Jennifer's negative thinking appeared to be specific to her relationship with David, she was also given a homework assignment that was more cognitive in nature: whenever she felt negative or suspicious towards David, she was to balance this thought with a positive one. (Jennifer was also instructed to keep a record of this list.)

To improve the quality of the marriage, other specific goals, based on the procedure of contingency contracting, were formulated in concrete terms as follows: David agreed to be home on time for dinner three nights a week and, in turn, Jennifer would have the house in order so that they could enjoy a peaceful dinner together. David was free to spend one night a week "out with the boys" when he would not have to worry about Jennifer being angry at him. Jennifer, for her part, would not nag David or question him as to his whereabouts. David was, of course, free to tell Jennifer where he had been if he chose to do so. One day each week at a mutually convenient time, David was to take total charge of their son; Jennifer was free to participate in this activity or to do something else. Jennifer agreed not to berate David in front of company, and David agreed to include Jennifer in more of his conversations when they were with friends. In addition, the couple agreed to plan one joint pleasurable activity in which they could participate each week.

Finally, David and Jennifer were both asked to make a list of these goals and to provide a rating for each one, both for themselves and for their spouse. A 4-point scale was agreed upon to rate how well they had completed their tasks. The couple was reminded to bring in all the sheets for the following session. The couple's level of resistance was so high that the therapist decided that at least 20 sessions would be necessary to make any reasonable gains. The therapist set this up in contract form along with the specified treatment objectives. She added that in all likelihood, all sessions would involve working with the couple together, but if a time arose when she would like to speak to one of them individually, they would always have a week's warning. (The therapist was reluctant to see one of these spouses on an individual basis because of their previous and repeated attempts to draw her in as judge and to take sides. Ultimately, the therapist decided it was not worth the risk and saw them throughout therapy only in couple sessions.) Both Jennifer and David stated that 20 sessions seemed a long time, yet both agreed that they had dug themselves in so deeply that they might not be able to get out more quickly than that.

Jennifer was evaluated by the clinic psychiatrist, who prescribed antidepressant medication for her. In combination with this somatic treatment, Jennifer and David continued in treatment with the therapist. The next few sessions were both challenging and stressful. Jennifer appeared to be making serious efforts to make the specified changes. Although she was using her afternoon each week for herself, David reacted to Jennifer's meeting of the marital goals with accusations that the changes were not really genuine and that she was just doing them to follow the therapist's instructions and did not really feel them in her heart. Jennifer denied this, stating that at first it was difficult to follow through with some of the goals, but that now she was actually starting to enjoy them. David then stated that he felt that in any case, they simply would not last. It became obvious that the more Jennifer tried, the more critical David became. To complicate this picture, it was also clear that David's positive changes were met with similar reactions from Jennifer, who indicated that they were "too little, too late." Both spouses were clearly making solid efforts and gains, but these were repeatedly being ambushed by their partner. The therapist decided that another reframing was in order:

> Something unusual is going on here that I feel I must point out to you. On the one hand, I see Jennifer struggling hard and coming up with some positive changes, only to be flattened by David's reactions. On the other hand, I see David digging in and carving out some truly positive gains, only to be deflated by Jennifer's difficulty in accepting them. It is beginning to look to me as if deep down in your hearts you both think the other wants out of this relationship. In fact, this feeling is so strong that you are afraid if the relationship continues to show the gains you have both made, then you are trapping your partner in the marriage. I am truly impressed by the sacrifice you are both willing to make for the other. You have both shown many strengths in getting this far. You have been creative, strong, compromising, and self-sacrificing, but you are definitely holding back from taking that final step into solving your difficulties. That suggests very strongly to me that you are not ready for this move, especially when both of you are probably feeling that the other wants out.

This portrayal of the couple's resistance to change caused each spouse to suddenly see the other from a different perspective. No longer did it feel like a greedy, self-protective relationship; suddenly, each was faced with an almost alien perception, namely, that the other person was prepared to make a sacrifice for them. This interpretation had a profound impact on the couple. They reacted first with denial, then disbelief, then surprise, and finally, with strong emotion. This session represented a turning point in the couple's treatment. There was an immediate increase in the level of affection, and for the first time in months Jennifer and David felt like a team. They started planning common goals and vacations together. Given this couple's history of problems and difficulties with control, the therapist warned them that they were trying to make too many gains too fast. They gently accused the therapist of being too cautious. After all, they were two intelligent people who knew what they were doing. Nevertheless, given this couple's history of resistance, the therapist felt it was important to restrain them from moving too quickly.

By the twentieth session, Jennifer and David both felt ready to terminate therapy. They had accomplished all their previous goals and more, and both felt strongly that their marriage at this point was a good one. David and Jennifer were both happier and feeling more productive with their lives. Jennifer's BDI score of 7 had been stable over the last four sessions, and was consistent with the fact that she no longer met DSM-III criteria for depression. Indeed, the clinic psychiatrist's recent evaluation of Jennifer corroborated this perception. David too ended therapy with a BDI score in the nondepressed range. Their scores on the DAS during this session showed marked improvement from their pre-treatment levels (Jennifer, 105; David, 109). These data indicated that termination was warranted, and a follow-up session was planned for 6 months.

The follow-up session with this couple revealed a marital relationship that was still intact. David had received a major promotion at work, which was a significant boost to both his ego and their bank account. Jennifer remained at home with their son, but had secured a part-time position outside the home. Neither Jennifer (BDI of 4) nor David (BDI of 7) was depressed. No mention was made of an affair and, indeed, the couple seemed to have settled in more with each other. Although their relationship lacked the "honeymoon" quality they had demonstrated at termination, they seemed more realistic in their expectations of marriage and of each other. Jennifer seemed somewhat more satisfied than did David, and this perception was corroborated by their DAS scores (Jennifer, 112; David, 105). Nevertheless, David felt that he was accepting his new parental role and for the most part was enjoying it. Both David and Jennifer indicated they were satisfied with their relationship and with themselves and did not feel the need for further treatment. Again, they were invited to do so if the need arose.

CONCLUDING COMMENTS

In these three case examples, we have attempted to illustrate how the interpersonal systems approach presented in this guidebook can be both useful and effective in the treatment of a variety of manifestations of depression. We have presented cases involving a depressed child and his parents, a depressed university student treated in individual therapy (within the context of this interpersonal systems perspective), and a depressed woman with concomitant marital difficulties, who also met diagnostic criteria for endogenous depression. In each case, the rationale underlying the use of various strategies derived from this interpersonal systems perspective has been described. It is important for the reader to note that not all of the procedures described in this guidebook are utilized in each case. Nevertheless, the therapist should be familiar and facile with all of these techniques to select the most appropriate strategy for a particular treatment objective. In our experience, in treating even a small number of diverse cases the therapist will make use of all of these techniques.

Although it may not have been apparent in our examples, most of these strategies are used repeatedly throughout the treatment of a particular case. This repetition, or "working through," is often necessary to emphasize the point being made, to overcome a patient's resistance to therapeutic change and, as we noted in Chapter 3, to promote generalization, transfer of training, and hence long-lasting treatment effects. Finally, these cases highlight the active involvement of the therapist in both designing and effecting change. Indeed, this therapy is a relatively short-term process partly because of the therapist's skill in actively identifying the families' strengths and in encouraging the family members themselves to mobilize these resources in reaching their treatment objectives.

In the Afterword we move beyond the treatment of depression to a brief examination of how the interpersonal systems approach may be applied to a diverse range of disorders.

Afterword

Beyond Depression: Further Applications of Interpersonal Systems Therapy

This guidebook has focused on the nature and treatment of depression. Although the prevalence of this disorder is such that it has been referred to as "the common cold of psychopathology," it is important to bear in mind that depression is only one of the many forms of dysfunction encountered by the practicing clinician. In this afterword, we will see that the interpersonal systems description of the assessment and treatment of depression presented in this guidebook is not limited to this disorder. Rather, this perspective (or very similar frameworks) has been used in the conceptualization and treatment of a broad range of maladjustments. In the following pages, we will briefly describe interpersonal conceptualizations and treatment studies of various disorders. Although it is beyond the scope of this guidebook to offer detailed descriptions of these papers, we hope that this afterword will serve as a springboard, stimulating clinicians to examine these and other related reports in greater detail.

Schizophrenic Disorders. Schizophrenia has received the greatest attention from family theorists and therapists. Early investigators noted disturbed functioning in families with schizophrenic members and coined such terms as *schizophrenogenic mother, double-bind,* and *schismatic* and *skewed* family structures to describe these families. These and other concepts and empirical findings led Waxler (1975) to conclude that the family is a dysfunctional system that supports the schizophrenic individual, and they provided the impetus for interpersonally-based treatment programs for this disorder.

Glick and Kessler (1980) described the various tasks that face a therapist treating a family with a schizophrenic member. It is instructive to note the similarity of these tasks, outlined for the treatment of schizophrenia, and those presented in this guidebook for the treatment of depression. For example, Glick and Kessler state that the therapist working with a family with a schizophrenic member must teach the identified patient to reduce hostile contact with his family and must encourage the family to develop more positive patterns of interaction. The therapist must also attempt to remove the focus from the identified patient and place it more on the family and its dysfunctional interactions. Although it remains an empirical question, it seems reasonable that given the similarities between the therapist's objectives in treating families with schizophrenic members and those goals used in treating families with depressed members, the strategies, techniques, and procedures described in this guidebook for the treatment of depression may profitably be used to accomplish the tasks described by Glick and Kessler in the treatment of schizophrenia.

Other Psychiatric Disorders. Several investigators recently applied systems-oriented approaches to the conceptualization and treatment of other psychiatric disorders. Schwoeri and Schwoeri (1982) present a systems description of borderline personality disorders and suggest that interpersonal systems-oriented therapy might be useful as an initial form of therapy in the treatment of these patients. Similarly, Bergner (1977) describes the structure and functioning of the marital system of individuals diagnosed as having a hysterical personality disorder, and emphasizes the therapeutic importance of such techniques as joining, altering marital or family myths or realities, and changing the nature of the couples' interactions.

From a similar perspective, Hafner, Badenoch, Fisher, and Swift (1983) compared the use of spouse-aided versus individual therapy in the treatment of patients with a wide range of severe, persisting psychiatric disorders. Mirroring Weisz and Bucher's (1980) findings with obese patients, Hafner et al. (1983) found that across diagnostic categories, involving the spouse in treatment was sufficient to produce superior results in a number of different measures, including improvement in target problems, psychological symptoms, and marital satisfaction. These results suggest that even without explicitly utilizing specific systems-oriented strategies, simply involving the spouse in the patient's treatment leads to greater change than does individual treatment.

Childhood Disorders. As we recommended in Chapter 4, systems-oriented therapy is often used when a child presents with symptomatic behavior. Tiller (1978) describes the use of family therapy in the treatment of Childhood Tic Syndrome, and Protinsky and Kersey (1983) and Wendorf (1984) report the successful use of systems-based family therapy in the treatment of encopresis. Smith, Smith, and L'Abate (1985) describe a systems conceptualization of hyperactivity and present a family-oriented intervention program for the assessment and treatment of this disorder. The tasks facing the therapist in this context include determining the reason the family is seeking treatment now, facilitating the development of different, more adaptive interpersonal boundaries within the family, improving the communication skills among the family members, reframing the child's behavior, and reducing the level of disengagement or enmeshment. Similarly, Dalton (1983) presents an interpersonal therapy for the treatment of obsessive-compulsive children and, as we have done here, describes the use of joining, restructuring the family boundaries, and disrupting dysfunctional interactional patterns to bring about therapeutic change. Finally, systems-oriented interventions have also been applied to the treatment of various types of psychogenic pain in children. White (1979) describes the application of a structural-systems treatment for families with children presenting with psychogenic abdominal pain. White obtained positive results through the use of such techniques as reframing the pain, changing the structure of the family, and resolving marital conflicts. Similar techniques have been successful in the treatment of children's headaches (e.g., O'Connor, 1984), and White (1979) also describes the use of these strategies in the treatment of anorexia nervosa, encopresis, and school phobia.

Psychosomatic Disorders. In a recent review of research examining the functioning of families in which individuals (most often children) are suffering from psychosomatic disorders, Haggerty (1983) concluded that "sufficient evidence is now available . . . to demonstrate unequivocal links between family interaction and somatic health" (p. 615). A number of studies have found that "psychosomatic families," compared with controls, exhibit restricted expression of affect, rigidity, enmeshment, overprotectiveness, and lack of conflict resolution among family members (e.g., Minuchin, Rosman, & Baker, 1978). Most interesting perhaps is Dysinger's (1961) observation, consistent with the tenets of systems theory presented earlier, that psychosomatic symptoms in one family member were often inversely related to the emotional health of another member, and further that the development of symptoms in one family member appeared to decrease conflict among the other family members. Drawing on these observations, Sargent (1983) concluded that, "in a circular fashion, the family organization maintains and is maintained by the involvement of the psychosomatic member" (p. 44).

Minuchin and his colleagues (e.g., Liebman, Minuchin, & Baker, 1974; Minuchin et al., 1978) developed intervention programs using structural family therapy in the treatment of families with children suffering from anorexia nervosa, diabetes, and asthma (see also Schilson and Van Valkenburg's [1984] interpersonal model of childhood obesity). Minuchin focuses on elucidating the dysfunctional family patterns that reinforce the patients' symptoms, improving the families' communication, interactions, and problem-solving abilities, and changing the structure and functioning of the family system. In accomplishing these objectives, Minuchin uses the techniques of joining, reframing, and altering both the family's boundaries and their myths. Minuchin's outcome data suggest that this interpersonal approach to therapy is effective in a high percentage of the cases treated.

Medical Disorders. Whereas in the past diseases were conceptualized as part of the patient, the recent development of systems theories and therapies has led medical practitioners to shift the focus of treatment from dealing with a patient in isolation, to involving the entire family. This change has occurred in part as a result of studies implicating the families, particularly the spouses of patients, in the development and maintenance of various "medical" disorders (e.g., cardiac disease: Croog & Fitzgerald, 1978; hemophilia: Simon, 1984; end-stage renal disease: Stewart & Johansen, 1976/77). Martindale and Bottomley (1980) and Phipps and Desplat (1984) describe an interpersonal systems-oriented approach to the treatment of Huntington's chorea. Consistent with the material presented in Chapter 3, these investigators encourage family support and frank, open discussion of the illness in intervening in the family system. In achieving these objectives, Phipps and Desplat report the use of reframing and restructuring, altering family myths about the illness, and improving the pattern of the family's interactions.

Binger (1984) and Sourkes (1977) stress the importance of treating the entire family of a child diagnosed with a potentially terminal illness such as cancer or leukemia. These authors maintain that practitioners must consider the coping ability of the family members, the life stressors with which the family is currently dealing, and the support systems available to the family. Binger (1984) and Sourkes (1977) particularly recommend that the therapist use the therapeutic techniques of joining, highlighting, and facilitating positive communication patterns among family members, and modeling coping skills for the parents.

Alcoholism. Self-report data indicate that the marriages of alcohol addicts are often problematic (Jacob, Dunn, & Leonard, 1983). In fact, Billings, Kessler, Gomberg, and Weiner (1979) found that the marital interactions of alcoholic couples were remarkably similar to those of nonalcoholic but maritally distressed couples: both were more negative and less positive than the interactions of normal couples. Based on such data, theorists have recently begun to conceptualize alcoholism as a systems problem involving the entire family (e.g., Finney, Moos, Cronkite, & Gamble, 1983; Kaufman and Pattison, 1981), and currently, as Stanton (1979) has recently noted, " . . . the majority of our nation's drug (and alcohol) programs employ some kind of family services—in many cases, family therapy—as part of their armamentarium" (p. 252).

Kaufman and Pattison (1981) describe specific techniques used in the systems-oriented treatment of alcoholism. They discuss such procedures as joining, using a contract, assigning homework tasks for the family, relabeling or reframing, restructuring, and enactment. Usher, Jay, and Glass (1982) also outline a systems-oriented intervention for families with an alcoholic member that involves reframing the alcoholism as a family problem. Usher et al. (1982) describe the formation of contracts involving the entire family that focus on altering interactions among the family members. The therapist works to increase the family's awareness of its communications and patterns of interaction, leading ultimately to more positive communication and a closer family unit. Again, it is instructive to observe that all of these are strategies we have outlined in this guidebook for the treatment of depression.

CONCLUDING COMMENTS

In this brief overview, we have illustrated some of the diverse ways in which interpersonal conceptualizations have been used in understanding and treating maladaptive behavior. We recognize that we have blurred somewhat the traditional distinctions among structural, strategic, and systems approaches to marital and family therapy. It is not our intent to minimize the significance of these distinctions; indeed, they are of considerable value in conducting meaningful outcome research and are necessary if we are to be able ultimately to successfully match the type of patient with the type of treatment.

We nevertheless believe that the commonalities of these various perspectives are more important than their differences. In particular, we would like to highlight two characteristics shared by these approaches. The first is their recognition of and attention to the critical role played by interpersonal factors in the development, maintenance, and treatment of dysfunctional behavior. Whether a structural, strategic, or systems perspective is adopted, the focus of both the conceptualization and the treatment of the disorder is clearly on the interpersonal dynamics of the system. The second characteristic common to these approaches is that they utilize strikingly similar strategies and techniques in their treatment of dysfunctional behavior. Joining, reframing, and enactment, for example, are techniques that are widely used across a number of schools of marital and family therapy. Consequently, in presenting these and other techniques, we have emphasized their appropriateness and applicability in the treatment of depression, regardless of whether the strategy was derived originally from a structural, strategic, or systems approach.

In this guidebook, we have focused on the phenomenon of depression. We have described an interpersonal systems approach to the understanding of depression and have outlined intervention strategies and procedures based on this conceptualization. Studies using procedures similar to those described in this guidebook have already reported successful results in the treatment of depression (e.g., Beach & O'Leary, 1986; Friedman, 1975; Hinchliffe et al., 1978; McLean et al., 1973). Although further empirical work is required to validate the efficacy of this particular intervention and to refine the use of the techniques presented herein, the results of these initial investigations—utilizing an interpersonal approach to the treatment of depression—are promising. We hope that this presentation has kindled in the reader a motivation not only to use the strategies described for the treatment of depression, but also to go beyond depression and attempt to conceptualize and treat other forms of dysfunctional behavior from an interpersonal systems perspective.

References

Abrahams, M.J., & Whitlock, F.A. (1969). Childhood experience and depression. *British Journal of Psychiatry, 115,* 883-888.

Abrams, R., & Taylor, M.A. (1980). The importance of mood-incongruent psychotic symptoms in melancholia. *Journal of Affective Disorders, 25,* 179-181.

Abramson, L.Y., Seligman, M.E.P., & Teasdale, J.D. (1978). Learned helplessness in humans: Critique and reformulation. *Journal of Abnormal Psychology, 87,* 49-74.

Ackerman, N.W. (1958). *The psychodynamics of family life: Diagnosis and treatment of family relationships.* New York: Basic Books.

American Psychiatric Association. (1980). *Diagnostic and statistical manual of mental disorders (3rd ed.).* Washington, DC: Author.

Aneshensel, C.S., Frerichs, R.R., & Clark, V.A. (1981). Family roles and sex differences in depression. *Journal of Health and Social Behavior, 22,* 379-393.

Arkowitz, H., Holliday, S., & Hutter, M. (1982). *Depressed women and their husbands: A study of marital interaction and adjustment.* Paper presented at the annual meeting of the Association for Advancement of Behavior Therapy, Los Angeles, CA.

Arthur, J.A., Hops, H., & Biglan, A. (1982). *LIFE (Living in familial environments) coding system.* Unpublished manuscript, Oregon Research Institute, Eugene, OR.

Beach, S.R.H., & O'Leary, K.D. (1986). The treatment of depression occurring in the context of marital discord. *Behavior Therapy, 17,* 43-49.

Beck, A.T. (1967). *Depression: Causes and treatments.* Philadelphia: University of Pennsylvania Press.

Beck, A.T., Rush, A.J., Shaw, B.F., & Emery, G. (1979). *Cognitive therapy of depression.* New York: Guilford Press.

Beck, A.T., Ward, C.H., Mendelson, M., Mock, J., & Erbaugh, J. (1961). An inventory for measuring depression. *Archives of General Psychiatry, 4,* 561-571.

Benjaminsen, S. (1981). Primary nonendogenous depression and features attributed to reactive depression. *Journal of Affective Disorders, 3,* 245-259.

Bergner, R.M. (1977). The marital system of the hysterical individual. *Family Process, 16,* 85-95.

Biglan, A., Hops, H., Sherman, L., Friedman, L.S., Arthur, J., & Osteen, V. (1985). Problem-solving interactions of depressed women and their husbands. *Behavior Therapy, 16,* 431-451.

Billings, A.B., Kessler, M., Gomberg, C., & Weiner, S. (1979). Marital conflict resolutions of alcoholic and nonalcoholic couples during drinking and nondrinking sessions. *Journal of Studies on Alcohol, 40,* 183-195.

Binger, C.M. (1984). Psychosocial intervention with the child cancer patient and family. *Psychosomatics, 25,* 899-902.

Birchler, G.R., Weiss, R.L., & Vincent, J.P. (1975). Multimethod analysis of social reinforcement exchange between maritally distressed and nondistressed spouse and stranger dyads. *Journal of Personality and Social Psychology, 31,* 349-360.

Bothwell, S., & Weissman, M. (1977). Social impairments four years after an acute depressive episode. *American Journal of Orthopsychiatry, 47*, 231-237.

Bowen, M. (1981). Theory in the practice of psychotherapy. In G. Berenson & H. White (Eds.), *Annual review of family therapy, Vol. 1.* New York: Human Sciences Press.

Boyer, J.L., & Guthrie, L. (1985). Assessment and treatment of the suicidal patient. In E.E. Beckham & W.R. Leber (Eds.), *Handbook of depression: Treatment, assessment, and research* (pp. 606-633). Homewood, IL: The Dorsey Press.

Bradburn, N.M. (1975). The measurement of psychological well-being. In J. Elinson (Ed.), *Health goals and health indicators* (pp. 84-94). Washington: American Association for the Advancement of Science.

Braverman, S. (1980). Family therapist: Technician or clinician? *Canadian Journal of Psychiatry, 25*, 666-670.

Brown, F. (1961). Depression and childhood bereavement. *Journal of Mental Science, 107*, 754-777.

Brown, G.W., & Harris, T. (1978). *Social origins of depression.* New York: Free Press.

Brumback, R.A., Dietz-Schmidt, S.G., & Weinberg, W.A. (1977). Depression in children referred to an educational diagnostic center: Diagnosis and treatment and analysis of criteria and literature review. *Diseases of the Nervous System, 38*, 529-535.

Carroll, B.J., Feinberg, J.M., Smouse, P.E., Rawson, S.G., & Greden, J.F. (1981). The Carroll Rating Scale for Depression: I. Development, reliability and validation. *British Journal of Psychiatry, 138*, 194-200.

Cautela, J.R. (1977). *Behavior analysis forms for clinical intervention.* Champaign, IL: Research Press Co.

Clark, J., Capel, W.C., Goldsmith, B.M., & Stewart, G.T. (1972). Marriage and methadone: Spouse behavior patterns in heroin addicts maintained on methadone. *Journal of Marriage and the Family, 34*, 496-501.

Cloninger, C.R., Christiansen, K.O., Reich, T., and Gottesman, I. (1978). Implications of sex differences in the prevalence of antisocial personality, alcoholism, and criminality for familial transmission. *Archives of General Psychiatry, 35*, 941-951.

Cohen, M.B., Baker, G., Cohen, R.A., Fromm-Reichman, F., & Weigart, E.V. (1954). An intensive study of twelve cases of manic-depressive psychosis. *Psychiatry, 17*, 103-137.

Collins, J., Kreitman, N., Nelson, B., & Troop, J. (1971). Neurosis and marital interaction. III. Family roles and functions. *British Journal of Psychiatry, 119*, 233-242.

Coyne, J.C. (1976a). Depression and the response of others. *Journal of Abnormal Psychology, 85*, 186-193.

Coyne, J.C. (1976b). Toward an interactional description of depression. *Psychiatry, 39*, 28-40.

Coyne, J.C., & Gotlib, I.H. (1983). The role of cognition in depression: A critical appraisal. *Psychological Bulletin, 94*, 472-505.

Coyne, J.C., & Gotlib, I.H. (1986). *Depression and parenthood: An integrative review.* Unpublished manuscript.

Coyne, J.C., & Gotlib, I.H. (in press). Studying the role of cognition in depression: Well-trodden paths and cul-de-sacs. *Cognitive Therapy and Research.*

Coyne, J.C., Kahn, J., & Gotlib, I.H. (in press). Depression. In T. Jacob (Ed.), *Family interaction and psychopathology.* New York: Plenum.

Coyne, J.C., & Segal, L. (1982). A brief, strategic interactional approach to psychotherapy. In J.C. Anchin & D.J. Kiesler (Eds.), *Handbook of interpersonal psychotherapy* (pp. 248-261). New York: Pergamon Press.

Croog, S.H., & Fitzgerald, E.F. (1978). Subjective stress and serious illness in a spouse: Wives of heart patients. *Journal of Health and Social Behavior, 19*, 166-178.

Crook, T., & Eliot, J. (1980). Parental death during childhood and adult depression: A critical review of the literature. *Psychological Bulletin, 87*, 252-259.

Crowther, J.H. (1985). The relationship between depression and marital maladjustment: A descriptive study. *Journal of Nervous and Mental Disease, 173*, 227-231.

Dalton, P. (1983). Family treatment of an obsessive-compulsive child: A case report. *Family Process, 22,* 99-108.

DeLongis, A., Coyne, J.C., Dakof, G., Folkman, S., & Lazarus, R.S. (1982). Relationship of daily hassles, uplifts, and major life events to health status. *Health Psychology, 1,* 119-136.

Dempsey, P.A. (1964). Unidimensional depression scale for the MMPI. *Journal of Consulting Psychology, 28,* 364-370.

Digdon, N., & Gotlib, I.H. (1985). Developmental considerations in the study of childhood depression. *Developmental Review, 5,* 162-199.

Dobson, K.S., & Joffe, R. (1986). The role of activity level and cognition in depressed mood in a university sample. *Journal of Clinical Psychology, 42,* 264-271.

Dysinger, R.H. (1961). A family perspective on the diagnosis of individual members. *American Journal of Orthopsychiatry, 31,* 61-68.

Endicott, J., Cohen, J., Nee, J., Fleiss, J., & Sarantakos, S. (1981). Hamilton Depression Rating Scale, extracted from regular and change versions of the Schedule for Affective Disorders and Schizophrenia. *Archives of General Psychiatry, 38,* 98-103.

Endicott, J., & Spitzer, R.L. (1978). A diagnostic interview: The Schedule for Affective Disorders and Schizophrenia. *Archives of General Psychiatry, 35,* 837-844.

Epstein, N.B., Bishop, D.S., & Levin, S. (1978). The McMaster model of family functioning. *Journal of Marriage and Family Counseling, 4,* 19-31.

Feldman, L.B. (1985). Integrative multi-level therapy: A comprehensive interpersonal and intrapsychic approach. *Journal of Marital and Family Therapy, 11,* 357-372.

Finney, J.W., Moos, R.H., Cronkite, R.C., & Gamble, W. (1983). A conceptual model of the functioning of married persons with impaired partners: Spouses of alcoholic patients. *Journal of Marriage and the Family, 45,* 23-34.

Friedman, A.S. (1975). Interaction of drug therapy with marital therapy in depressive patients. *Archives of General Psychiatry, 32,* 619-637.

Frommer, E.A., & O'Shea, G. (1973). Antenatal identification of women liable to have problems in managing their infants. *British Journal of Psychiatry, 123,* 149-156.

Garfinkel, P.E., Garner, D.M., Rose, J., Barby, P.L., Brandes, J.S., O'Hanlon, J., & Walsh, N. (1983). A comparison of characteristics in the families of patients with anorexia nervosa and normal controls. *Psychological Medicine, 13,* 821-828.

Gibson, R.W. (1957). *Comparison of the family background and early life experience of the manic-depressive and schizophrenic patient.* Final Report on Office of Naval Research Contract (Nonr-751(00)). Washington, DC: Washington School of Psychiatry.

Glick, I.D., & Kessler, D.R. (1980). *Marital and family therapy* (2nd ed.). New York: Grune & Stratton.

Gotlib, I.H. (1982). Self-reinforcement and depression in interpersonal interaction: The role of performance level. *Journal of Abnormal Psychology, 91,* 3-13.

Gotlib, I.H. (1983). Perception and recall of interpersonal feedback: Negative bias in depression. *Cognitive Therapy and Research, 7,* 399-412.

Gotlib, I.H. (1986). *Depression and marital interaction: A longitudinal perspective.* Presented at the Third International Conference on Personal Relationships, Tel Aviv, Israel.

Gotlib, I.H., & Asarnow, R.F. (1979). Interpersonal and impersonal problem-solving skills in mildly and clinically depressed university students. *Journal of Consulting and Clinical Psychology, 47,* 86-95.

Gotlib, I.H., & Beatty, M.E. (1985). Negative responses to depression: The role of attributional style. *Cognitive Therapy and Research, 9,* 91-103.

Gotlib, I.H., & Cane, D.B. (1986). *Construct accessibility and clinical depression: A longitudinal approach.* Unpublished manuscript.

Gotlib, I.H., & Hooley, J.M. (in press). Marital relationships and depression. In S. Duck (Ed.), *Handbook of Personal Relationships: Theory, research and interventions.* New York: John Wiley.

Gotlib, I.H., & McCann, C.D. (1984). Construct accessibility and depression: An examination of cognitive and affective factors. *Journal of Personality and Social Psychology, 47*, 427-439.

Gotlib, I.H., & Meltzer, S.J. (in press). Depression and the perception of social skill. *Cognitive Therapy and Research.*

Gotlib, I.H., & Robinson, L.A. (1982). Responses to depressed individuals: Discrepancies between self-report and observer-rated behaviour. *Journal of Abnormal Psychology, 91*, 231-240.

Gottman, J.M. (1979). *Marital interaction: Experimental investigations.* New York: Academic Press.

Gottman, J.M., & Lieblum, S.R. (1973). *How to do psychotherapy and how to evaluate it.* New York: Holt, Rinehart and Winston.

Gove, W.R., & Geerkin, M.R. (1977). Response bias in surveys of mental health: An empirical investigation. *American Journal of Sociology, 82*, 1289-1317.

Gove, W.R., Hughes, M., & Briggs Style, C. (1983). Does marriage have positive effects on the psychological well-being of the individual? *Journal of Health and Social Behavior, 24*, 122-131.

Gove, W.R., & Tudor, J.F. (1973). Adult sex roles and mental illness. *American Journal of Sociology, 78*, 51-73.

Haas, G.L., Clarkin, J.F., & Glick, I.D. (1985). Marital and family treatment of depression. In E.E. Beckham & W.R. Leber (Eds.), *Handbook of depression: Treatment, assessment, and research* (pp. 151-183). Homewood, IL: The Dorsey Press.

Hafner, J., Badenoch, A., Fisher, J., & Swift, B. (1983). Spouse-aided versus individual therapy in persisting psychiatric disorders: A systematic comparison. *Family Process, 22*, 385-399.

Haggerty, J.J. (1983). The psychosomatic family: An overview. *Psychosomatics, 24*, 615-623.

Haley, J. (1976). *Problem-solving therapy: New strategies for effective family therapy.* San Francisco: Jossey-Bass.

Hamilton, M. (1960). A rating scale for depression. *Journal of Neurology, Neurosurgery and Psychiatry, 12*, 56-62.

Hammen, C.L. (1981). Assessment: A clinical and cognitive emphasis. In L.P. Rehm (Ed.), *Behavior therapy for depression: Present status and future directions.* New York: Academic Press.

Hautzinger, M., Linden, M., & Hoffman, N. (1982). Distressed couples with and without a depressed partner: An analysis of their verbal interaction. *Journal of Behavior Therapy and Experimental Psychiatry, 13*, 307-314.

Helms, P.M., & Smith, R.E. (1983). Recurrent psychotic depression: Evidence of diagnostic stability. *Journal of Affective Disorders, 5*, 51-54.

Henderson, S., Byrne, D.G., & Duncan-Jones, P. (1981). *Neurosis and the social environment.* New York: Academic Press.

Hersen, M., Bellack, A.S., Himmelhoch, J.M., & Thase, M.E. (1984). Effects of social skill training, amitriptyline, and psychotherapy in unipolar depressed women. *Behavior Therapy, 15*, 21-40.

Hinchliffe, M., Hooper, D., & Roberts, F.J. (1978). *The melancholy marriage.* New York: John Wiley.

Hodges, K., Kline, J., Stern, L., Cytryn, L., & McKnew, D. (1982). The development of a child assessment interview for research and clinical use. *Journal of Abnormal Child Psychology, 10*, 173-189.

Hoffman, L. (1981). *Foundations of family therapy: A conceptual framework for systems change.* New York: Basic Books.

Hops, H., Wills, T., Patterson, G.R., & Weiss, R.L. (1972). *Marital interaction coding system (MICS).* Eugene, OR: University of Oregon and Oregon Research Institute (NAPS Document #02077).

Howes, M.J., & Hokanson, J.E. (1979). Conversational and social responses to depressive interpersonal behavior. *Journal of Abnormal Psychology, 88*, 625-634.

Jacob, T., Dunn, N.J., & Leonard, K. (1983). Patterns of alcohol abuse and family stability. *Alcoholism: Clinical and Experimental Research, 7*, 382-385.

Jacobson, N.S., Follette, W.C., & Revenstorf, D. (1984). Psychotherapy outcome research: Methods for reporting variability and evaluating clinical significance. *Behavior Therapy, 15,* 336-352.

Jacobson, S., Fasman, J., & DiMascio, A. (1975). Deprivation in the childhood of depressed women. *Journal of Nervous and Mental Diseases, 166,* 5-16.

Kahn, J., Coyne, J.C., & Margolin, G. (1985). Depression and marital disagreement: The social construction of despair. *Journal of Social and Personal Relationships, 2,* 447-461.

Karpel, M.A., & Strauss, E.S. (1983). *Family evaluation.* New York: Gardner Press.

Kaufman, E., & Pattison, M. (1981). Differential methods of family therapy in the treatment of alcoholism. *Journal of Studies on Alcohol, 42,* 951-971.

Kiesler, D.J. (1975/1984). *Research manual for the Impact Message Inventory.* Richmond, Virginia: Virginia Commonwealth University.

Klerman, G.L., Weissman, M.M., Rounsaville, B.J., & Chevron, E. (1984). *Interpersonal psychotherapy of depression.* New York: Basic Books.

Kovacs, M. (1983). *The Interview Schedule for Children (ISC): Interrater and parent-child agreement.* Unpublished manuscript.

Kowalik, D.L., & Gotlib, I.H. (in press). Depression and marital interaction: Concordance between intent and perception of communication. *Journal of Abnormal Psychology.*

Leber, W.R., Beckham, E.E., & Danker-Brown, P. Diagnostic criteria for depression. In E.E. Beckham & W.R. Leber (Eds.), *Handbook of depression: Treatment, assessment, and research* (pp. 343-371). Homewood, IL: The Dorsey Press.

Lehmann, H.E. (1971). Epidemiology of depressive disorders. In R.R. Fieve (Ed.), *Depression in the 70's: Modern theory and research.* Princeton, NJ: Excerpta Medica.

Lehmann, L. (1985). The relationship of depression to other DSM-III Axis I disorders. In E.E. Beckham & W.R. Leber (Eds.), *Handbook of depression: Treatment, assessment, and research* (pp. 669-699). Homewood, IL: The Dorsey Press.

Lewinsohn, P.M. (1974). A behavioral approach to depression. In R.J. Friedman & M.M. Katz (Eds.), *The psychology of depression: Contemporary theory and research* (pp. 157-178). Washington, DC.: V.H. Winston.

Lewinsohn, P.M., & Atwood, G.E. (1969). Depression: A clinical research approach. *Psychotherapy: Theory, Research, and Practice, 6,* 166-171.

Lewinsohn, P.M., Biglan, A., & Zeiss, A.M. (1976). Behavioral treatment of depression. In P.O. Davidson (Ed.), *The behavioral management of anxiety, depression and pain.* New York: Brunner/Mazel.

Lewinsohn, P.M., Lobitz, W.C., & Wilson, S. (1973). "Sensitivity" of depressed individuals to aversive stimuli. *Journal of Abnormal Psychology, 81,* 259-263.

Lewinsohn, P.M., & Schaffer, M. (1971). The use of home observations as an integral part of the treatment of depression: Preliminary report of case studies. *Journal of Consulting and Clinical Psychology, 37,* 87-94.

Lewinsohn, P.M., & Teri, L. (1982). Selection of depressed and nondepressed subjects on the basis of self-report data. *Journal of Consulting and Clinical Psychology, 50,* 590-591.

Liebman, R., Minuchin, S., & Baker, L. (1974). An integrated treatment program for anorexia nervosa. *American Journal of Psychiatry, 131,* 432-435.

Lloyd, C. (1980). Life events and depressive disorder reviewed. I. Events as predisposing factors. *Archives of General Psychiatry, 37,* 529-535.

Locke, H.J., & Wallace, K.M. (1959). Short marital-adjustment and prediction tests: Their reliability and validity. *Marriage and Family Living, 21,* 251-255.

MacPhillamy, D.J., & Lewinsohn, P.M. (1982). The Pleasant Events Schedule: Studies on reliability, validity and scale intercorrelations. *Journal of Consulting and Clinical Psychology, 50,* 363-380.

Martindale, B., & Bottomley, V. (1980). The management of families with Huntington's chorea. A case study to illustrate some recommendations. *Journal of Child Psychology and Psychiatry and Allied Disciplines, 21,* 343-351.

McLean, P.D., & Hakstian, A.R. (1979). Clinical depression: Comparative efficacy of outpatient treatments. *Journal of Clinical and Consulting Psychology 47*, 818-836.

McLean, P.D., Ogston, L., & Grauer, L. (1973). Behavioral approach to the treatment of depression. *Journal of Behaviour Therapy and Experimental Psychiatry, 4*, 323-330.

Merikangas, K.R. (1984). Divorce and assortative mating among depressed patients. *American Journal of Psychiatry, 141*, 74-76.

Merikangas, K.R., Ranelli, C., & Kupfer, D. (1979). Marital interaction in hospitalized depressed patients. *Journal of Nervous and Mental Disease, 167*, 689-695.

Merikangas, K.R., Weissman, M.M., & Pauls, D.L. (1985). Genetic factors in the sex ratio of major depression. *Psychological Medicine, 15*, 63-69.

Miller, I.W., Bishop, S., Norman, W.H., & Maddever, H. (1985). The Modified Hamilton Rating Scale for Depression: Reliability and validity. *Psychiatry Research, 14*, 131-142.

Miller, I.W., Epstein, N.B., Bishop, D.S., & Keitner, G.I. (1985). The McMaster Family Assessment Device: Reliability and validity. *Journal of Marital and Family Therapy, 11*, 345-356.

Minuchin, S., & Fisman, C. (1981). *Family therapy techniques.* Cambridge, MA: Harvard University Press.

Minuchin, S., Rosman, B.L., & Baker, L. (1978). *Psychosomatic families: Anorexia nervosa in context.* Cambridge, MA: Harvard University Press.

Mitchell, R.E., Cronkite, R.C., & Moos, R.H. (1983). Stress, coping and depression among married couples. *Journal of Abnormal Psychology, 92*, 443-448.

Monroe, S.M., Imhoff, D.F., Wise, B.D., & Harris, J.E. (1983). Prediction of psychological symptoms under high-risk psychosocial circumstances: Life events, social support, and symptom specificity. *Journal of Abnormal Psychology, 92*, 338-350.

Moos, R.H., & Fuhr, R. (1982). The clinical use of social-ecological concepts: The case of an adolescent girl. *American Journal of Orthopsychiatry, 52*, 111-122.

Moos, R., & Moos, B. (1981). *Family Environment Scale Manual.* Palo Alto, CA: Consulting Psychologists Press.

Munro, A. (1966). Some familial and social factors in depressive illness. *British Journal of Psychiatry, 112*, 429-441.

Nelson, G. (1982). Parental death during childhood and adult depression: Some additional data. *Social Psychiatry, 17*, 37-42.

Nuckolls, K.B., Cassel, J., & Kaplan, B.H. (1972). Psychosocial assets, life crisis, and the prognosis of pregnancy. *American Journal of Epidemiology, 95*, 431-441.

O'Connor, J.J. (1984). The resurrection of a magical reality: Treatment of functional migraine in a child. *Family Process, 23*, 501-509.

O'Hara, M.W. (1986). Social support, life events, and depression during pregnancy and the puerperium. *Archives of General Psychiatry, 43*, 569-573.

Olson, D.H., Bell, R., & Portner, J. (1978/1983). *FACES Item Booklet.* St. Paul, MN: Family Social Science, University of Minnesota.

Olson, D.H., Sprenkle, D.H., & Russell, C.S. (1979). Circumplex model of marital and family systems: I. Cohesion and adaptability dimensions, family types, and clinical applications. *Family Process, 18*, 3-28.

Papp, P. (1981). Paradoxes. In S. Minuchin & C. Fisman (Eds.). *Family therapy techniques.* Cambridge, MA: Harvard University Press.

Parker, G. (1981). Parental reports of depressives: An investigation of several explanations. *Journal of Affective Disorders, 3*, 131-140.

Paykel, E.S., Emms, E.M., Fletcher, J., & Rassaby, E.S. (1980). Life events and social support in puerperal depression. *British Journal of Psychiatry, 136*, 339-346.

Paykel, E.S., Myers, J.K., Dienelt, M.N., Klerman, G.L., Lindenthal, J.J., & Pepper, M.P. (1969). Life events and depression: A controlled study. *Archives of General Psychiatry, 21*, 753-760.

Paykel, E.S., & Tanner, L. (1976). Life events, defensive relapse, and maintenance treatment. *Psychological Medicine, 6*, 481-485.

Pearlin, L.I., Lieberman, M.A., Menaghan, E.G., & Mullan, J.T. (1981). The stress process. *Journal of Health and Social Behavior, 22,* 337-356.

Petty, F., & Nasrallah, H.A. (1981). Secondary depression in alcoholism: Implications for future research. *Comprehensive Psychiatry, 22,* 587-595.

Phipps, E., & Desplat, P. (1984). The intertwining of the family system in Huntington's disease. *Family Systems Medicine, 1,* 298-308.

Pokorny, A.D. (1964). Suicide rates in various psychiatric disorders. *Journal of Nervous and Mental Diseases, 139,* 499-506.

Protinsky, H., & Kersey, B. (1983). Psychogenic encopresis: A family therapy approach. *Journal of Clinical Child Psychology, 12,* 192-197.

Prusoff, B.A., Weissman, M.M., Klerman, G.L., & Rounsaville, B.J. (1980). Research diagnostic criteria subtypes of depression. *Archives of General Psychiatry, 38,* 902-907.

Puig-Antich, J., Blau, S., Marx, N., Greenhill, L.L., & Chambers, W. (1978). Prepubertal major depressive disorders: A pilot study. *Journal of the American Academy of Child Psychiatry, 17,* 695-707.

Radloff, L.S. (1975). Sex differences in depression: The effects of occupation and marital status. *Sex Roles, 1,* 249-265.

Radloff, L.S. (1977). The CES-D Scale: A self-report depression scale for research in the general population. *Applied Psychological Measurement, 1,* 385-401.

Raskin, A., Boothe, H.H., Reatig, N.A., Schulterbrandt, J.G., & Odle, D. (1971). Factor analyses of normal and depressed patients' memories of parental behavior. *Psychological Reports, 29,* 871-879.

Rehm, L.P. (1976). Assessment of depression. In M. Hersen & A.S. Bellack (Eds.), *Behavioral assessment: A practical handbook.* New York: Pergamon Press.

Renne, K.S. (1971). Health and marital experience in an urban population. *Journal of Marriage and the Family, 33,* 338-350.

Richman, J. (1979). The family therapy of attempted suicide. *Family Process, 18,* 131-142.

Robins, E., & Guze, S.B. (1972). Classification of affective disorders: The primary-secondary, the endogenous-reactive, and the neurotic-psychotic concept. In T.A. Williams, M.M. Katz, & J.A. Shield (Eds.), *Recent advances in the psychobiology of the depressive illnesses* (DHEW Publication No. [HSM] 79-9053). Washington, DC: U.S. Government Printing Office.

Rounsaville, B.J., Weissman, M.M., Prusoff, B.A., & Herceg-Baron, R.L. (1979). Marital disputes and treatment outcomes in depressed women. *Comprehensive Psychiatry, 20,* 483-489.

Rush, A.J., Shaw, B.F., & Khatami, M. (1980). Cognitive therapy for depression: Utilizing the couples system. *Cognitive Therapy and Research, 4,* 103-113.

Sager, C.J., Gundlach, R., & Kremer, M. (1968). The married in treatment. *Archives of General Psychiatry, 19,* 205-217.

Sargent, J. (1983). The family and childhood psychosomatic disorders. *General Hospital Psychiatry, 5,* 41-48.

Sartorius, N. (1979). Research on affective psychoses within the framework of the WHO programme. In M. Schon & E. Stromgren (Eds.), *Origin, prevention and treatment of affective disorders.* London: Academic Press.

Schilson, E.A., & Van Valkenburg, M. (1984). Childhood obesity: A family systems perspective. *Family Therapy, 11,* 105-113.

Schless, A.P., Schwartz, L., Goetz, C., & Mendels, J. (1974). How depressives view the significance of life events. *British Journal of Psychiatry, 125,* 406-410.

Schwoeri, L., & Schwoeri, F. (1982). Interactional and intrapsychic dynamics in a family with a borderline patient. *Psychotherapy: Theory, Research and Practice, 19,* 198-204.

Seagraves, R.T. (1982). *Marital therapy: A combined psychodynamic-behavioral approach.* New York: Plenum.

Secunda, S.K., Katz, M.M, Friedman, R.J., & Schuyler, D. (1973). *Special Report 1973: The depressive disorders.* Washington, DC: U.S. Government Printing Office.

Simon, R. (1984). Hemophilia and the family system. *Psychosomatics, 25,* 845-849.

Sinaikin, P.M. (1985). A clinically relevant guide to the differential diagnosis of depression. *Journal of Nervous and Mental Disease, 173,* 199-211.

Smith, M.T., Smith, M.P., & L'Abate, L. (1985). Systems interventions with hyperactive children: An interdisciplinary perspective. In L. L'Abate (Ed.), *The handbook of family psychology and therapy* (pp. 1152-1178). Homewood, IL: The Dorsey Press.

Sourkes, B. (1977). Facilitating family coping with childhood cancer. *Journal of Pediatric Psychology, 2,* 65-67.

Spanier, G.B. (1976). Measuring dyadic adjustment: New scales for assessing the quality of marriage and similar dyads. *Journal of Marriage and the Family, 38,* 15-28.

Spitzer, R.L., Endicott, J., & Robins, E. (1980). *Research diagnostic criteria for a selected group of functional disorders.* New York: Biometric Research Unit, New York Psychiatric Institute.

Stanton, M.D. (1979). Family treatment approaches to drug abuse problems: A review. *Family Process, 18,* 251-280.

Stewart, S., & Johansen, R. (1976/77). A family systems approach to home dialysis. *Psychotherapy and Psychosomatics, 27,* 86-92.

Strack, S., & Coyne, J.C. (1983). Social confirmation of dysphoria: Shared and private reactions to depression. *Journal of Personality and Social Psychology, 44,* 798-806.

Temoche, A., Pugh, T.F., & MacMahon, B. (1964). Suicide rates among current and former mental institution patients. *Journal of Nervous and Mental Diseases, 136,* 124-130.

Tennant, C., Bebbington, P., & Hurry, J. (1980). Parental death in childhood and risk of adult depressive disorder: A review. *Psychological Medicine, 10,* 289-299.

Teuting, P., Koslow, S.H., & Hirschfeld, R.M.A. (1981). *Special report on depression research.* Rockville, MD: National Institute of Mental Health.

Tiller, J. (1978). Brief family therapy for Childhood Tic Syndrome. *Family Process, 17,* 217-223.

Tisher, M., & Lang, M. (1983). The children's depression scale: Review and further developments. In D.P. Cantwell & G.A. Carlson (Eds.), *Affective disorders in childhood and adolescence: An update.* New York: Spectrum Publications.

Usher, M., Jay, J., & Glass, D. (1982). Family therapy as a treatment modality for alcoholism. *Journal of Studies on Alcohol, 43,* 927-938.

Vaughn, C.E., & Leff, J.P. (1976). The influence of family and social factors on the course of psychiatric illness: A comparison of schizophrenic and depressed neurotic patients. *British Journal of Psychiatry, 129,* 125-137.

von Bertalanffy, L. (1950). An outline of general systems theory. *British Journal of the Philosophy of Science, 1,* 134-165.

von Bertalanffy, L. (1968). *General systems theory.* New York: Braziller.

Waldron, S., Shrier, D.K., Stone, B., & Tobin, F. (1975). School phobia and other childhood neuroses: A systematic study of the children and their families. *American Journal of Psychiatry, 132,* 802-808.

Waldron-Skinner, S. (1978). Indications and contra-indications for the use of family therapy. *Journal of Child Psychology and Psychiatry, 19,* 57-62.

Watzlawick, P., Weakland, J., & Fisch, R. (1974). *Change: Principles of problem formation and problem resolution.* New York: Norton.

Waxler, N. (1975). The normality of deviance: An alternate explanation of schizophrenia in the family. *Schizophrenia Bulletin, 14,* 38-47.

Weiss, R.L., Hops, H., & Patterson, G.R. (1973). A framework for conceptualizing marital conflict, technology for altering it, some data for evaluating it. In L.A. Hamerlynck, L.C. Handy, & E.J. Mash (Eds.), *Behavior change: Methodology, concepts, and practice.* Champaign, IL: Research Press.

Weissman, M.M. (1979). The psychological treatment of depression. *Archives of General Psychiatry, 36,* 1261-1269.

Weissman, M.M., & Boyd, J.H. (1983). The epidemiology of affective disorders: Rates and risk factors. In L. Grinspoon (Ed.), *Psychiatry update, Vol. II.* Washington, DC: American Psychiatric Press.

Weissman, M.M., & Klerman, G.L. (1973). Psychotherapy with depressed women: An empirical study of content themes and reflection. *British Journal of Psychiatry, 123,* 55-61.

Weissman, M.M., & Klerman, G.L. (1977). Sex differences in the epidemiology of depression. *Archives of General Psychiatry, 34,* 98-111.

Weissman, M. M., Myers, J.K., & Harding, P.S. (1978). Psychiatric disorders in a U.S. urban community: 1975-1976. *American Journal of Psychiatry, 135,* 259-462.

Weissman, M. M., Myers, J.K., & Thompson, W.D. (1981). Depression and its treatment in a U.S. urban community. *Archives of General Psychiatry, 38,* 417-421.

Weissman, M.M., & Paykel, E.S. (1974). *The depressed woman: A study of social relationships.* Chicago: University of Chicago Press.

Weisz, G., & Bucher, B. (1980). Involving husbands in treatment of obesity: Effects on weight loss, depression, and marital satisfaction. *Behavior Therapy, 11,* 643-650.

Wendorf, R.J. (1984). Family therapy with an enuretic, encopretic child. *Family Systems Medicine, 2,* 46-52.

Wetzel, J.W., & Redmond, F.C. (1980). A person-environment study of depression. *Social Service Review, 54,* 363-375.

White, M. (1979). Structural and strategic approaches to psychosomatic families. *Family Process, 18,* 303-314.

Wiggins, J.S. (1982). Circumplex models of interpersonal behavior in clinical psychology. In P.C. Kendall & J.N. Butcher (Eds.), *Handbook of research methods in clinical psychology.* New York: John Wiley.

Zung, W. (1965). A self-rating depression scale. *Archives of General Psychiatry, 12,* 63-70.

Author Index

Abrahams, M.J., 11, 13, 171
Abrams, R., 7, 171
Abramson, L.Y., 32, 171
Ackerman, N.W., 84, 171
Aneshensel, C.S., 9, 171
Arkowitz, H., 19, 60, 171
Arthur, J.A., 89, 171
Asarnow, R.F., 16, 173
Atwood, G.E., 20, 175

Badenoch, A., 167, 174
Baker, G., 12, 172
Baker, L., 168, 175, 176
Barby, P.L., 173
Beach, S.R.H., 20, 170, 171
Beatty, M.E., 17, 173
Bebbington, P., 11, 178
Beck, A., 14, 32, 60, 74, 171
Beckham, E.E., 7, 175
Bell, R., 86, 176
Bellack, A.S., 63, 174
Benjaminsen, S., 7, 171
Bergner, R.M., 167, 171
Biglan, A., 16, 18, 19, 59, 60, 89, 171, 175
Billings, A.B., 169, 171
Binger, C.M., 169, 171
Birchler, G.R., 88, 171
Bishop, D.S., 78, 87, 173, 176
Blau, S., 13, 176
Boothe, H.H., 12, 177
Bothwell, S., 21, 63, 172
Bottomley, V., 169, 175

Bowen, M., 26, 172
Boyd, J.H., 8, 179
Boyer, J.L., 83, 172
Bradburn, N.M., 8, 172
Brandes, J.S., 173
Braverman, S., 83, 172
Briggs Style, C., 9, 174
Brown, F., 11, 172
Brown, G.W., 10, 15, 17, 172
Brumback, R.A., 13, 172
Bucher, B., 167, 179
Byrne, D.G., 15, 174

Cane, D.B., 35, 173
Capel, W.C., 32, 172
Carroll, B.J., 73, 172
Cassel, J., 15, 176
Cautela, J.R., 60, 172
Chambers, W., 13, 177
Chevron, E., 31, 63, 78, 175
Christiansen, K.O., 9, 172
Clark, J., 32, 172
Clark, V.A., 9, 171
Clarkin, J.F., 82, 174
Cloninger, C.R., 9, 172
Cohen, J., 73, 173
Cohen, M.B., 12, 172
Cohen, R.A., 12, 172
Collins, J., 10, 172
Coyne, J.C., 14, 15, 16, 17, 19, 32, 33, 35, 68, 86, 93, 136, 172, 173, 175, 178
Cronkite, R.C., 86, 169, 173, 176
Croog, S.H., 169, 172

181

Crook, T., 11, 172
Crowther, J.H., 17, 172
Cytryn, L., 73, 174

Dakof, G., 15, 173
Dalton, P., 168, 173
Danker-Brown, P., 7, 175
DeLongis, A., 15, 173
Dempsey, P.A., 75, 173
Desplat, P., 169, 177
Dienelt, M.N., 176
Dietz-Schmidt, S.G., 13, 172
Digdon, N., 2, 13, 173
DiMascio, A., 11, 175
Dobson, K.S., 59, 173
Duncan-Jones, P., 15, 174
Dunn, N.J., 169, 174
Dysinger, R.H., 168, 173

Eliot, J., 11, 172
Emery, G., 14, 60, 171
Emms, E.M., 14, 176
Endicott, J., 72, 73, 81, 82, 173, 178
Epstein, N.B., 87, 173, 176
Erbaugh, J., 74, 171

Fasman, J., 11, 175
Feinberg, J.M., 73, 172
Feldman, L.B., 31, 32, 173
Finney, J.W., 169, 173
Fisch, R., 27, 178
Fisher, J., 167, 174
Fisman, C., 49, 176
Fitzgerald, E.F., 169, 172
Fleiss, J., 73, 173
Fletcher, J., 14, 176
Folkman, S., 15, 173
Follette, W.C., 95, 175
Frerichs, R.R., 9, 171
Friedman, A.S., 20, 82, 170, 173
Friedman, R.J., ix, 177
Fromm-Reichmann, F., 12, 172
Frommer, E.A., 11, 173
Fuhr, R., 86, 176

Gamble, W., 169, 173
Garfinkel, P.E., 32, 173

Garner, D.M., 173
Geerkin, M.R., 9, 174
Gibson, R.W., 12, 173
Glass, D., 169, 178
Glick, I.D., 82, 166, 167, 173, 174
Goetz, C., 17, 177
Goldsmith, B.M., 32, 172
Gomberg, C., 169, 171
Gotlib, I.H., 2, 13, 14, 16, 17, 19, 32, 35, 86, 172, 173, 174, 175
Gottesman, I., 9, 172
Gottman, J.M., 32, 88, 95, 174
Gove, W.R., 9, 174
Grauer, L., 20, 176
Greden, J.F., 73, 172
Greenhill, L.L., 13, 177
Gundlach, R., 17, 177
Guthrie, L., 83, 172
Guze, S.B., 7, 177

Haas, G.L., 82, 83, 174
Hafner, J., 167, 174
Haggerty, J.J., 168, 174
Hakstian, A.R., 74, 176
Haley, J., 67, 68, 70, 92, 93, 101, 174
Hamilton, M., 72, 174
Hammen, C.L., 74, 75, 174
Harding, P.S., 1, 179
Harris, J.E., 15, 176
Harris, T., 10, 15, 17, 172
Hautzinger, M., 18, 174
Helms, P.M., 7, 174
Henderson, S., 15, 174
Herceg-Baron, R.L., 18, 177
Hersen, M., 63, 174
Himmelhoch, J.M., 63, 174
Hinchliffe, M., 18, 20, 170, 174
Hirschfeld, R.M.A., ix, 178
Hodges, K., 73, 174
Hoffman, L., 22, 174
Hoffman, N., 18, 174
Hokanson, J.E., 17, 174
Holliday, S., 19, 171
Hooley, J.M., 19, 173
Hooper, D., 18, 174
Hops, H., 85, 88, 89, 171, 174, 178
Howes, M.J., 17, 174

Hughes, M., 9, 174
Hurry, J., 11, 178
Hutter, M., 19, 171

Imhoff, D.F., 15, 176

Jacob, T., 169, 174
Jacobson, N.S., 95, 175
Jacobson, S., 11, 13, 175
Jay, J., 169, 178
Joffe, R., 59, 173
Johansen, R., 169, 178

Kahn, J., 17, 19, 86, 172, 175
Kaplan, B.H., 15, 176
Karpel, M.A., 113, 175
Katz, M.M., ix, 177
Kaufman, E., 169, 175
Keitner, G.I., 87, 176
Kersey, B., 167, 177
Kessler, D.R., 166, 167, 173
Kessler, M., 169, 171
Khatami, M., 17, 177
Kiesler, D.J., 85, 175
Klerman, G.L., 8, 21, 31, 63, 78, 81,
    175, 176, 177, 179
Kline, J., 73, 174
Koslow, S.H., ix, 178
Kovacs, M., 73, 74, 75, 175
Kowalik, D.L., 19, 175
Kreitman, N., 10, 172
Kremer, M., 17, 177
Kupfer, D., 18, 176

L'Abate, L., 167, 178
Lang, M., 75, 178
Lazarus, R.S., 15, 173
Leber, W.R., 7, 175
Leff, J.P., 17, 178
Lehmann, H.E., 1, 175
Lehmann, L., 83, 175
Leonard, K., 169, 174
Levin, S., 87, 173
Lewinsohn, P.M., 16, 19, 20, 35, 59, 60,
    74, 175
Lieberman, M.A., 15, 176
Lieblum, S.R., 95, 174

Liebman, R., 168, 175
Linden, M., 18, 174
Lindenthal, J.J., 176
Lloyd, C., 11, 175
Lobitz, W.C., 35, 175
Locke, H.J., 85, 175

MacMahon, B., 2, 178
MacPhillamy, D.J., 60, 175
Maddever, H., 78, 176
Margolin, G., 19, 86, 175
Martindale, B., 169, 175
Marx, N., 13, 177
McCann, C.D., 35, 174
McKnew, D., 73, 174
McLean, P.D., 20, 74, 170, 176
Meltzer, S.J., 17, 174
Menaghan, E.G., 15, 176
Mendels, J., 17, 177
Mendelson, M., 74, 171
Merikangas, K.R., 9, 17, 18, 176
Meyer, A., 22
Miller, I.W., 78, 87, 176
Minuchin, S., 49, 168, 175, 176
Mitchell, R.E., 86, 176
Mock, J., 74, 171
Monroe, S.M., 15, 176
Moos, B., 86, 176
Moos, R.H., 86, 169, 173, 176
Mullan, J.T., 15, 176
Munro, A., 7, 11, 176
Myers, J.K., 1, 9, 176, 179

Nasrallah, H.A., 9, 177
Nee, J., 73, 173
Nelson, B., 10, 172
Nelson, G., 11, 176
Norman, W.H., 78, 176
Nuckolls, K.B., 15, 176

O'Connor, J.J., 168, 176
O'Hanlon, J., 173
O'Hara, M.W., 14, 176
O'Leary, K.D., 20, 170, 171
O'Shea, G., 11, 173
Odle, D., 12, 177
Ogston, L., 20, 176

Olson, D.H., 26, 86, 87, 176

Papp, P., 55, 176
Parker, G., 13, 176
Patterson, G.R., 85, 88, 174, 178
Pattison, M., 169, 175
Pauls, D.L., 9, 176
Paykel, E.S., 14, 17, 18, 176, 179
Pearlin, L.I., 15, 176
Pepper, M.P., 176
Petty, F., 9, 177
Phipps, E., 169, 177
Pokorny, A.D., 2, 177
Portner, J., 86, 176
Protinsky, H., 167, 177
Prusoff, B.A., 18, 81, 177
Pugh, T.F., 2, 178
Puig-Antich, J., 13, 177

Radloff, L.S., 9, 10, 74, 177
Ranelli, C., 18, 176
Raskin, A., 12, 177
Rassaby, E.S., 14, 176
Rawson, S.G., 73, 172
Reatig, N.A., 12, 177
Redmond, F.C., 86, 179
Rehm, L.P., 75, 177
Reich, T., 9, 172
Renne, K.S., 10, 177
Revenstorf, D., 95, 175
Richman, J., 83, 177
Roberts, F.J., 18, 174
Robins, E., 7, 81, 82, 177
Robinson, L.A., 16, 17, 174, 178
Rose, J., 173
Rosman, B.L., 168, 176
Rounsaville, B.J., 18, 31, 63, 78, 81,
    175, 177
Rush, A.J., 14, 17, 20, 60, 171, 177
Russell, C.S., 26, 86, 176

Sager, C.J., 17, 177
Sarantakos, S., 73, 173
Sargent, J., 168, 177
Sartorius, N., 1, 177
Schaffer, M., 20, 175
Schilson, E.A., 168, 177

Schless, A.P., 17, 177
Schulterbrandt, J.G., 12, 177
Schuyler, D., ix, 177
Schwartz, L., 17, 177
Schwoeri, F., 167, 177
Schwoeri, L., 167, 177
Seagraves, R.T., 30, 177
Secunda, S.K., ix, 177
Segal, L., 68, 93, 136, 172
Seligman, M.E.P., 32, 171
Shaw, B.F., 14, 17, 60, 171, 177
Shrier, D.K., 32, 178
Simon, R., 169, 177
Sinaikin, P.M., 7, 178
Smith, M.P., 167, 178
Smith, M.T., 167, 178
Smith, R.E., 7, 174
Smouse, P.E., 73, 172
Sourkes, B., 169, 178
Spanier, G.B., 85, 178
Spitzer, R.L., 72, 81, 82, 173, 178
Sprenkle, D.H., 26, 86, 176
Stanton, M.D., 169, 178
Stern, L., 73, 174
Stewart, G.T., 32, 172
Stewart, S., 169, 178
Stone, B., 32, 178
Strack, S., 17, 178
Strauss, E.S., 113, 175
Sullivan, H.S., 22, 23
Swift, B., 167, 174

Tanner, L., 14, 176
Taylor, M.A., 7, 171
Teasdale, J.D., 32, 171
Temoche, A., 2, 178
Tennant, C., 11, 178
Teri, L., 74, 175
Teuting, P., ix, 178
Thase, M.E., 63, 174
Thompson, W.D., 9, 179
Tiller, J., 167, 178
Tisher, M., 75, 178
Tobin, F., 32, 178
Troop, J., 10, 172
Tudor, J.F., 9, 174

Usher, M., 169, 178

Van Valkenburg, M., 168, 177
Vaughn, C.E., 17, 178
Vincent, J.P., 88, 171
Von Bertalanffy, L., 24, 178

Waldron, S., 32, 178
Waldron-Skinner, S., 91, 178
Wallace, K.M., 85, 175
Walsh, N., 173
Ward, C.H., 74, 171
Watzlawick, P., 27, 178
Waxler, N., 166, 178
Weakland, J., 27, 178
Weigart, E.V., 12, 172
Weinberg, W.A., 13, 172

Weiner, S., 169, 171
Weiss, R.L., 85, 87, 88, 171, 174, 178
Weissman, M.M., 1, 8, 9, 10, 18, 21,
   31, 63, 64, 78, 81, 82, 172, 175, 176,
   177, 178
Weisz, G., 167, 179
Wendorf, R.J., 167, 179
Wetzel, J.W., 86, 179
White, M., 168, 179
Whitlock, F.A., 11, 13, 171
Wiggins, J.S., 85, 179
Wills, T., 88, 174
Wilson, S., 35, 175
Wise, B.D., 15, 176

Zeiss, A.M., 59, 60, 175
Zung, W., 74, 179

Subject Index

Adaptability, 26, 114
Alcohol abuse. *See* Substance abuse
Anorexia nervosa, 32, 168
Areas of Change Questionnaire, 84, 85
Assessment of depression
  assessment of symptoms, 77–81
  cautions
    alcohol/drug abuse, 83–84
    endogenous features, 81–83
    potential for suicide, 83
  determining who to assess, 63–66, 93,
    147–148, 153–154
  initial interview, 66–70, 76–81, 92–95,
    153
  interview measures
    Carroll Rating Scale for Depression,
      73
    Child Assessment Schedule, 73, 76
    Hamilton Rating Scale for
      Depression, 72–73, 76, 78
    Interview Schedule for Children,
      73–74
    Schedule for Affective Disorders and
      Schizophrenia, 72, 76, 78,
      109, 143, 153
  self–report measures
    Beck Depression Inventory, 74, 76,
      78, 109, 114, 134, 143, 146,
      149–150, 152, 153, 154, 157,
      158–159, 163–164
    Center for Epidemiological Studies
      Depression Scale, 74–75
    Child Depression Inventory, 75, 76,
      109, 110, 114, 134, 136, 143,

    149–150, 152
    MMPI-D-30, 75
    MMPI-D Scale, 75
    Zung Self–Rating Depression Scale,
      75
  utilizing the assessment data, 94–95,
    110–117, 134–136
Assessment of the marital/family system
  cautions, 91–92
  determining who to assess, 63–66, 93,
    147–148, 153–154
  direct observation measures
    Couples Interaction Scoring System,
      88
    Living in Familial Environments
      Coding System, 89
    Marital Interaction Coding System,
      88
    Spouse Observation Checklist,
      87–88
  initial interview, 66–70, 84–95
  self–report measures
    Areas of Change Questionnaire,
      84, 85
    Dyadic Adjustment Scale, 84, 85,
      109, 110, 134, 136, 143, 146,
      147, 148, 149–150, 152, 158–
      159, 163
    Family Adaptability and Cohesion
      Evaluation Scales, 84, 86–87
    Family Assessment Device, 87
    Family Environment Scale, 84, 86,
      109, 110, 111, 143–144, 146,
      154, 156

Impact Message Inventory, 84, 85–86
Marital Adjustment Test, 85
utilizing the assessment data, 94–95,
110–117, 134–136

Beck Depression Inventory, 74, 76, 78,
109, 114, 134, 143, 146, 149–150,
152, 153, 154, 157, 158–159,
163–164
Borderline personality disorders
treatment of, 167
Boundaries, 53–54, 113, 134, 150

Carroll Rating Scale for Depression, 73
Case examples, 38–41, 147–165
Center for Epidemiological Studies
Depression Scale, 74–75
Chaos, 27, 53
Child Assessment Schedule, 73, 76
Child Depression Inventory, 75, 76, 109,
110, 114, 134, 136, 143, 149–150,
152
Childhood Tic Syndrome
treatment of, 167
Children of depressed parents, 14, 63–65
Circumplex model, 26–27
Classification. See Diagnosis of
depression
Cognitive factors in depression, 13–14,
32, 34–35, 58–59, 132–133
Cognitive therapy, 20
Cognitive triad, 32
Cohesion, 26, 114
Contracts, 117, 118–119, 139, 150, 157,
162, 169
Couples Interaction Scoring System, 88

Depression
assessment, 38, 62–84, 94–95
cognitive factors, 13–14, 32, 34–35,
58–59, 132–133
DSM–III, 4–6, 62, 73, 77, 109, 114,
146, 157, 159, 163
development, 33–38, 128–129, 170
diagnosis, 4–8, 62
endogenous–reactive, 7, 81–83, 110,
159

epidemiology, 1, 8–10
interpersonal risk factors, 11–16
learned helplessness model, 32, 34
life events, 14–15, 17, 34, 35–36
loss, 11
marital discord, 17–21, 36–37, 63–64,
104, 114, 160
marital/family therapy outcome,
19–21
pharmacotherapy, 20–21, 162
primary–secondary, 7
social behavior, 16–17
social support, 15–16
suicide, 2, 10, 83
symptoms, 2–4, 159
systems conceptualization, 30–38
unipolar–bipolar, 4–7
Development of depression, 33–38, 128–
129, 170
Diagnosis of depression
DSM–III, 4–6, 62, 73, 77, 109, 114,
146, 157, 159, 163
endogenous–reactive, 7, 81–83, 110,
159
primary–secondary, 7
unipolar–bipolar, 4–7
Disengagement, 26, 53
Double–bind theory, 23
DSM–III, 4–6, 62, 73, 77, 109, 114, 146,
157, 159, 163
Dyadic Adjustment Scale, 84, 85, 109,
110, 134, 136, 143, 146, 147–148,
149 150, 152, 158–159, 163

Emphasizing strengths, 57–58, 122–123,
145, 151–152, 161, 164–165
Enactment, 51–52, 61, 121, 141, 148,
154, 159–160, 169, 170
Encopresis
treatment of, 167, 168
Enmeshment, 26, 53
Epidemiology of depression
age, 9
divorce, 17
gender, 8–9
marital status, 9–10
socioeconomic status, 10

suicide, 10

Family Adaptability and Cohesion
      Evaluation Scales, 84, 86–87
Family Assessment Device, 87
Family Environment Scale, 84, 86, 109,
      110, 111, 143–144, 146, 154, 156
Family therapy. See Marital/family
      therapy
Follow–up, 95, 143, 145–146, 152,
      157, 164

Generalization, 60–61, 164
Ground rules of therapy, 46–47, 67,
      93–94, 116–117

Hamilton Rating Scale for Depression,
      72–73, 76, 78
Homework tasks, 59, 61, 112, 115,
      119–120, 124–127, 134–136,
      137–139, 140, 156, 161–162, 169
Hyperactivity
      treatment of, 167

Impact Message Inventory, 84, 85–86
Initial interview
      ending the interview, 93–94
      goal–definition stage, 92–93, 110–117
      interaction stage, 70, 106–110
      problem identification stage, 68–70,
            101–106
      social stage, 67–68, 99–100, 148
Integrative Multi–Level Therapy, 31–32
Interpersonal description of depression,
      16–17, 21, 27–29, 33, 35,
      37–38, 170
Interpersonal Psychotherapy for
      depression (IPT), 31, 63, 81–82
Interpersonal risk factors
      early family environment, 12–14
      early loss, 11
      life events, 14–15, 17
      social support, 15–16
Interview Schedule for Children, 73–74

Joining, 49–50, 131, 139–140, 148, 154,
      159, 167, 168, 169, 170

Learned helplessness model of depression,
      32, 34
Life events, 14–15, 17, 34, 35–36
Living in Familial Environments Coding
      System, 89

Marital Adjustment Test, 85
Marital discord, 17–21, 32, 36–37,
      63–64, 104, 114, 116, 160
Marital/family therapy
      assessment, 62–66, 84–92
      concepts, 25–30
      depression and, 19–21, 31–32
      goals, 43, 48–49, 92–93, 103, 116
      historical perspective, 22–24
      principles, 42–45
      tasks, 45–49
      techniques, 49–58
      termination, 95
Marital Interaction Coding System, 88
Measurement of depression. See
      Assessment of depression
Measurement of marital/family
      functioning. See Assessment of
      the marital/family system
Medical disorders
      treatment of, 168–169
MMPI–D Scale, 75
MMPI–D–30, 75

Obesity
      treatment of, 167
Obsessive–compulsive disorder
      treatment of, 168

Pain disorders
      treatment of, 168
Paradoxical techniques
      redefining, 55–56, 129–130
      restraining, 56–57, 136, 156
Parental loss, 11–12
Parental rejection, 12–14
Pharmacotherapy, 20–21, 81–83,
      110, 162
Pleasant Events Schedule, 60, 143, 156
Postpartum depression, 14
Psychosomatic disorders

treatment of, 168

Redefining, 55–56, 129–130
Reframing, 50–51, 61, 121–122,
    129–130, 150–151, 155,
    160–161, 163, 168, 169, 170
Reinforcement Survey Schedule, 60
Resistance to treatment, 55–57, 59,
    63–64, 96–98, 114
Restraining, 56–57, 136, 156
Restructuring, 52–53, 168, 169
Rigidity, 26–27, 53

Schedule for Affective Disorders and
    Schizophrenia, 72, 76, 78, 109,
    143, 153
Schizophrenic disorders
    treatment of, 166–167
School phobia, 32, 168
Social skills, 16–17, 34
Social support, 15–16
Sources of Self-Esteem Inventory, 60
Spouse Observation Checklist, 87–88
Substance abuse, 32, 83–84, 169
Suicide, 2, 10, 83
Symptoms of depression
    behavioral, 2
    cognitive, 3
    physiological, 3–4, 159
Systems conceptualization of depression,
    30–38
Systems theory
    adaptation to change, 26–27
    concepts, 23, 24–30
    function of the symptom, 27–29, 168
    involvement of the family, 29–30, 168
    mutual causality, 25, 133
    system rules, 25–26, 52
    treatment principles, 42–45

Termination of therapy, 95, 142–145, 163
Therapy goals, 43, 48–49, 58, 92–93,
    143, 150, 154, 161
Therapy tasks

determining who to see, 45–46,
    153–154
educating the family, 47–48, 150
formulating treatment goals, 43,
    48–49, 92–93, 103, 143, 150,
    154, 161
structuring the sessions, 46–47
Therapy techniques
Individual therapy
    educating the patient, 58,
        130–133, 156
    generalization, 60–61, 164
    homework tasks, 59, 133, 137–139,
        156, 161–162
    increasing pleasurable activities,
        59–60, 61, 138, 156, 161
    organizing a daily schedule, 60,
        138, 156
    self-monitoring, 58–59, 133,
        137–139, 156
    self-reinforcement, 60
Marital/family therapy
    altering boundaries, 53–54, 134,
        150, 168
    constructing alternate realities,
        54–55
    dealing with resistance, 55–57, 59,
        63–64, 96–98, 114
    emphasizing strengths, 57–58,
        122–123, 145, 151–152, 161,
        164–165
    enactment, 51–52, 61, 121, 141,
        148, 154, 159–160, 169, 170
    joining, 49–50, 131, 139–140, 148,
        154, 159, 167, 168, 169, 170
    reframing, 50–51, 61, 121–122,
        129–130, 150–151, 155,
        160–161, 163, 168, 169, 170
    restructuring, 52–53, 168, 169

Utilizing assessment data, 94–95,
    110–117, 134–136

Zung Self-Rating Depression Scale, 75

About the Authors

Dr. Ian H. Gotlib is an Associate Professor in the Department of Psychology at The University of Western Ontario, and is Co-Director of the Clinical Training Program. He is a graduate of the Clinical Psychology Program at the University of Waterloo. Actively involved in both research and clinical practice, Dr. Gotlib is the principal investigator on research grants examining the marital and family relationships of depressed patients. He has published numerous articles and chapters on cognitive and interpersonal aspects of depression, and has presented treatment workshops and papers at local and international meetings. Dr. Gotlib currently serves as associate editor of *Cognition and Emotion*, and is on the editorial boards of *The Journal of Abnormal Psychology, Cognitive Therapy and Research*, and *The Journal of Social and Personal Relationships*.

Dr. Catherine A. Colby completed her graduate training at the University of Western Ontario. She is currently Program Director of an inpatient adolescent treatment unit at Children's Psychiatric Research Institute. Dr. Colby has been instrumental in shaping this program to include a strong focus on family involvement in the treatment of troubled adolescents. As an adjunct faculty member of the Psychology Department at the University of Western Ontario, she has taught a graduate course in Marital and Family Therapy, provided clinical supervision for graduate students, and conducted research on memory functioning in depressed persons. Dr. Colby is also strongly involved in community programs concerned with child abuse, family violence, and increased accessibility of mental health services.

Psychology Practitioner Guidebooks

Editors
Arnold P. Goldstein, Syracuse University
Leonard Krasner, SUNY at Stony Brook
Sol L. Garfield, Washington University

Elsie M. Pinkston & Nathan L. Linsk—CARE OF THE ELDERLY: A Family Approach

Donald Meichenbaum—STRESS INOCULATION TRAINING

Sebastiano Santostefano—COGNITIVE CONTROL THERAPY WITH CHILDREN AND ADOLESCENTS

Lillie Weiss, Melanie Katzman & Sharlene Wolchik—TREATING BULIMIA: A Psychoeducational Approach

Edward B. Blanchard & Frank Andrasik—MANAGEMENT OF CHRONIC HEADACHES: A Psychological Approach

Raymond G. Romanczyk—CLINICAL UTILIZATION OF MICROCOMPUTER TECHNOLOGY

Philip H. Bornstein & Marcy T. Bornstein—MARITAL THERAPY: A Behavioral-Communications Approach

Michael T. Nietzel & Ronald C. Dillehay—PSYCHOLOGICAL CONSULTATION IN THE COURTROOM

Elizabeth B. Yost, Larry E. Beutler, M. Anne Corbishley & James R. Allender—GROUP COGNITIVE THERAPY: A Treatment Approach for Depressed Older Adults

Lillie Weiss—DREAM ANALYSIS IN PSYCHOTHERAPY

Edward A. Kirby & Liam K. Grimley—UNDERSTANDING AND TREATING ATTENTION DEFICIT DISORDER

Jon Eisenson—LANGUAGE AND SPEECH DISORDERS IN CHILDREN

Eva L. Feindler & Randolph B. Ecton—ADOLESCENT ANGER CONTROL: Cognitive-Behavioral Techniques

Michael C. Roberts—PEDIATRIC PSYCHOLOGY: Psychological Interventions and Strategies for Pediatric Problems

Daniel S. Kirschenbaum, William G. Johnson & Peter M. Stalonas, Jr.—TREATING CHILDHOOD AND ADOLESCENT OBESITY

W. Stewart Agras—EATING DISORDERS: Management of Obesity, Bulimia and Anorexia Nervosa

Ian H. Gotlib—TREATMENT OF DEPRESSION: An Interpersonal Systems Approach

Walter B. Pryzwansky & Robert N. Wendt—PSYCHOLOGY AS A PROFESSION: Foundations of Practice

Cynthia D. Belar, William W. Deardorff & Karen E. Kelly—THE PRACTICE OF CLINICAL HEALTH PSYCHOLOGY

Paul Karoly & Mark P. Jensen—MULTIMETHOD ASSESSMENT OF CHRONIC PAIN

William L. Golden, E. Thomas Dowd & Fred Friedberg—HYPNOTHERAPY: A Modern Approach

Patricia Lacks—BEHAVIORAL TREATMENT FOR PERSISTENT INSOMNIA